921191

Patterns of Civilization

volume 2

Burton F. Beers
Professor of History
North Carolina State University

Prentice-Hall Canada Inc., Scarborough, Ontario

Burton F. Beers

Burton F. Beers is Professor of History at North Carolina State University. In the course of his career, Dr. Beers has taught European history, Asian history, and American history. He has published numerous articles in historical journals and has written several books on East Asia, including *The Far East: A History of Western Impacts and Eastern Responses* with Paul H. Clyde and *China in Old Photographs*. As a consultant to the North Carolina Department of Public Instruction for many years, Dr. Beers has developed social studies curriculum in western and nonwestern studies. He has also planned and directed numerous workshops for social studies teachers.

Area Specialists

Early Modern Europe	Helen Nader, Indiana University, Bloomington, Indiana
Nineteenth-Century Europe	Charles F. Delzell, Vanderbilt University, Nashville, Tennessee
Twentieth-Century Europe	Marian Nelson, University of Nebraska, Omaha, Nebraska
Africa	Marylee Crofts Wiley, African Studies Center, Michigan State University, East Lansing, Michigan
Asia	Burton F. Beers, North Carolina State University, Raleigh, North Carolina
Latin America	Stanley R. Ross, University of Texas, Austin, Texas
Middle East	Helen Rivlin, State University of New York, Binghamton, New York

Canadian Cataloguing in Publication Data

Beers, Burton F.
    Patterns of civilization

For use in schools.
Includes bibliographies and indexes.
ISBN 0-13-653908-4 (v. 1) ISBN 0-13-653924-6 (v. 2)

1. Civilization – Juvenile literature.   I. Title.

CB69.2.B43 1984   909   C84-098761-7

Original American Edition published by Prentice-Hall Inc., Englewood Cliffs, New Jersey, U.S.A. Copyright © 1983 by Prentice-Hall, Inc. This edition is authorized for sale in Canada.

Prentice-Hall, Inc., Englewood Cliffs, New Jersey
Prentice-Hall International, Inc., London
Prentice-Hall of Australia, Pty., Ltd., Sydney
Prentice-Hall of India, Pvt., Ltd., New Delhi
Prentice-Hall of Japan, Inc., Tokyo
Prentice-Hall of Southeast Asia (Pte.) Ltd., Singapore
Editora Prentice-Hall do Brasil Ltda., Rio de Janeiro
Prentice-Hall Hispanoamericana, S.A., Mexico

ISBN 0-13-653924-6

Production Editor: Paula Pettitt
Production: Joanne Matthews

Printed and bound in Canada by Ronalds Printing

4   5   6   RP   92   91   90

Contents

Special Features

Skill Lessons

Charts and Graphs

Maps

Reference Section Maps

To the Student

Through a study of world history, you will become familiar with the varied experiences of people throughout history as well as with the common patterns of civilization. You will learn about the political, social, and economic developments that have created the world as you know it. As you study the past, you will begin to better understand the challenges of the present and the major issues of the future.

Many features have been included in this book to assist you during your course of study:

1. **Unit Overview.** Each unit begins with a brief overview identifying major themes you will read about in the unit.
2. **Chapter Outline.** Each chapter begins with an outline of the contents to give you an overview of the chapter.
3. **Chapter Introduction.** The chapter introduction opens with a story or an excerpt from a primary source that tells you about a person or an event from the time period covered in the chapter. The introduction also provides you with a setting for the material in the chapter.
4. **Important Terms.** Historical terms and vocabulary words are italicized and clearly defined the first time they appear in the text. Often you will be asked to define these terms in a section review. Important historical terms also appear in a glossary at the end of the book.
5. **Maps, Graphs, Charts.** Numerous maps, graphs, and charts appear throughout the book to help you understand major historical developments and events. Their clarity makes them useful reinforcements of the narrative. Captions provide background information and relate the maps, graphs, and charts to what you are reading.
6. **Illustrations.** The text contains many paintings and photographs to enliven the study of each historical period. The captions contain useful information about the illustrations and the people and events pictured.
7. **Special Features.** Boxed features give you a close look at people and events in world history. They include biographies and descriptions of events, as well as selections from diaries, literature, and other contemporary sources.
8. **Skill Lessons.** Special boxed lessons help you understand and practice important skills, such as reading maps and graphs, using visual evidence and statistics, and analyzing conflicting sources.
9. **Section Reviews.** Each section ends with a set of review questions to test your understanding of what you have read. They include locating places on maps, identifying people and events, and defining vocabulary terms.
10. **In Perspective.** The chapter summary, called In Perspective, reviews the developments you read about in the chapter and puts them in perspective.
11. **Time Line.** A time line appears at the end of each chapter. By highlighting major events and developments, it will help you understand how events discussed in the chapter are related in time.
12. **End-of-Chapter Materials.** Four sets of questions end each chapter. The questions called Recalling Facts help you remember basic facts from the chapter. The Chapter Checkup questions help you review the content of the chapter. The questions called For Further Thought ask you to consider historical issues, offer your interpretation of them, and relate past issues to the present. In Developing Basic Skills, you will learn and practice such basic skills as classifying, comparing, map and graph reading, placing events in time, researching, and analyzing source material.
13. **Reference Section.** At the back of the book, you will find a special section of reference material to be used throughout the course. The reference section includes maps, a chronology, a pronunciation key, a glossary, and a list of suggested readings for each chapter.
14. **Index.** An index at the end of the book helps you find references to important people, places, and events discussed in the book.

Unit Overview The battle of Bunker Hill, illustrated in this painting by John Trumbull, was an early battle in the American Revolution. In June 1775, British troops attacked American forces defending Bunker Hill, the heights overlooking the city of Boston. The heroic stand of American patriots in this battle inspired the colonists in their struggle for independence.

In the 1600s and 1700s, revolutionary forces shaped events in Western Europe as well as in the New World. A revolution in thinking gradually changed the way people saw the world. This revolution in thinking was part of the Scientific Revolution. Many people began to think that once they understood the laws governing natural events, they could master the world. This confidence in people's ability to dominate their world would have far-reaching consequences.

The revolution in thinking contributed to political revolutions. Revolutions strengthened Parliament in Britain, helped create the United States of America, and toppled an absolute monarch in France. In all three nations, citizens demanded a larger role in government. The growth of democratic institutions allowed citizens to take an active part in government and gradually closed the gap between rulers and the people.

Unit One

An Age of Revolution

1 Revolution in England and North America

(1509–1791)

Signing the American Declaration of Independence.

In the 1600s and 1700s, new *technology* and improved methods of scientific research led to an explosion in knowledge known as the Scientific Revolution. Discoveries about the physical world affected philosophers as well as scientists. They applied scientific principles to the study of government and society. During this period, named the *Enlightenment*, philosophers emphasized the use of reason. They thought that people should use reason to free themselves from ignorance and superstition and thereby become enlightened. They were convinced that enlightened people could perfect themselves and society.

England had developed a strong, centralized government during the 1600s and 1700s. This government had begun to limit the power of the *monarch* and had evolved into a *limited monarchy* rather than an *absolute monarchy*. The English accepted many of the ideas of John Locke, an Enlightenment philosopher. They believed that government should protect certain basic liberties. They also felt that that power to govern came from the consent of the governed. The ideas and institutions that emerged in England became the basis for more democratic forms of government in both England and North America.

During the 1770s, the British government angered its 13 American *colonies* by introducing new tax laws. In January 1776, a pamphlet entitled *Common Sense* created a great stir. The author, an Englishman named Thomas Paine, had settled in Pennsylvania less than two years earlier. He argued that the American colonists should solve their dispute with Britain by declaring independence.

Paine helped convince many colonists to support the Declaration of Independence. After winning their independence, the colonists had to decide who should govern them and how. Ironically, 100 years earlier, the people of England had debated the same questions.

1 Enlightenment Thinkers: A Review

In the late 1600s and the 1700s, philosophers reexamined society using the *scientific method*, a new approach developed during the Scientific Revolution to study the natural world. During the Enlightenment, philosophers felt confident that they could use reason to discover natural laws that governed human behavior. As a result, this period is also called the Age of Reason.

Hobbes and Locke

The ideas of two English philosophers, Thomas Hobbes and John Locke, had a significant impact on how people viewed the individual's role in society. During the 1640s, Hobbes witnessed the violent upheavals of a civil war in England.* Hobbes became convinced that if people were left alone they would constantly fight among themselves. In 1651, he published his ideas in *Leviathan*. In this work, he described a state of nature in which people had no laws or government. Hobbes claimed that such a life would be "nasty, brutish, and short."

According to Hobbes, to escape the chaos of their natural state, people entered into a contract, or agreement. They gave up their freedom and agreed to obey a ruler. In exchange, the ruler ensured peace and order. The best government, Hobbes said, was one in which the ruler had absolute power to keep order. Furthermore, Hobbes insisted, once people entered into such a contract, they could not rebel, even if they thought the ruler was a tyrant. Hobbes' ideas, therefore, supported the rule of absolute monarchs.

In 1690, John Locke published *Two Treatises on Government*. Locke agreed with Hobbes that the purpose of government was to establish order in society. He also saw government as a contract between the ruler and the ruled. However, Locke's other ideas about government differed greatly from those of Hobbes.

Locke had a more optimistic view of human nature than Hobbes. He thought people were basically reasonable and would cooperate with each other. Moreover, Locke argued that rulers could stay in power only as long as they had the consent of those they governed. If a ruler were a tyrant, then he or she had broken the contract. In such a case, the people had the right to rebel and set up a new government.

Locke presented some very important ideas. He believed people had natural rights, including the right to life, liberty, and property. Government was responsible for protecting these rights, but its power should be limited. After Locke's death, his ideas became popular in France and in North America.

Social and Economic Ideas

Many writers and thinkers, especially in France, expanded on Locke's idea of natural rights. They became known as *philosophes*, a French word meaning philosophers. The philosophes had great confidence that the use of science and reason would lead to continued human progress.

Many philosophes gathered in Paris, where they helped to make Enlightenment ideas popular. Often, they came from middle class families. They were well-educated and valued clear thinking as well as wit and humor.

The philosophes were concerned about many social issues. They urged religious toleration and condemned wars of religion. They claimed people had the right to believe as they wished. The philosophes called for freedom of speech and the press, and they criticized the strict censorship that most governments imposed. They believed censorship was harmful because it prevented people from learning about new ideas. They encouraged education as the way to end ignorance, prejudice, and superstition.

The philosophes denounced slavery because it deprived people of their most basic rights. They spoke out against torture and cruel punishments for crimes. Some philosophes campaigned for more humane treatment of the mentally ill.

One group of philosophes, known as *physiocrats*, searched for natural laws to explain economics. Mercantilism influenced the economic policies of most governments at the time. *Mercantilism* was an economic philosophy maintaining that a nation's economic strength depends on exporting more goods than it imports. Physiocrats opposed mercantilism. They argued that land was the true source of national wealth, not hoards of gold and silver. They urged rulers to encourage farming.

Furthermore, physiocrats believed that restrictions on trade should be removed so farmers could sell their products wherever there was a market. They favored a *free market*, that is, a market in which all goods can be bought and sold without restraint. They argued that the resulting increase in trade would mean greater wealth for everyone.

Josiah Wedgwood: A Practical Man of the Enlightenment

During the Enlightenment, middle class businesspeople, lawyers, and scientists tried to apply the scientific method and the principles of reason to everyday life. One such person was Josiah Wedgwood, who lived in England from 1730 to 1795. Wedgwood is best known for producing Wedgwood pottery, which is still sold all over the world.

Wedgwood was no ordinary potter. He combined science and art as few in his field had done before. He taught himself chemistry so he could understand the chemical changes that took place when clay was heated. He invented special thermometers to measure the high temperatures required for glazing clay. An experimenter, he frequently tried new materials and designed new ovens to improve the quality of his products.

Like many artists of this period, Wedgwood admired the simple, elegant designs of classical Greece and Rome. As a result, his pottery often carried Greek or Roman figures.

As his pottery business prospered, Wedgwood pursued other interests. He joined the Lunar Society, a group of businesspeople and scientists who met to discuss scientific developments. Among Wedgwood's friends in the Lunar Society was Joseph Priestley, the scientist who discovered oxygen. Wedgwood helped support Priestley's work financially. He also invented special laboratory equipment for Priestley.

Wedgwood used his pottery to spread ideas about social justice. Like many Enlightenment thinkers, he campaigned vigorously against the slave trade. Wedgwood designed and produced thousands of anti-slavery medallions like the one shown here. The slave in chains utters the words: "Am I not a man and a brother?" Wedgwood distributed the medallions in Britain and shipped many across the Atlantic to the American colonies. Fashionable people wore the medallions or put them on display at home, thereby expressing their support for the antislavery cause. In his own way, Wedgwood helped to channel Enlightenment ideas into the homes of many people.

Three Influential Views on Government

Among the most influential Enlightenment thinkers were Montesquieu (MAHN tuhs kyoo), Voltaire, and Rousseau (roo SOH). Each formed his own ideas about the best way to organize governments. Yet all three shared the basic beliefs of the philosophes.

Montesquieu. Born to a noble family, the Baron de Montesquieu was a keen student of government. He read the works of Newton and Locke. In *The Spirit of Laws*, he discussed various forms of government.

Montesquieu was especially impressed with the system of government that had developed in England by the mid-1700s. He believed that English government preserved the liberty of the people by the separation of power among three branches of government: the legislature, executive, and judiciary. Montesquieu thought that in England Parliament, as the legislature, made the laws; the king, as the executive, enforced the laws; and the courts, as the judiciary, interpreted the laws if disputes arose. The English system did not work that way in reality, but Montesquieu's ideas were widely discussed.

Montesquieu also thought that the power of each branch of government should be carefully defined to provide a system of checks and balances. That way no branch of government could dominate another. Montesquieu's ideas on checks and balances and the separation of powers would later influence the men who wrote the Constitution of the United States.

Voltaire. Probably the best known philosophe was François Marie Arouet, who used the pen name Voltaire. Voltaire came from a French middle class family. He traveled widely and became popular for his witty plays and novels as well as for his pamphlets attacking evils in society.

Voltaire spent much of his life arguing for religious toleration and freedom of thought. He is credited with saying, "I do not agree with a word you say but I will defend to the death your right to say it."

Voltaire praised English liberties and the works of Newton and Locke. He favored the idea of a strong monarch. To Voltaire, the best ruler was an "enlightened monarch." By that he meant a monarch who studied the science of government and protected the basic rights of the people.

Rousseau. The Swiss philosophe Jean Jacques Rousseau came from a poor and unhappy family. When he went to Paris, he always felt out of place among the sophisticated intellectuals who gathered there. A complainer and constant critic of others, Rousseau quarreled with many philosophes. Yet his political and social ideas were an important part of Enlightenment thought.

Rousseau believed that human nature was basically good. In his opinion, society corrupted people. He also argued that all people were equal and that all titles of rank and nobility should be abolished. "Man is born free," he wrote, "and everywhere is in chains."

Rousseau admired what he called the "noble savage," who lived in a natural state, free from the influences of civilization. How-

The French honored their greatest writers, including Voltaire and Rousseau, by electing them to the French Academy. Members of the French Academy were called "the immortals." This picture shows a winged spirit conducting Rousseau, on the left, and Voltaire, on the the right, to the temple of glory and immortality. The writings of Rousseau and Voltaire shaped Enlightenment thinking in France and elsewhere.

ever, Rousseau realized that people could not return to the natural state.

In *The Social Contract*, Rousseau described an ideal society. In this society, people would form a community and make a contract with each other, not with a ruler. People would give up some of their freedom in favor of the "general will," or the decisions of the majority. The community would vote on all decisions, and everyone would accept the community decision.

Rousseau's beliefs in equality and in the will of the majority made him a spokesman for the common people. Revolutionaries in many countries would later adopt his ideas.

SECTION REVIEW

1. Identify: Thomas Hobbes, John Locke, Montesquieu, Voltaire, Jean Jacques Rousseau.

2. Define: scientific method, philosophe, physiocrat, mercantilism, free market.

3. (a) What kind of government did Hobbes support? (b) According to Locke, when did people have a right to rebel?

4. Describe three concerns of the philosophes.

5. Why did Montesquieu support a government system with checks and balances?

6. (a) Who did Voltaire think should govern? (b) What did Rousseau mean by the "general will"?

The first English coffee house opened around 1650. London coffee houses, like the one shown here, became gathering places for writers, scientists, businessmen, and politicians. At these coffee houses, men discussed politics and the new ideas of the Enlightenment.

2 Clashes Between King and Parliament

Unlike other European monarchs, English kings and queens had limits on their power. They were obliged to respect the tradition that the ruler must obey the law, and they had to deal with Parliament.

A Balance With Parliament

By the 1500s, the English Parliament had won several important rights. Parliament approved new taxes, passed laws proposed by the monarch, and advised monarchs. However, monarchs had more power than Parliament. They named officials and judges, summoned and dismissed Parliament, and conducted foreign policy. After 1534, monarchs also headed the *Church of England*.

The Tudor rulers, Henry VIII and his daughter Elizabeth I, were forceful personalities, but they both recognized the value of good relations with Parliament. Henry, for example, sought and obtained Parliament's approval to establish the Church of England.

Elizabeth followed a cautious policy in her dealings with Parliament. She lived simply so she would not have to ask for money too often. But she also clearly established her rights as monarch. She sometimes scolded Parliament for interfering in matters that she felt did not concern it. However, she also knew when to keep quiet and not to offend Parliament. During most of her reign, Elizabeth was a popular queen, and she managed to maintain a balance between exercising her power and deferring to Parliament. In this way, she preserved unity and stability.

In 1603, Elizabeth died without any direct heir. The English throne passed to the Stuarts, the ruling family of Scotland. When James VI of Scotland traveled south to London to be crowned James I of England, he knew little about English politics.

James I and the Divine Right of Kings

James I was a well-meaning ruler and a scholar. He supervised a new translation of the Bible, known as the King James version. He also wrote a book called *The True Law of Free Monarchies*. In it, he presented his belief that monarchs ruled by divine right. "Kings are called gods," he declared "because they sit upon God's throne on earth." Furthermore, he argued that the monarch should have no restraints on his or her power but should be able to rule for the good of all the people. James's belief in his divine right to rule soon led to conflict with Parliament.

Parliament was made up of two houses: the House of Lords, in which nobles served for life, and the House of Commons, whose members were elected.* Most representatives in the House of Commons were wealthy landowners, called gentry. Many of the gentry had bought *monastery* lands that Henry VIII had seized from the church and sold. The gentry raised sheep for wool,

Elizabeth I was queen of England for 45 years, between 1558 and 1603.

* Only a small number of property owners had the right to vote for members of the House of Commons.

James I was a well-educated monarch. He published articles on such subjects as witchcraft, the dangers of smoking tobacco, and rules for writing Scottish poetry. Unfortunately, he had little skill as a statesman. A contemporary described James as "the most learned fool in Christendom."

which helped build a prosperous textile industry. The growing merchant class in England also had some representatives in the House of Commons.

James I and Parliament quarreled over three main issues: religion, money, and foreign policy. A major religious issue involved the demands of the Puritans. Puritans wanted to see the Anglican Church "purified" of Catholic rituals and ceremonies. They also demanded that local congregations be allowed to rule themselves rather than be ruled by bishops and archbishops appointed by the king. Among the Puritans were many powerful merchants, some of whom served as members of Parliament.

The House of Commons sympathized with the Puritans' demands. However, the king refused to make any changes in the church organization. Whereas Elizabeth had tolerated most Puritans, James vowed to "harry them out of the land." His per-

secution of Puritans forced some of them to leave England.

James was constantly in need of money. He spent lavishly on his court and gave generous gifts to his friends. In addition, England owed many debts to bankers for its wars against Catholic Spain. When the king summoned Parliament to approve new taxes, Parliament often refused unless he would accept its wishes on religious matters. James would angrily lecture Parliament on the divine right of kings and send the representatives home.

James would then have to bolster his income in other ways. He revived feudal fines and raised customs duties, which went directly to the crown. Although such moves were technically legal, James's actions angered Parliament.

Parliament criticized the king's foreign policy, especially when he made peace with Spain and tried to arrange a marriage between his son and a Spanish princess. Furthermore, many people in England felt that James did not give enough help to Protestants in Europe during the wars of religion there.

Charles I and Parliament

James's son Charles I inherited the throne in 1625. Like his father, Charles believed in the divine right of kings. When Parliament refused to give him enough money, Charles dismissed it and demanded loans from individual people. He imprisoned anyone who refused to pay the forced loans.

By 1628, Charles had to summon Parliament because he needed funds desperately. Parliament refused his financial demands until he signed the Petition of Right. In the petition, Charles promised not to collect forced loans or levy taxes without the consent of Parliament. He also agreed not to imprison a person without cause or house soldiers in private homes without the owner's consent. Through the Petition of Right, Parliament hoped to end the king's arbitrary actions.

However, once Parliament approved the funds he needed, Charles dissolved it. For the next 11 years, he ruled without calling another Parliament. He ignored the Petition of Right and returned to the policies of James I.

During the 1630s, Charles made many enemies because of his arbitrary rule. He appointed unpopular officials, such as William Laud to be Archbishop of Canterbury. Laud persecuted Puritans and other dissenters, Protestants who would not accept Anglican practices. Charles and his advisors also used special courts such as the Court of High Commission and the Court of Star Chamber to suppress opposition. These courts did not have to follow *common law* or use juries.

The gulf between the king and the country grew wider. A revolt in Scotland finally brought matters to a head. In 1638, Charles tried to impose the Anglican Church on Scotland, where the official religion was Presbyterian. The Scots resisted and invaded England. Because Charles needed money to equip and pay an army, he summoned Parliament in 1640.

The Long Parliament

The Parliament that was called in 1640 would meet in one form or another until 1660. Known as the Long Parliament, it would eventually lead a revolution against the monarchy. But in 1640, Parliament was chiefly concerned with limiting the king's power and removing unpopular officials.

Before granting Charles's request for money, Parliament demanded the trial of Charles's chief ministers, Archbishop Laud and the Earl of Strafford, for abusing their power. Both men were found guilty and executed.

Parliament abolished the Court of High Commission and the Court of Star Chamber. It also passed the Triennial Act, which stated that the king must call a parliament at least once every three years. As the Long Parliament continued to meet, critics of the king grew more outspoken. Eventually they pushed through a bill condemning Charles as a tyrant.

Charles struck back by leading a band of armed supporters into Parliament and arresting five outspoken members. The king's use of force made compromise impossible. In 1642, the king and Parliament raised their own armies, and civil war began.

The English Civil War

The civil war lasted from 1642 to 1649. People of all classes fought on both sides. In general, the king rallied to his side nobles and people in rural areas, especially in northwestern England. The king's supporters were called Cavaliers because the aristocratic leaders were mounted horsemen, or cavalry.

Parliament recruited its troops mostly from the middle class, especially from towns in southeastern England. Many Puritans fought for Parliament. Supporters of Parliament were called Roundheads because the men cut their hair close to their heads to show that they rejected the aristocratic style of long hair.

In 1645, Oliver Cromwell, a strong-minded Puritan officer, reorganized Parliament's army as the New Model Army. Under his energetic leadership, the New Model Army became a well-disciplined force, and it defeated the Cavaliers and captured Charles I.

The Long Parliament, which had continued to meet during the civil war, decided the

This contemporary political cartoon reflects the views of royalists, who supported the monarchy and despised Cromwell, shown at left. Cromwell's supporters are cutting down the "Royall Oake," the source of English law and institutions.

During the English civil war, Cromwell purged the House of Commons of the king's supporters. After Charles I was captured by Cromwell, the remaining members of the House of Commons met as a court to try the king. At the trial, shown here, Charles, seated in the center, refused to recognize the authority of the court. He claimed "a king cannot be tried by any superior jurisdiction on earth." Nevertheless, he was condemned to die.

king should be put on trial. In January 1649, a court ordered the execution of Charles I. The House of Commons then voted to abolish the monarchy and the House of Lords and proclaimed England a *republic*. Thus, the civil war resulted in a revolution in English government.

The Commonwealth under Cromwell

Oliver Cromwell was chosen to head the English republic, which became known as the Commonwealth. Cromwell was a man with high moral principles. He supported a policy of religious toleration for all Protestants but not for Catholics. He hoped that he could restore peace with the help of Parliament.

Yet the civil war had left England bitterly divided. Presbyterians, Anglicans, and Puritans had differing views about the kind of government England should have. In addition, some extreme reformers wanted to push the revolution further. One group, the Levellers, led by John Lilburne, demanded an end to all titles of nobility. They also thought all English men should have the right to vote, a startling idea at a time when only a small number of property owners could vote.

Parliament itself was so seriously divided that Cromwell dissolved it in 1653. He then took the title Lord Protector and ruled England as a dictator until his death in 1658. As Lord Protector, Cromwell depended on the army to govern the country. Army officials imposed strict Puritan rule. They closed theaters, banned newspapers and dancing, and enforced laws against other forms of popular entertainment.

Cromwell tried to bring Scotland and Ireland under tighter English control, but he met strong resistance. Therefore, he crushed the Scots and brutally suppressed Catholic rebels in Ireland. He then encouraged Protestants to settle in Ireland. The new settlers replaced Catholic landlords, especially in the north.*

Cromwell's rule became increasingly unpopular, and people began to long for the restoration of the monarchy. After Cromwell's death, the Long Parliament reconvened. It asked the son of Charles I, who was living in France, to return to England and be crowned Charles II.

Although the monarchy was thus restored, the civil war and the Commonwealth had lasting effects. The new king would rule with the memory of what had happened to his father and would be careful in his dealings with Parliament. Moreover, Parliament took steps to prevent Charles II and future rulers from exercising power arbitrarily.

---

* Both Henry VIII and Elizabeth I had given Protestants lands taken from Catholics in Ireland. Cromwell and later English rulers continued this policy.

SECTION REVIEW

1. Identify: William Laud, Long Parliament, Cavalier, Roundhead, Oliver Cromwell, Commonwealth.
2. How did Elizabeth I deal with Parliament?
3. Describe one of the issues that created conflict between James I and Parliament.
4. What limits did the Petition of Right put on the monarch's power?
5. Describe two actions taken by the Long Parliament.
6. What problems did Cromwell face in trying to rule England?

3 Establishing a Limited Monarchy

Charles II received a warm welcome upon his return to England in 1660. In contrast to Cromwell's stern Puritan policies, Charles, a charming and lively man, held lavish court banquets. He reopened theaters and encouraged other entertainments, such as horse-racing, which the Puritans had forbidden.

The Restoration Under Charles II

Charles II had spent his years in exile at the French court. Although he admired the absolute power enjoyed by Louis XIV, he knew he must accept limits on his own power. Before taking the throne, Charles agreed to respect the Magna Carta and the Petition of Right. He dealt cautiously with Parliament and generally had its support.

Meanwhile, members of Parliament protected their own interests. Most were landowners, and they passed laws abolishing the feudal dues that landowners paid to the monarch. In place of the feudal dues, Parliament granted the monarch a yearly income to be paid from taxes.[†]

Charles II secretly preferred the Catholic Church to the Anglican Church, but he knew Parliament would not accept a return to Catholicism. Thus, he urged toleration of all religions. However, the English were not ready to accept religious toleration. In 1673, Parliament passed the Test Act, which required any person holding public office to belong to the Anglican Church. The Test Act also excluded Protestant dissenters and Catholics from the army, the navy, and universities.

In foreign policy, Charles cooperated with France. He entered into a secret treaty with Louis XIV, in part because he needed money. In return for Louis's financial support, Charles pledged to restore Catholicism in England as soon as it was practical. He

---

† In England, unlike other parts of Europe, nobles as well as commoners paid taxes.

also agreed to join France in a war against the Dutch. Under Charles, the English seized the Dutch colony of New Netherland.

Emergence of Political Parties

During Charles's reign, two political parties emerged in England: the Tories and the Whigs. The Tories generally supported the king and the Anglican Church, while the Whigs wanted to strengthen Parliament.

The Whigs tended to favor toleration of all Protestants, but they were fiercely anti-Catholic. As a result, they worried that when Charles died, his brother James would inherit the throne. Unlike Charles, who hid his religious opinions, James openly admitted to being Catholic. To prevent James from inheriting the throne, the Whigs tried to pass the Exclusion Act.

In 1679, the Tories were able to defeat the Exclusion Act, but only by accepting another piece of legislation, the Habeas Corpus Act. The Habeas Corpus Act is still considered one of the most basic guarantees of individual rights because it protects a citizen from arbitrary arrest. The act provided that if a person were arrested, a judge would issue a "writ of habeas corpus." The "writ" was an order to bring the prisoner before a judge and state the charges against the person. The judge would then decide whether or not the person should be held for trial.

The Habeas Corpus Act thus made it illegal for an individual to be held in prison without a trial. It also decreed that a person could not be imprisoned twice for the same crime. Today, the Constitution of Canada includes the right of habeas corpus.

James II and the Glorious Revolution

In 1685 James II became king. He was determined to make Parliament grant tolerance for Catholics. Ignoring the Test Act, James placed Catholics in high government posts and in the army. Parliament protested but took no action. The king's opponents believed James would be succeeded by his daughter Mary, a Protestant. In 1688, James's second wife, a Catholic, gave birth to a son. The boy became heir to the throne and was to be raised a Catholic.

Mary's husband, Prince William of Orange, encouraged by promises of support from powerful men in England, promptly organized an invasion. In November 1688, William landed in England with an army of 15,000. James and his family fled to France.

When parliament agreed to William's demand that he be declared King in his own right, he and Mary became rulers of England. In 1689, the new monarchs signed the Bill of Rights which ensured the powers of Parliament and protected English liberties. The signing of the Bill of Rights marked the end of what is known as the Glorious Revolution.

The English Bill of Rights

The Bill of Rights included several provisions making Parliament stronger than the monarchs. It stated that the monarchs could not suspend any laws without the consent of Parliament. The king and queen also needed the approval of Parliament to raise taxes and maintain an army. Furthermore, they had to summon Parliament frequently and could not interfere in its elections.

In addition to making Parliament supreme, the Bill of Rights protected the rights of individuals. It guaranteed the right of trial by jury for anyone accused of a crime. It also outlawed cruel and unusual punishments and limited the amount of bail that could be imposed on a person being held for trial.

Despite the limits Parliament placed on the power of the monarchs, English government and society were not democratic. Few people had the right to vote. Members of Parliament were not paid, so only the wealthy could afford to run for office. Religious toleration also remained limited. In 1689, Parliament passed the Act of Toleration. It assured all Protestants freedom of worship, but it did not give the same right to Catholics.

British Isles, 1707

☐ Great Britain

0 — 200 Miles
0 — 300 km

■ *The Act of Union joined Scotland and England in 1707. Ireland remained a separate nation, but it was ruled by England. Wales had been united with England in the early 1500s.*

Ireland and Scotland

Even after the Glorious Revolution, Parliament worried that James II or his heirs might reclaim the throne. This concern influenced relations between England and Ireland.

In 1689, James II led a rebellion in Ireland, hoping to regain the English throne. But he was defeated at the battle of the Boyne. In an effort to prevent James or any other Catholic from claiming the throne, Parliament passed the Act of Settlement in 1701. It stated that only an Anglican could inherit the English throne.

To prevent any future rebellion, the English Parliament imposed harsh penalties on Catholics in Ireland. English policies in Ireland bred a deep-seated resentment among the Catholic Irish. Even though the Catholics were a majority in Ireland, they could not buy or inherit land from Protestants. Furthermore, Catholics could not be elected to the Irish Parliament, making it easy for the Protestant minority to rule.

Since James II had also been king of Scotland, Parliament also worried that he or his heirs might reclaim the Scottish throne. To prevent this from happening, Parliament negotiated the Act of Union, which the Scots reluctantly accepted in 1707. The Act of Union joined the kingdoms of England and Scotland into the United Kingdom of Great Britain.

Although James and his heirs hatched plots to seize the throne, their efforts failed. After the deaths of William and Mary, Anne, James's other Protestant daughter, ruled Britain. The Act of Settlement provided that on Queen Anne's death the throne should pass to the nearest Protestant relative. Thus, in 1714, George, the German Elector of Hanover, became King George I of Britain. The peaceful transition from the Stuart to the Hanover dynasty was evidence that the Glorious Revolution had created stable government in Britain.

Growth of Constitutional Government

The English civil war and the Glorious Revolution established Britain as a limited constitutional monarchy—that is, the power of the monarchy was limited by laws and traditions. The British did not have a formal written constitution. Instead, the British constitution was composed of all acts of Parliament and documents such as the Magna Carta, the Petition of Right, and the Bill of Rights. It also included traditions and customs. The relationship between the monarch and Parliament, for example, was based largely on tradition.

In the late 1600s and throughout the 1700s, three developments affected constitutional government in England. First,

13

Major Events in England 1603-1701

1603	James I inherits the throne
1628	Charles I signs the Petition of Right
1642	English civil war begins
1649	Parliament declares England a republic; Charles I executed
1660	Restoration of the monarchy; Charles II agrees to respect the Magna Carta and Petition of Right
1679	Habeas Corpus Act passed
1688-1689	Glorious Revolution; William and Mary sign the Bill of Rights
1701	Act of Settlement passed

political parties acquired a more well-defined role in Parliament. Second, a cabinet system evolved. Third, the office of prime minister came into existence.

Political parties. As you read earlier in this section, the Whigs and Tories had begun to emerge as political parties after the restoration of Charles II. By the late 1600s, the differences between the two parties had become more distinct.

During the Glorious Revolution, the Whigs supported laws that limited royal power. Most Whigs were wealthy landowners who thought their power would increase as the monarch's power declined. Some Whigs were successful merchants. They favored policies, such as a strong navy, that would help promote British trade.

The Tories usually defended royal power against challenges by Parliament. Although most Tories were landowners, they usually owned less land than Whigs.

The cabinet. During the late 1600s, King William I chose his chief ministers, or advisors, from both political parties in Parliament.

But he soon realized that Whig and Tory ministers did not get along. As a result, he began to appoint ministers from the party that held the majority of seats in Parliament. The practice of appointing ministers from the majority party eventually led to the cabinet system of government.

The cabinet was made up of the ministers appointed by the monarch. Each cabinet member was responsible for a department of government, such as the navy or finance. Cabinet members remained members of Parliament. Therefore, they could vote for their own policies and try to convince others to do the same.

Eventually, a cabinet would stay in power as long as Parliament approved its policies. If Parliament rejected government policies, the monarch would call for new elections to Parliament. The new majority party would then form the next cabinet.

The prime minister. The cabinet acquired much of its power during the reign of George I in the early 1700s. Born and raised in Hanover, the king spoke only German and did not understand English politics. Therefore, he relied heavily on his English advisors. Sir Robert Walpole, an able and powerful Whig member of Parliament, became the king's chief advisor. Although Walpole did not use the title, he is usually considered the first *prime minister*, or head of the cabinet.

Between 1721 and 1742, Walpole skillfully steered legislation through Parliament. He gradually took over from the king the job of appointing many government officials, including other cabinet members. He managed government finances well, avoided costly wars, and supported laws that encouraged trade and industry. He allowed the English colonies in North America to develop on their own and avoided taking a stand on controversial issues. In fact, Walpole's motto was "Let sleeping dogs lie."

Personal Rule of George III

When George III came to the throne in 1760, he felt that the cabinet and Parliament under the Whigs had taken too much power from the monarch. Many small landowners agreed with the king, and they supported his efforts to regain control of the government.

For 12 years from 1770 to 1782, George III personally supervised the government and appointed his own ministers. Lord North, George's prime minister, rallied a group in Parliament known as "the king's friends" to support George's policies. As you will read in the next section, some of the king's policies angered the American colonists, who declared their independence from England in 1776.

During the American Revolution, George lost support at home, and Parliament reasserted its power. It eventually forced the king to accept a new cabinet that would make peace with the United States. Parlia-ment also passed a reform bill that limited the monarch's right to appoint officials.

SECTION REVIEW

1. Identify: Tories, Whigs, Habeas Corpus Act, Glorious Revolution.
2. Define: prime minister.
3. Describe the major provision of each of the following acts of Parliament: (a) Test Act; (b) Act of Toleration; (c) Act of Settlement; (d) Act of Union.
4. What limits did the Bill of Rights place on royal power?
5. What policy did Parliament follow in Ireland?
6. What duties did Sir Robert Walpole take on as prime minister?

---

4 Revolution in Colonial America

Events in England and Enlightenment ideas greatly influenced people in the 13 American colonies. The colonists believed they should have the same rights that people in England won during the Glorious Revolution. When the British government appeared to violate these rights, the American colonists raised a storm of protest.

Governing the Colonies

Between 1700 and 1763, the American colonies expanded rapidly along the eastern seaboard. Busy with wars in Europe, Britain allowed the colonies to develop largely on their own. In most colonies, royal governors appointed by the king controlled trade and appointed judges and other officials. Each colony also had its own elected assembly.* Colonial assemblies had the right to approve laws related to local affairs. They also approved salaries for officials, including the governor, and levied taxes to meet local government expenses.

Although colonists controlled local affairs, Britain regulated colonial trade. During the 1600s, Parliament had passed the Navigation Acts, which reflected mercantilist ideas. For example, one act required colonial merchants to ship goods only on colonial or English vessels.

Other Navigation Acts forbade the colonies to import goods from Europe unless these goods first went to England, where a customs duty was paid to the crown. In addition, certain colonial products, such as sugar, cotton, tobacco, and naval supplies, could be shipped only to England.

In general, the Navigation Acts benefited the colonies as well as England. The colonies developed their own shipbuilding industries to construct ships for carrying goods to England. In addition, freedom from foreign competition helped colonial merchants develop their businesses.

Some New England merchants, however, did not like the Navigation Acts. These merchants relied heavily on sugar and molasses imported from the West Indies.

---

* As in European countries, voting in the colonies was usually limited to men who owned property or paid taxes. However, land was more plentiful in North America, so more people were landowners. Therefore, a much larger percentage of the male population in the colonies could vote than in any European nation.

According to the acts, they could buy sugar and molasses only from the British West Indies. In practice, they ignored the law and smuggled sugar and molasses from the French West Indies.

The Road to Revolution

Between 1756 and 1763 seven major European powers were involved in a war, known as the Seven Years' War, which was fought in Europe, Asia, and North America. When this war ended, British policy toward the American colonies changed. The war had been expensive and left Britain deeply in debt. Furthermore, the British had to keep troops in North America to defend the vast territories it acquired from France. George III and his ministers felt that the American colonies should help pay the costs of their own defense. Therefore, the king urged Parliament to pass a series of laws to raise revenue from the colonies. One of these was the Stamp Act, passed by parliament in 1765.

The Stamp Act taxed a variety of items, from newspapers, deeds, and wills to dice and playing cards. People in Britain and in other parts of Europe had been paying such taxes for centuries. But in the American colonies, the Stamp Act caused an angry reaction.

Delegates from 9 of the 13 colonies met in New York to protest the Stamp Act. They claimed that the colonists had the same rights as other British subjects, including the right to consent to any taxes. They argued that Parliament did not have the right to tax them because they did not send representatives to Parliament. Only colonial assemblies, they declared, had the right to impose taxes on the colonies.

When the British government tried to enforce the Stamp Act, riots erupted in the major colonial cities. For months, the colonists successfully boycotted British goods, fi-

On March 5, 1770, a crowd of angry Bostonians gathered at the Boston customs house. The crowd jeered and threw snowballs at the British soldiers guarding the building. A shot was heard, causing the British to open fire on the crowd. Five colonists were killed in the "Boston Massacre." This engraving of the scene was made by Boston silversmith and patriot Paul Revere. It was widely circulated in the colonies and stirred resentment against the British.

nally forcing Parliament to repeal the unpopular act. However, Parliament still insisted that it had the right to tax the colonies.

Between 1765 and 1775, relations between Britain and its American colonies worsened as Parliament imposed new taxes and tried to reassert British control over the colonies. In 1773, a group of Bostonians openly expressed their contempt for British policies. Disguised as Indians, they dumped a shipment of tea into Boston harbor. Many colonists cheered when they heard of the "Boston Tea Party," as the event was called. The British government was outraged by what it saw as an act of rebellion.

In 1774, to punish the colonists, Parliament passed a series of laws that the colonists called the "Intolerable Acts." Parliament closed the port of Boston, forbade the Massachusetts assembly from holding regular sessions, and imposed military rule on the colony. Parliament also passed the Quebec Act, which provided a government for the territories Britain had acquired from France. The act extended the boundaries of Quebec south to the Ohio River. The colonists saw the Quebec Act as an effort to prevent them from moving westward.

In reaction to these acts, delegates from all the colonies except Georgia met at a Continental Congress in Philadelphia. They urged residents of Boston to ignore the Intolerable Acts, and they voted to boycott all British goods. The delegates agreed to meet in a second Continental Congress in the spring of 1775. However, by that time, fighting had broken out between the colonists and British soldiers.

In April 1775, some British troops from Boston were sent to Concord to search for illegal weapons said to be stored there. At Lexington, they met armed colonists, and the first shots of the American Revolution were fired.

The Declaration of Independence

A month later, in May 1775, the Second Continental Congress met in Philadelphia. Some delegates still hoped to reach a compromise with Britain. The more radical delegates argued for independence. Finally on July 4, 1776, the delegates agreed on a Declaration of Independence that explained the reasons for their separation from Britain.

The Declaration of Independence was drafted largely by Thomas Jefferson, a patriot from Virginia. A scholar, Jefferson was familiar with the ideas of Newton, Locke, and the French philosophes.

Like Locke, Jefferson wrote that people had certain natural rights, including "life, liberty and the pursuit of happiness." Jefferson also argued that government arose from an agreement between the ruler and the ruled. A ruler had power only as long as he or she had the consent of the governed. While people could not overthrow their rulers for minor reasons, the Declaration of Independence stated that Britain had consistently and deliberately oppressed the colonists. Therefore, the colonists had the right to rebel.

An American Victory

The American Revolution lasted from 1776 to 1783. At first, the British appeared to have the military advantage. They had welltrained troops, and their armies occupied the major American cities. The Americans had few trained officers and little military equipment when the war began. Moreover, individual colonies did not always cooperate with one another, and some colonists did not support the revolution.

Yet the Americans enjoyed several important advantages. They were patriots, fighting on their own territory for their families and homes. The British, in contrast, were thousands of kilometres from home, and it took weeks or even months for supplies to arrive from England. Furthermore, although the British held the cities, the colonists could retreat into the countryside and then reappear to ambush the British.

Finally, the Americans found a brilliant military leader in George Washington, a Virginia landowner. Washington was able to unite the colonies in their common cause. At first, Washington suffered defeats, but he learned quickly. He successfully reorganized the colonial forces, which won important victories at Trenton and Princeton in December 1776.

The winter of 1777 to 1778 marked a turning point in the war. Armed with weapons secretly supplied by France, an American army defeated the British at Saratoga in October 1777. This victory convinced France to give the colonies its official support. In February 1778, France recognized the colonies' independence and signed an alliance with them. France then declared war on Britain and sent money and troops to the Americans.

In 1781, with the help of the French navy, Washington captured a British army at Yorktown, Virginia. Although George III wanted to continue the war, Parliament forced him to negotiate a peace treaty that recognized the independence of the United States.

Framing a Constitution

The newly independent nation faced many challenges. It had to form a government that would preserve the liberties the people had just won. Between 1781 and 1789, the United States operated under a constitution called the Articles of Confederation. The Articles created a congress that had limited powers. For example, it could not collect taxes. Most of the political power remained with the individual states.

Washington and other leaders warned that the nation faced great dangers if the states did not cooperate. For example, Britain refused to withdraw its troops from several military posts. In 1787, leaders met in Philadelphia to revise the Articles of Confederation. They soon decided to draft a new constitution. In 1788, after much debate and compromise, the individual states ratified the Constitution of the United States.

Benjamin Franklin: An American in Paris

In September 1776, the Continental Congress named Benjamin Franklin minister to France. His mission was to secure French loans and arms for the revolutionary army. With help from France, the most powerful nation in Europe, the Americans felt sure they could achieve victory in their war against Britain.

In choosing Franklin, the Americans selected a successful diplomat and experienced statesman. Between 1757 and 1775, Franklin had spent almost 18 years in London. During those years, Franklin's reputation for intelligence and humor had spread throughout Europe.

Thus, when the 70-year-old Franklin reached Paris in 1776, he was already well-known. The French had heard about his experiments with electricity, and they knew about his inventions, including bifocal lenses and the Franklin stove. Described by a French noble as "the sage whom two worlds claimed as their own," Franklin received a warm welcome wherever he went.

In the salons of Paris, where people were eager to meet the famous Dr. Franklin, the American negotiator cut an unusual figure. Amid the French, in their curled and powdered wigs, Franklin wore his own hair long and straight under an unfashionable fur cap. He dressed in a plain brown cloth coat, a somber contrast to the colorful silks and satins favored by wealthy Parisians. Yet the French were charmed by his appearance. To them, he was an American frontiersman.

Franklin owed his popularity in Paris as much to his courteous, diplomatic manner as to his style of dress. However, it took more than personality and style to secure French aid. During months of patient negotiations, Franklin urged the French king Louis XVI to make loans to the Americans. Finally, in February 1778, after the battle of Saratoga, Franklin signed the first treaty of alliance between the United States and France.

After the war ended, Franklin remained as the American minister to France until 1785. When Thomas Jefferson arrived to take his place, the French asked, "Is it you, sir, who replaces Dr. Franklin?" Jefferson replied, "No one can replace him. I am only his successor."

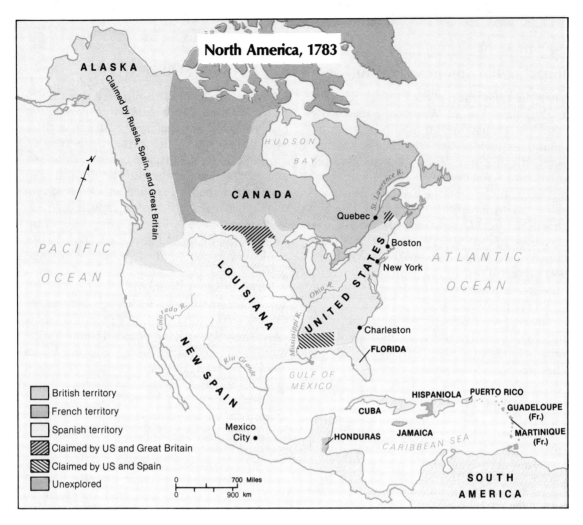

North America, 1783

ALASKA

Claimed by Russia, Spain, and Great Britain

HUDSON BAY

CANADA

St. Lawrence R.

Quebec

PACIFIC OCEAN

ATLANTIC OCEAN

Boston

New York

LOUISIANA

Ohio R.

UNITED STATES

Colorado R.

NEW SPAIN

Mississippi R.

Charleston

FLORIDA

Rio Grande

GULF OF MEXICO

Mexico City

HISPANIOLA PUERTO RICO

CUBA

GUADELOUPE (Fr.)

HONDURAS JAMAICA

MARTINIQUE (Fr.)

CARIBBEAN SEA

SOUTH AMERICA

British territory
French territory
Spanish territory
Claimed by US and Great Britain
Claimed by US and Spain
Unexplored

0   700 Miles
0   900 km

■ *In November 1782, the British and the Americans signed the Treaty of Paris, which ended the American Revolutionary War. The American Congress ratified the treaty in April 1783. According to the treaty, the British recognized the independence of the United States. They also recognized American control of the land from the Atlantic coast to the Mississippi River and from Canada to Florida.*

The men who wrote the Constitution were inspired by the works of Locke and Montesquieu. Both philosophers had suggested that the separation of powers would prevent tyranny in government. The Constitution therefore established three separate branches of government: a legislature, the Congress made up of the House of Representatives and the Senate; an executive, the President; and a judiciary, the system of national courts.

In *The Spirit of Laws*, Montesquieu had proposed that no one branch of government should have more power than the others. Therefore, the framers of the Constitution established a system of checks and balances.

For example, the President was given the power to appoint officials and negotiate treaties, but the Senate had to approve these actions. Before a bill could become law, it had to be passed by both houses of Congress and signed by the President. The Supreme Court had the power to decide if a law was constitutional.

When the Constitution was sent to the states for approval, several states asked for a bill of rights to guarantee the personal liberties of citizens. In 1791, the Bill of Rights was added as the first ten amendments to the Constitution. The Bill of Rights protected such basic rights as freedom of speech, press, and religion.

Impact of the American Revolution

When the states ratified the Constitution, the revolutionary era in America ended. The United States had established itself as an independent, democratic republic that protected the liberties of its citizens. But the American Revolution would have consequences far beyond the United States.

To many people in Europe and other parts of the world, the events in North America symbolized a dramatic struggle for freedom. The colonists had broken away from their powerful British rulers and had created a government that put the ideas of the Enlightenment into practice.

In the years ahead, the Declaration of Independence and the Constitution of the United States would be used as models by other peoples of the world.

SECTION REVIEW

1. Identify: Stamp Act, Boston Tea Party, Intolerable Acts, Thomas Jefferson, George Washington, Articles of Confederation.
2. (a) How did the Navigation Acts help the colonies? (b) What effect did they have on New England merchants who imported molasses from the West Indies?
3. Why did the colonists object to paying taxes to Britain?
4. List three factors that helped the Americans defeat the British.
5. Why did the framers of the Constitution establish a system of checks and balances?

IN PERSPECTIVE

In the early 1600s, the Stuart kings of England clashed repeatedly with Parliament over religious and financial issues as well as over the Stuarts' belief in the divine right of kings. By 1642, the dispute between Charles I and Parliament resulted in the English civil war. Under the Puritan general Oliver Cromwell, Parliamentary forces captured, tried, and executed the king. During the Commonwealth, Cromwell governed England but could not restore unity to a bitterly divided country.

On Cromwell's death, the English restored the monarchy. However, Parliament made the king Charles II accept limits on his power. By 1688, King James II and Parliament were at odds over religion. When James fled from England, Parliament invited William and Mary to take the throne.

After the Seven Years' War, Parliament started taxing its American colonies to help pay for their own defense. The colonists rejected Parliament's authority to tax them and declared their independence from Britain. During a long, hard struggle against Britain, the colonies united to form a republic.

The newly independent United States established a constitution that reflected Enlightenment ideas. The Constitution of the United States soon became a model for other peoples seeking a republican system of government.

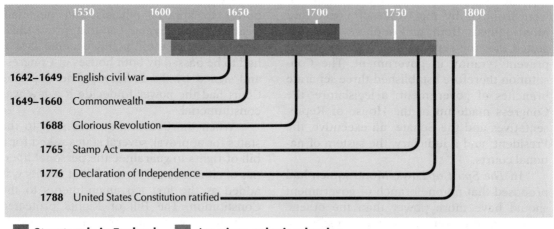

1642–1649	English civil war	
1649–1660	Commonwealth	
1688	Glorious Revolution	
1765	Stamp Act	
1776	Declaration of Independence	
1788	United States Constitution ratified	

■ Stuarts rule in England   ■ American colonies develop

Choose the word or phrase that best completes each of the following statements.

1. Elizabeth I was a popular queen in part because she (a) restored the Catholic Church; (b) kept on good terms with Parliament; (c) reconquered English lands in France.

2. In 1628, Parliament granted money to Charles I only after he signed the (a) Petition of Right; (b) Triennial Act; (c) Test Act.

3. During the Commonwealth, England was a (a) monarchy; (b) republic; (c) democracy.

4. The Habeas Corpus Act protected individual rights by granting (a) freedom of speech; (b) freedom of religion; (c) freedom from unjust arrest.

5. The English Bill of Rights signed in 1688 limited the power of (a) Parliament; (b) the monarchy; (c) the prime minister.

6. The first British prime minister was (a) Lord North; (b) Archbishop Laud; (c) Robert Walpole.

7. The framers of the United States Constitution adopted the idea of checks and balances that had been proposed by (a) Montesquieu; (b) Hobbes; (c) Newton.

8. The Stamp Act angered many American colonists because it (a) limited their trade with other countries; (b) taxed them without their consent; (c) prevented them from moving westward.

6. Describe the role of each of the following in British government during the 1700s: (a) political parties; (b) the cabinet; (c) the prime minister.

7. (a) In what ways were the American colonies relatively free from British control before 1763? (b) Why did British policy toward the colonies change after 1763? (c) How did the colonists react to the change?

8. Describe the Enlightenment ideas included in the Constitution of the United States.

For Further Thought

1. *Expressing an Opinion* In the 1600s, the Stuart rulers in England admired the absolute power of monarchs in France. Yet when they tried to rule as absolute monarchs they failed. In your opinion, why did England become a limited monarchy?

2. *Evaluating* (a) Which English monarchs that you read about in this chapter dealt most successfully with Parliament? Why? (b) Which were least successful? Why? (c) What characteristics do you think would have helped a ruler get along with Parliament?

3. *Applying Information* (a) What ideas about government do you think English settlers brought with them to America? (b) How might these ideas have contributed to the American Revolution?

4. *Relating Past to Present* How do you think the success of the American Revolution might still affect people in the world today?

Chapter Checkup

1. (a) How were the ideas of Hobbes and Locke similar? (b) How were their ideas different? (c) What social and economic changes did the philosophes want?

2. (a) Describe James I's views on the power of monarchs. (b) How did his views contribute to conflict with Parliament?

3. (a) What policies of Charles I angered Parliament? (b) What steps did Parliament take to limit the king's power? (c) How did Charles I respond to the actions of Parliament?

4. (a) What was the outcome of the Engish civil war? (b) Describe English government during the Commonwealth.

5. (a) Describe the political parties that emerged in Parliament during the Restoration. (b) Which party wanted to prevent James II from becoming king? (c) Did it succeed? Explain.

Developing Basic Skills

1. *Ranking* List the events and acts of Parliament that led to the establishment of a limited constitutional monarchy in England. Then rank them according to which you think was most important in limiting the power of the monarch. Explain why you ranked them in that order.

2. *Comparing* Make a chart with three columns and three rows. Label the columns English civil war, Glorious Revolution, and American Revolution. Label the rows Date, Causes, Results. Use what you read in this chapter to complete the chart. Then answer the following questions: (a) How were the causes of each struggle similar? (b) How were they different? (c) How were the results of the Glorious Revolution and the American Revolution similar? (d) How were they different?

See page 203 for suggested readings.

2 The French Revolution and Napoleon

(1789–1815)

The storming of the Bastille on July 14, 1789.

In the early summer of 1789, bread and other foods were scarce all over Paris. Talk of revolution filled the air. At Versailles, representatives of all classes had been meeting since May to find solutions to the economic problems that troubled France. But in Paris, many poor citizens focused their anger toward the government on the Bastille, where they believed hundreds of French citizens had been unjustly imprisoned.

On July 14, 1789, Louis de Flue was expecting trouble. De Flue was an officer in the Swiss guards who protected the Bastille, a huge prison fortress in Paris. By 3:00 P.M. that day, a large mob had surrounded the Bastille, demanding its surrender.

Still, Louis de Flue was not worried. He knew that the Bastille could be defended until reinforcements arrived. But to de Flue's surprise, as the mob grew, the commander of the Bastille, the Marquis de Launay, did not defend the outer drawbridge. Instead, de Launay offered to surrender the fortress if his troops were allowed to leave peacefully. But the crowd replied, "No surrender! Lower the bridge!"

Louis de Flue watched helplessly as the second drawbridge was lowered, and the mob swarmed into the courtyard. Armed with axes, the crowd ran to the prison cells and freed the astonished inmates. The mob found only seven prisoners in the entire fortress.

Louis de Flue was led roughly along the streets of Paris while angry citizens called for his death. "Swords, bayonets, and pistols were being continually pressed against me. . . . I felt that my last moment had come." Fortunately for de Flue, the guards held back the crowd. But de Launay and many others died that night.

To the common people of Paris, the Bastille symbolized the tyranny of the absolute monarchy in France. The fall of the Bastille signaled the central role that the people of Paris would take in the French Revolution. The French Revolution went through many stages and had far-reaching effects, not only on France but on all of Europe.

1 The French Monarchy in Crisis

In 1715, when the Sun King Louis XIV died, France was the richest, most powerful nation in Europe. It remained so throughout the 1700s. The French army was the most powerful in Europe, and its navy was rivaled only by that of Britain. French philosophers led the Enlightenment, and people across Europe followed French fashions in clothes, art, and even cooking.

At the same time, France suffered from a growing economic crisis that would eventually shake the foundations of the French monarchy. Attempts to solve the economic problems of the country were hampered by the traditional political and social system of France, which historians call the Old Regime.

Structure of the Old Regime

Under the Old Regime, the monarch had absolute power. Louis XIV had centralized power in the royal *bureaucracy*, the government departments which administered his policies. Louis's successors lacked his abilities to govern. Nevertheless, they worked to preserve royal authority and maintained the rigid social structure of the Old Regime.

The people of France were divided by law into three estates or classes: clergy, nobility, and commoners. The first two estates enjoyed many privileges. In general, they opposed any reforms that would threaten their privileges. The Third Estate, however, had many grievances against the Old Regime.

The First and Second Estates. The First Estate included the higher clergy, who were nobles, as well as the parish priests, who were commoners. Some of the higher clergy lived in luxury at Versailles or in Paris. Parish priests usually lived a simple, hardworking life. Many of them criticized social injustices in France and resented the privileges enjoyed by the higher clergy.

The clergy administered the church, ran schools, kept birth and death records, and cared for the poor. To support these activities, the clergy collected the tithe, a tax on income. The church owned vast amounts of land and other property on which it paid no taxes.

The Second Estate, or nobility, made up less than 2 percent of the French population. Many nobles enjoyed great wealth and privileges. Only nobles could become officers in the army or fill high offices of the church. In addition, nobles were exempt from most taxes.

Not all French nobles were wealthy. Some lived in near poverty in the country. However, they firmly defended their traditional privileges. When rising prices reduced their income, they made peasants on their estates pay long forgotten feudal dues.

After Louis XIV's death, French nobles tried to regain the political power they had lost during his reign. Leading the effort were the wealthy and influential "nobles of the robe," who had received noble status for their service to the royal government. Many were judges in the parlements, or high courts. The parlements had to register, or approve, the monarch's orders in order for these orders to become laws. Nobles of the robe sometimes exercised this power and refused to approve the monarch's orders if the orders limited their power.

The Third Estate. The vast majority of French people were commoners belonging to the Third Estate. The Third Estate included the *bourgeoisie*, or middle class, peasants, and city workers.

The bourgeoisie was small in numbers, but it was the wealthiest, most outspoken group within the Third Estate. The bourgeoisie included successful merchants and manufacturers, educated lawyers and doctors, as well as small storekeepers and *artisans*. They resented the privileges enjoyed by nobles. Many criticized the Old Regime because they believed in the Enlightenment ideas of equality and social justice. The bourgeoisie called for extensive reform of the tax system because the Third Estate carried the burden of paying most taxes.

Peasants made up the largest group within the Third Estate. In general, French peasants were better off than peasants in other parts of Europe. *Serfdom* had largely disappeared in France, although French peasants still paid many feudal dues dating back to the Middle Ages. French peasants also had to perform unpaid services for their landlords and the monarch. For example, if peasants lived near a royal road, they had to spend as much as a month every year repairing the road.

Peasants were burdened by heavy taxes, the tithe to the church, and rents to their landlords. The privileges of nobles further added to the peasants' troubles. For example, only nobles could hunt. Peasants were forbidden to kill rabbits and birds that ate their crops. Nobles also damaged crops by galloping across fields during a hunt.

■ These graphs clearly show the unequal distribution of land in France. Moreover, within the Third Estate, a small number of bourgeoisie owned much of the land. Thus, peasants ended up with only 45 percent of the land. Both peasants and bourgeoisie resented paying taxes while the First and Second Estates paid none.

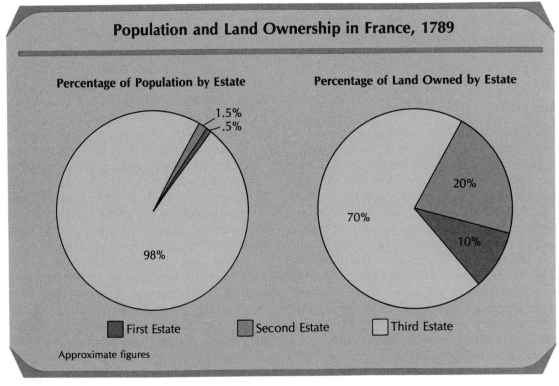

Population and Land Ownership in France, 1789

Percentage of Population by Estate

1.5%
.5%
98%

Percentage of Land Owned by Estate

20%
70%
10%

■ First Estate   ■ Second Estate   □ Third Estate

Approximate figures

24

Source: Alfred Cobban, *A History of Modern France*, Vol. 1.

Another group within the Third Estate was city workers. In the towns and cities of France, thousands of men and women earned wages as servants, apprentices, and day laborers. Workers suffered when inflation hit because food prices rose faster than their wages. Like the bourgeoisie and peasants, city workers resented the privileges enjoyed by the First and Second Estates.

The Growing Economic Crisis

During much of the 1700s, the French economy prospered. The population grew from about 18 million people in 1715 to about 25 million in 1789. Farmers produced food surpluses that fed the growing population and supported economic expansion. Mercantilist policies helped manufacturers in the textile and mining industries.

In the 1770s, however, economic activity slowed. Poor harvests hurt the economy. In addition, regulations surviving from the *Middle Ages* hampered any further expansion of trade and manufacturing. For example, a merchant who shipped a wagonload of wine from the upper Loire Valley to Paris had to pay 11 separate customs duties and 12 different tolls. Furthermore, *guilds* still had *monopolies* over the production of certain goods. As a result, *entrepreneurs* could not set up their own businesses.

However, the most serious economic problem facing the French government during the 1770s and 1780s was the huge debt it owed to bankers. The government had borrowed large amounts of money to pay for the wars of Louis XIV. Louis XV and Louis XVI continued to borrow money to support the court at Versailles and to fight wars to maintain French power in Europe and overseas. French support of the American Revolution alone nearly doubled the government's debt.

Attempts at Reform

When Louis XVI came to the throne in 1774, he recognized the need for economic reform. But Louis was not a very determined

This cartoon illustrates some of the burdens of the Third Estate. The clergyman and nobleman represent the First and Second Estates. They are riding on the back of an aged peasant, representing the Third Estate.

or able ruler. He preferred to spend his days hunting or tinkering with puzzles rather than coping with economic problems. Moreover, Louis lacked the strength of will to back his ministers when they pressed for reforms.

Louis's first finance minister, Robert Turgot (ter GOH), eased the financial crisis for a time by controlling government spending and reducing expenses at Versailles. He also removed some internal customs duties on food and tried to limit the power of the guilds. But he had little success when he proposed a major reform—taxing the nobles.

The king could not tax the nobles unless the parlements approved new tax laws. But these law courts were controlled by the nobles of the robe, and they stubbornly rejected Turgot's suggestion that they should be taxed. As one noble said, "All public financial burdens should be borne by the lower classes."

When Turgot came under attack, the king dismissed him. As he left office in 1776, Turgot ominously warned the king, "Remember, sire, that it was weakness which brought the head of Charles I to the block."

For a time, the government limped along on new bank loans. Then, in 1786, as the government debts mounted, bankers refused to lend more money to the French treasury. In 1787 and 1788, poor harvests caused bread shortages all over France. The economic situation worsened, and Louis XVI went before the Parlement of Paris to try to make it register a new tax law. "Sire, this is illegal!" one member exclaimed. "It is legal," countered Louis XVI, "because I wish it!" But even royal wishes could not prevail.

The desperate economic crisis and the opposition of the privileged classes to any reform convinced the king to take a bold action. In the fall of 1788, he summoned the Estates General to meet the following May. The Estates General was an assembly that represented the three estates in France.

SECTION REVIEW

1. Identify: Old Regime, Robert Turgot.
2. (a) What groups made up each of the three estates in France? (b) What privileges did the First and Second Estates enjoy?
3. List three factors that contributed to the French economic crisis of the 1770s and 1780s.
4. (a) What major reform did Turgot recommend? (b) Was he able to make the reform? Why or why not?

2 A Moderate Start to the Revolution

When Louis XVI summoned the Estates General, he hoped to win support for reforms that would restore economic stability. The Estates General had not met since 1614, and no one could predict what would happen when deputies representing the three estates met at Versailles.

From Estates General to National Assembly

Each estate elected its own deputies to the Estates General. Within the Third Estate, almost all adult men had the right to vote for representatives to local assemblies. These assemblies, in turn, elected the Third Estate's deputies to the Estates General. A similar procedure was followed by the First and Second Estates.

When the Estates General met in May 1789, deputies from the Third Estate demanded that the three estates meet together, with each deputy having an equal vote. In the past, the three estates had met separately. Each estate voted as a group and had one vote. That way the First and Second Estates could outvote the Third Estate two to one. Deputies from the Third Estate hoped that if the estates met together and deputies voted individually, sympathizers among the clergy and nobles would give the Third Estate a majority.

When the king insisted that the estates meet separately, the Third Estate took matters into its own hands. On June 17, deputies from the Third Estate declared themselves the National Assembly and claimed the right to write a constitution for France. Louis XVI promptly banished the rebellious deputies from their meeting hall.

Joined by many of the lower clergy and some reform-minded nobles, delegates of the Third Estate gathered at a nearby tennis court. There, they swore an oath, known as the Tennis Court Oath, promising not to disband until they had written a constitution. Louis XVI hesitated, but then he ordered the other two estates to join the Third Estate in the National Assembly. The Third Estate had taken a peaceful first step in a revolution that would eventually transform France.

Although the three estates met as one body, there were deep divisions among the estates and within each one. Many clergy and nobles sought to protect their privileges. However, some nobles and lower clergy, along with many commoners, wanted to establish a limited, constitutional monarchy like the one in Britain. A few radical reformers demanded equality for all classes

The leading artist of the French Revolution, Jacques Louis David, painted this work, The Tennis Court Oath. *The actual scene was even more chaotic. Members of the Third Estate along with some clergy and nobles pledged "never to separate but to meet in any place that circumstances may require, until the constitution of the kingdom is established on firm foundations."*

before the law. They wanted to abolish titles of nobility and all feudal obligations. They distrusted the king and opposed any constitution that would leave him with significant powers.

Popular Uprisings

The National Assembly had scarcely begun work on a constitution in July 1789 when the people of Paris and peasants in the countryside took the French Revolution along a new, more radical course. Peasants and workers had expected quick relief from taxes and poverty when the Estates General met. But little had happened. Instead, they still faced inflation, unemployment, and food shortages. Reports that the king was concentrating troops around Paris added to unrest in the capital.

When Louis brought troops to Versailles, many citizens feared that he planned to dissolve the National Assembly and crush the revolution. In reaction, on July 14, 1789, a Paris crowd stormed the Bastille, as you read at the beginning of the chapter. They saw the attack on the Bastille as an attack on the injustice and inequality of the Old Regime. (Today, the French celebrate July 14 as their national holiday.)

Disturbances soon broke out in the countryside. During the summer of 1789, peasants were caught up in what was called the "Great Fear." Rumors passed from village to village that brigands, or robbers, were destroying crops and homes all over France. Peasants took up arms to defend themselves.

When no brigands appeared, the frightened peasants turned on their landlords. They raided grain storehouses, destroyed tax records, and swore never again to pay ancient feudal dues. Like the people of Paris, the peasants were conducting their own revolution against the Old Regime.

Reforms of the National Assembly

The events in Paris and the countryside forced the National Assembly into action. During a long session on the night of August 4, many delegates rose to make impassioned speeches in support of reform. One noble urged that nobles be taxed. Another proposed that nobles give up their hunting rights. The clergy promised to end its tithes.

By the end of the evening, the Assembly had abolished most feudal customs. It ended serfdom and the tax exempt privileges of the nobles. It also made all male citizens eligible for government and church positions. "Just like our Frenchmen," commented the Comte de Mirabeau, a moderate leader. "They spend an entire month wrangling over syllables, and in a night overturn the whole of the ancient order of the kingdom!"

Before the end of August, the National Assembly adopted the Declaration of the Rights of Man. (See below.) The Declaration stated the democratic principles that would be the basis for French government. It called for equality for all citizens under the law and protection of personal property. However, the task of turning these ideals into a constitution remained.

While lawyers debated the wording of a constitution, angry Paris crowds rioted, forcing the National Assembly to take note of their demands. Many rioters were middle class shopkeepers and artisans.

The march on Versailles. In October 1789, a Paris crowd led by thousands of women marched in the rain to Versailles. The women were angry about high food prices. They also suspected that the king and the queen, Marie Antoinette, were plotting against the National Assembly. They demanded that Louis XVI and his family return with them to Paris, where they could watch over the king's activities. To prevent violence, the king agreed.

The return to Paris presented a striking scene. The king rode on horseback, escorted by a cheering crowd. He wore the tricolor, the red, white, and blue ribbon that the revolutionaries had adopted as their symbol. By forcing the king to wear the tricolor, the people proved that they were directing events in France. A few days later, the National Assembly also moved to Paris and resumed its work under the watchful eye of revolutionaries in the capital.

Religious reforms. All over France, the revolution swept away ancient customs and privileges. The National Assembly declared freedom of worship and abolished the special privileges of the Catholic Church. In 1790, it passed the Civil Constitution of the Clergy, which gave the French government control of the church and allowed citizens to elect bishops and priests. To raise badly needed money, the government began selling church lands. This action caused many Catholics who had supported the revolution up to this point to condemn it.

The Declaration of the Rights of Man

On August 26, 1789, the National Assembly adopted the Declaration of the Rights of Man. The Declaration echoed many ideas of the philosophes. It also showed the influence of the English Bill of Rights and the American Declaration of Independence. The Declaration of the Rights of Man was translated into many languages, so it broadcast the principles of the French Revolution across Europe.

From the *Declaration*

The representatives of the French people, organized as a national assembly, believing that the ignorance, neglect or contempt of the rights of man are the sole causes of public misfortunes and the corruption of governments, have determined to set forth in a solemn declaration, the natural, inalienable and sacred rights of man....

The aim of all political association is the preservation of the natural ... rights of man.

These rights are liberty, property, security, and resistance to oppression.

Liberty consists of being able to do everything which injures no one else....

Law can only prohibit such actions as are hurtful to society....

Law is the expression of the general will. Every citizen has a right to participate personally or through his representative in its formation....

No person shall be accused, arrested or imprisoned except in the cases and according to the forms prescribed by law....

As all persons are held innocent until they shall have been declared guilty....

The free communication of ideas and opinions is one of the most precious of the rights of man. Every citizen may, accordingly, speak, write and print with freedom, being responsible, however, for such abuses of this freedom as shall be defined by law.

Women played a major role in the French Revolution. This picture shows the women's march on Versailles. On October 5, 1789, a rumor that the king had worn the white symbol of his family, the Bourbons, rather than the revolutionary tricolor sent Parisian women hurrying to Versailles. Faced with the crowd of angry women, Louis XVI agreed to accompany them back to Paris.

The Constitution of 1791. In 1791, the National Assembly finally gave France its first constitution. The Constitution of 1791 made France a limited monarchy and established a system of separation of powers. At the head of the executive branch was the monarch. A legislature made the laws. The monarch could veto laws, but the legislature could override the monarch's veto. A new system of courts was set up as the judicial branch. The constitution also divided France into 83 departments, or regions, and replaced the old provincial governments with locally elected officials.

Under the constitution, the old distinctions between clergy, nobles, and commoners disappeared. "The feudal system is forever abolished in France," it declared. The constitution guaranteed equal rights under the law to all citizens.

Responses to the First Stage of the Revolution

Few people were satisfied with the new constitutional monarchy. Radical revolutionaries wanted a republic rather than a monarchy. For many nobles, the Constitution of 1791 went too far. Frightened by angry crowds in Paris and in the countryside, a growing number of nobles fled France. These *émigrés*, or political exiles, urged European rulers to oppose the revolutionaries in France.

Louis XVI grew increasingly alarmed at the actions of the National Assembly. He sought outside help, and Marie Antoinette appealed to her brother, the emperor of Austria, for support. In June 1791, the royal family decided to flee the country. When they fled toward the border, however, the king was recognized. The National Assembly sent officers to arrest the royal family and bring them back to the capital. A virtual prisoner of the Assembly, the king reluctantly accepted the new constitution in September.

In October 1791, the Legislative Assembly, elected under the new constitution, met for the first time. The seating arrangements in the Assembly reflected divisions among the revolutionaries. Moderate revolutionaries sat on the right side of the meeting hall, and radical revolutionaries sat on the left side.*

---

* The seating arrangement in the Assembly led to the use of "right" and "left" to describe political views. The right came to refer to people who wanted to preserve tradition. The left came to refer to people who supported far-reaching changes. People with views between the right and left were called the center.

The king's attempt to flee the country had deepened the divisions among the revolutionaries. Moderates were embarrassed by the king's attempted flight, but they wanted to preserve the constitutional monarchy. Radicals claimed that the king could not be trusted. They demanded the establishment of a republic.

However, the radicals themselves were further split. The most radical group, the Jacobins, demanded a true democracy in which all male citizens had the right to vote. As the French Revolution unfolded, the Jacobins and their leader, Maximilien Robespierre (ROHBS pyehr), would gain the upper hand.

SECTION REVIEW

1. Identify: Tennis Court Oath, National Assembly, Declaration of the Rights of Man, Civil Constitution of the Clergy.
2. Define: émigré.
3. Why did the Third Estate want the Estates General to meet as a single body?
4. (a) What conditions led to unrest among workers and peasants in the summer of 1789? (b) How did the National Assembly react to that unrest?
5. How did many French Catholics respond to the Civil Constitution of the Clergy?
6. What two groups were dissatisfied with the Constitution of 1791? Why?

3 The Revolution Deepens

Revolutionary ideas spread from France to other parts of Europe. Faced with unrest at home and abroad, European monarchs felt they had to take steps to turn back the tide of revolution. French émigrés urged Austria and Prussia to invade France and restore Louis XVI to full power. At the same time, many revolutionary leaders in France wanted war because they thought it would unite the people in defense of their homeland.

France at War

France declared war on Austria in April 1792. At first, the war went badly for France. French armies were disorganized and poorly led. Many army officers, who were nobles, had left France. Revolutionary ideas also caused some problems. For example, in the heat of battle, one regiment demanded to vote on whether or not to attack the enemy.

By August 1792, Austrian and Prussian armies were advancing on Paris. The Prussian commander, the Duke of Brunswick, issued a declaration, known as the Brunswick Manifesto. He warned that if Paris did not surrender peacefully Austrian and Prussian troops would burn the city and put its leaders to the "tortures which they have deserved."

Far from being frightened by the duke's message, the people of Paris angrily declared that no émigrés or foreign troops would crush the revolution. All over France, people rallied to defend the revolution and chanted the slogan: "Liberty, Equality, and Fraternity." Soldiers from Marseille hurried to Paris singing a patriotic marching song, the "Marseillaise," which was adopted as the national anthem of France. In September, the French defeated the Duke of Brunswick at Valmy. In the months that followed, revolutionary armies forced the invaders to retreat from France.

The war against Austria and Prussia caused high prices and desperate food shortages in France. Even while foreign troops threatened Paris, angry Parisians and sympathetic troops from the provinces joined in an uprising that has been called the second French Revolution.

Early in the morning of August 10, revolutionaries took over the Paris city government and established a new administration, the Commune. A large force of revolutionary troops marched on the Tuileries (TWEE ler eez), where the king and his family lived. The troops attacked the palace, killing many of the king's Swiss guards.

The king and queen fled to the Legislative Assembly, hoping for protection. But the radicals also seized control of the Assembly. They removed the king from office and voted to imprison the royal family. They then called for a national convention to write a new constitution.

The National Convention

The elections for delegates to the National Convention took place in a tense atmosphere. Austrian and Prussian troops were not far from Paris. In early September, mobs of poor working people roamed the streets of the capital, killing anyone they suspected of being an enemy of France. The Convention delegates elected in such an atmosphere were far more radical than the population in general.

The National Convention met in late September. As its first act, the Convention voted to abolish the monarchy and make France a republic. The Convention then had to decide what to do with the king. The radical Jacobins demanded that Louis be tried for treason. More moderate revolutionaries thought he should be imprisoned until the war ended.

In November, the Convention discovered a trunk containing letters written by the king. The letters showed that Louis was plotting with émigrés to crush the revolution. The damaging evidence sealed the king's fate. The Convention tried and convicted Louis XVI of treason. By a majority of one vote, the delegates sentenced him to death. On January 21, 1793, Louis mounted the steps of the guillotine. "People, I die innocent!" were the king's last words to the watching crowd. (See page 32.)

Attacks on the Revolution

News of Louis XVI's execution sent waves of shock and horror through the capitals of Europe. Monarchs had every reason to fear the spread of the revolution. By 1793, French armies seemed to be fighting effectively. They had captured the Austrian Netherlands and were threatening the Dutch Netherlands and Prussia. Moreover, the National Convention issued a proclamation promising to aid "all peoples wishing to recover their liberty."

In March 1793, Great Britain, the Dutch Netherlands, and Spain joined Prussia and Austria in the war against France. With five nations fighting them, the French were hard pressed. The Prussians and Dutch pushed the French back across the Rhine. Spain sent troops into southern France, and British forces captured the port of Toulon.

Trouble at home also threatened the revolution. The war caused starvation and

■ The armies of revolutionary France had expanded French territory by 1793, as you can see on this map. In 1793, however, five European nations banded together to fight the French. At the same time, the revolutionary government had to contend with uprisings in the province of Vendée and in several cities, including Marseille.

The Execution of Louis XVI: Analyzing Conflicting Sources

Primary sources are first-hand, or original, accounts of the experiences of people who were involved in an event, or who lived in a particular society. They provide useful information about historical events or developments. However, primary sources, such as eyewitness accounts and official documents, can give conflicting views of an event or development.

Two descriptions of the execution of Louis XVI follow. The first is an official announcement published by the National Convention on January 23, 1793. The second is a letter written on January 23 by a noble living in Paris to a friend in England. Read both sources. Then use the following steps to analyze their value as historical sources.

1. **Read the sources to find out what information is given.** Answer the following questions about each of the sources: (a) What does each source say about the attitude of the French people toward the king's execution? (b) What does each source say about conditions in France in 1793? (c) According to each source, what was the outcome of the king's execution?

2. **Compare the two sources.** Answer the following questions: (a) Do the sources agree on any points about the execution of Louis XVI? Explain. (b) On what points do the sources disagree?

3. **Evaluate the reliability of each source.** Answer the following questions to see if the writer is presenting a complete, accurate picture: (a) How might the fact that the National Convention voted for Louis XVI's execution affect its proclamation? (b) How might the noble's background affect his view of the king's execution? (c) Which source do you think is more reliable? Why?

4. **Use the sources to draw conclusions about a historical event or development.** (a) Based on the sources and what you read in this chapter, what conclusions would you draw about reaction to the execution of Louis XVI? (b) How do the differences between the sources reflect divisions in France during the revolution?

Proclamation of the National Convention

Citizens, the tyrant is no more. For a long time, the cries of the victims, whom war and domestic discord have spread over France and Europe, loudly protested his existence. He has paid his penalty, and only approval for the Republic and for liberty have been heard from the people.

We have had to combat deep-seated prejudices, and the superstition of centuries concerning monarchy. Uncertainties and disturbances always accompany great changes and revolutions as profound as ours. . . . [But] respect for liberty of opinion must cause these disturbances to be forgotten; only the good which they have produced through the death of the tyrant and of tyranny now remains . . . The National Convention and the French people are now to have only one mind, only one sentiment, that of liberty and fraternity.

Now above all we need peace in the Republic, and the most active surveillance of the domestic enemies of liberty. . . . Let us unite to avert the shame that domestic discord [civil war], would bring upon our newborn republic.

A Noble's Report on the Death of the King

Monsieur . . . the frightful event of the 21st has spread dismay everywhere, and it is worth noting that even the most zealous supporters of the revolution found this measure both excessive and dangerous. It will not save us from the untold ills which threaten us, the reality and length of which are now all the more sure. We must make up our minds to sacrifice peace, security, and fortune . . . I very much fear that civil war will come as a finishing touch to the horrible crimes and all the misfortunes which now assail us. I doubt, moreover, whether this crime, added to so many others, has the universal approval of France. Even if we thought that the king were guilty, we would not wish for his death, especially after he has endured such a long and sorrowful captivity . . . Meanwhile, prudence must silence criticism because under the empire of secret accusations, of inquisition, or even more, of tyranny, it is dangerous to speak one's thoughts.

economic hardships. In many parts of France, people felt the revolution had gone too far. Counterrevolutionaries, people who oppose revolution, led uprisings in the region of the Vendée and in the cities of Marseille, Bordeaux, and Lyon.

The Reign of Terror

In the face of domestic and foreign threats, the National Convention took drastic action. It set aside a constitution that had been approved in 1793 and created a Committee of Public Safety. The Committee of Public Safety had almost dictatorial powers. It waged a brutal campaign against people it considered enemies of France. This campaign, known as the Reign of Terror, lasted from July 1793 to July 1794.

Maximilien Robespierre led the Committee of Public Safety during the Reign of Terror. He was determined to create a "Republic of Virtue," in which "our country assures the welfare of each individual and where each individual enjoys with pride the prosperity and the glory of our country . . ."

Robespierre was utterly honest and dedicated to his ideals, but he was also inflexible and narrowminded. He believed the state must be ruthless against its enemies.

The Committee of Public Safety sent agents across France to help local revolutionary committees uncover traitors. A Law of Suspects declared that people suspected of being counterrevolutionaries could be arrested for "their conduct, their relations, their remarks, or their writings." Such a vague law allowed revolutionary courts to imprison and condemn citizens on very little evidence.

During the Reign of Terror, trials were held almost daily throughout France. Between 20,000 and 40,000 men, women, and children were condemned to the guillotine. The former queen, Marie Antoinette, was one victim. Many nobles and clergy also went to the guillotine. But most victims were commoners, including peasants, laborers, shopkeepers, and merchants. The ruthlessness of the Terror had its effect, and the revolts subsided.

The Committee of Public Safety dealt with the threat of foreign invasion by organizing the nation for war. New French armies were raised, drilled, and equipped. A national draft law made every French man, whatever his age or occupation, eligible to be drafted into the army.

The Committee set strict limits on prices and wages, rationed food, and outlawed the use of scarce white flour. Citizens were asked to use whole wheat flour to make "equality bread."

By the spring of 1794, the total national effort had paid off. French forces were again victorious on the battlefield. However, even supporters of the revolution were beginning to question the need for constant executions at home. In July 1794, the National Convention ordered Robespierre's arrest. He was quickly tried and executed. With his death, the Reign of Terror ended.

This sketch shows a dignified Marie Antoinette on her way to the guillotine. Before the Revolution, the queen had been known for her beauty and grace. To many, however, she symbolized the extravagance of the French court and its indifference to the needs of the people. During the Reign of Terror, she was accused of plotting with Austria against France. She was executed in October 1793.

Impact of the Revolution on Daily Life

Between 1789 and 1794, French life had been transformed. The monarchy was gone, and the king was dead. French society had become more democratic. In place of the privileged estates of the Old Regime, the revolution had declared equality of all people. The National Convention had abolished all remaining feudal dues and customs and ended slavery in the French colonies. In addition, it had confiscated the land of émigrés.

Styles in fashion and art changed. Among the wealthy, simple dresses and long trousers replaced the elaborate gowns and knee breeches of the Old Regime. Playwrights and painters produced patriotic works that supported the revolution.

Revolutionary leaders established a uniform system of weights and measures, known as the metric system. They also called for free public schools so all citizens could receive an education. However, the schools were never set up.

After Robespierre's death in July 1794, a tide of reaction swept across France. The radical phase of the revolution had ended.

SECTION REVIEW

1. Locate: Vendée, Marseille, Bordeaux, Lyon.
2. Identify: Brunswick Manifesto, Committee of Public Safety, Robespierre, Republic of Virtue.
3. What two nations invaded France in 1792?
4. What were the National Convention's first actions in September 1792?
5. What events and developments increased the fear of revolution among European monarchs early in 1793?
6. Why did the Committee of Public Safety begin the Reign of Terror?
7. Describe three ways in which the revolution affected daily life.

4 The Rise of Napoleon Bonaparte

During the summer of 1794, the people of France reacted against the excesses of the Reign of Terror. They hunted down and executed many leaders of the Terror. In 1795, the National Convention wrote yet another constitution that reflected the more conservative mood of the country.

The Directory

The Constitution of 1795 established a new government known as the Directory. The Directory included an elected legislature and an executive branch with five directors. The Constitution restricted the right to vote to men who could read and who owned a certain amount of property. As a result, the middle class and wealthy landowners gained influence in the new government.

The Directory, which lasted from 1795 to 1799, faced many problems. The five-man executive did not function efficiently, and corrupt deputies in the legislature bargained for political favors. Furthermore, when the government removed the controls on prices imposed during the Terror, prices rose sharply. As bread prices rose, poor workers rioted in the streets of Paris.

Despite economic problems and widespread discontent, the Directory pursued an aggressive foreign policy. During the revolution, France had built the largest army in Europe. French soldiers continued to fight for "liberty, equality, and fraternity." The military successes of one young officer, Napoleon Bonaparte, won the admiration and attention of the French public.

"I am no ordinary man."

Born on the island of Corsica in 1769, Napoleon Bonaparte was the son of a minor noble family. He trained to become an army officer at a French military academy. Napoleon rose quickly in the army during the revolution because so many officers fled France.

In 1793, Napoleon commanded the French troops that ousted the British from Toulon. Two years later, he broke up a Paris mob by ordering his troops to fire a "whiff of grapeshot," small pellets shot from cannons. This action brought Napoleon to the attention of the Directory. His marriage to Joséphine de Beauharnais (boh ahr NEH) also helped him because his wife had influential friends among the directors. By age 27, Napoleon was a general.

The young general soon received command of a French army for an invasion of Italy. He won several brilliant victories over the Austrians who ruled northern Italy. Napoleon's successes forced Austria to withdraw from the war in 1797 and left Britain the only country still fighting France.

In 1798, Napoleon invaded Egypt because it was a vital lifeline to British outposts in India. Napoleon quickly defeated the Egyptian army.* However, he suffered a disastrous setback at sea. The British fleet, under Admiral Horatio Nelson, destroyed the French fleet in the battle of the Nile. The loss of their fleet meant the French could not supply their troops in Egypt or take them home.

Leaving the army in Egypt, Napoleon returned to Paris. The French people were not fully aware of the losses in Egypt, and they welcomed him as a hero.

In Paris, Napoleon found that many people were dissatisfied with the Directory. With the help of troops loyal to him, he and two directors overthrew the government in 1799. They drew up another constitution, the fourth since the revolution had begun. Under the new government, Napoleon was named First Consul.

"I am no ordinary man," Napoleon once boasted. He certainly was a person who could command the attention of friends as well as enemies, and he was admired by soldiers all over Europe. Napoleon had a sharp mind. He quickly sized up a situation and decided on a course of action. He thought and spoke so fast that he could dictate let-

---

* Napoleon asked French archaeologists and scientists to study the ancient monuments of Egypt. Among their discoveries was the Rosetta Stone, which held the clue to Egyptian *hieroglyphics*.

Major Events of the French Revolution, 1789-1799	
1789	Estates General meets; Tennis Court Oath; fall of the Bastille; Declaration of the Rights of Man
1790	Civil Constitution of the Clergy
1791	Royal family tries to leave France; Louis XVI accepts the Constitution of 1791; Legislative Assembly meets
1792	France declares war on Austria; Brunswick Manifesto issued; royal family imprisoned; National Convention meets
1793	Louis XVI executed; European allies invade France; Reign of Terror begins
1794	Robespierre executed; Reign of Terror ends
1795	Directory established
1799	Napoleon overthrows the Directory

ters to four secretaries on four separate topics, all at the same time. Personal qualities and military talent helped Napoleon win widespread popular support. At age 30, Napoleon was the virtual dictator of France.

Napoleon's Domestic Policy

Between 1799 and 1804, Napoleon centralized power in his own hands. In 1802, he had himself made First Consul for life. A plebiscite, or popular vote, overwhelmingly approved this move. Two years later, Napoleon Bonaparte proclaimed himself "Emperor of the French." Once again, the majority of French voters endorsed his actions.

By 1804, Napoleon had gained almost absolute power. He knew the French would never stand for a return to the Old Regime. Therefore, he continued many reforms of the revolution. But at the same time, he kept firm personal control of the government. For

In 1804, Napoleon became "Emperor of the French." Jacques Louis David painted this picture of Napoleon's coronation. Pope Pius VII officiated at the ceremony, which took place in the Cathedral of Notre Dame. As the pope prepared to crown the emperor, Napoleon took the crown and placed it on his head himself. By this gesture, Napoleon showed that he did not bow to any authority.

example, he kept the system of dividing France into departments. But, he appointed local officials to replace the elected councils that had ruled during the revolution. He also allowed many émigrés to return home, but they had to agree not to demand the privileges they had enjoyed before the revolution.

The Napoleonic Code. Napoleon's greatest achievement in government was the Napoleonic Code, which has influenced French law to the present. This law code brought together many reforms of the revolution into a single, unified legal system. It recognized that all men were equal before the law and guaranteed freedom of religion as well as a person's right to work in any occupation.

The code did not always preserve the ideals of the revolution, however. It put the interests of the state above those of individual citizens. In addition, it dropped laws passed during the revolution that had protected the rights of women and children. The Napoleonic Code reflected ancient Roman law and made the man absolute head of the household with control over all family property.

Other reforms. To strengthen the French economy, Napoleon enforced a law requiring all citizens to pay taxes. He also created the national Bank of France, in which the tax money was deposited. The bank, in turn, issued paper money and made loans to businesses. Napoleon's economic policies gradually brought inflation under control.

To fill the need for educated, loyal government officials, Napoleon set up *lycées* (lee SAYZ), government-run schools. The lycées encouraged extreme patriotism, and the same courses were taught at each school. Usually, only the children of wealthy parents attended the lycées because of the tuition costs. However, some students received scholarships. Thus, the lycées represented a first step toward a system of public education—a long-standing goal of Enlightenment thinkers and the French revolutionary leaders.

In dealing with religion, Napoleon shrewdly combined reform and tradition. He realized that most French people were strongly Roman Catholic and despised the

Civil Constitution of the Clergy. (See page 28.) In the Concordat of 1801, an agreement between the French government and the pope, Napoleon ended the election of bishops. Under this agreement, the French government appointed Catholic bishops and paid the clergy, but the pope had authority over them. The Concordat also stated that the Catholic Church would not demand the return of church property seized during the revolution. Thus, Napoleon did not lose the support of people who had acquired church lands.

SECTION REVIEW

1. Identify: Horatio Nelson, Concordat of 1801.
2. Define: lycée.
3. What problems did the Directory face?
4. Describe the results of each of the following: (a) Napoleon's invasion of Italy; (b) Napoleon's invasion of Egypt.
5. (a) Give one example of how the Napoleonic Code reflected the ideas of the French Revolution. (b) Give one example of how it reflected older traditions.

5 Napoleon in Triumph and Defeat

Between 1792 and 1815, France was almost constantly at war. At first, French armies fought defensively to keep a coalition of European monarchs from crushing the revolution. Then, under Napoleon, France fought several wars of conquest. Napoleon created an empire that spanned the continent of Europe.

The Empire of Napoleon

In the early 1800s, France fought all the major European powers, including Austria, Prussia, Britain, and Russia. A skilled military leader, Napoleon moved his troops rapidly and in unexpected ways. For example, in 1805, he massed his troops against the Austrian army at Ulm. The Austrians expected Napoleon to attack head-on, but in a surprise move, French troops attacked the Austrians from the rear, cutting off any retreat. A few months later, Napoleon defeated Austria and Russia at Austerlitz. Both countries then made peace on Napoleon's terms.

Through shrewd diplomacy, Napoleon usually kept the European powers divided so they could not unite against him. Thus, he managed to keep Prussia neutral during his war with Austria and Russia. But Napoleon's victories made the Prussians fearful of French power. They became even more anxious when Napoleon dissolved the Holy Roman Empire and reorganized the German states into the Confederation of the Rhine.

Finally, in 1806, Prussia declared war on France. Napoleon easily overpowered the poorly led Prussian army and occupied Berlin.

Europe under French rule. From 1807 to 1812, Napoleon was at the height of his power. He controlled an empire that stretched from France to the borders of Russia. (See the map on page 38.) He governed France and the Netherlands directly as emperor. Other nations, such as Spain, Italy, and the Confederation of the Rhine, were satellite states—that is, their rulers followed Napoleon's policies. In Spain, Napoleon made his brother, Joseph, king. In addition, he tied Austria and Prussia to France as allies.

While ruling this vast empire, Napoleon helped spread the ideas of the French Revolution across Europe. Throughout the empire, Napoleon introduced religious toleration, abolished serfdom, and reduced the power of the Catholic Church. He also made the Napoleonic Code the basis of law in many countries.

At first, some people welcomed the French emperor as a liberator. However, Napoleon lost much support when he imposed high taxes to finance his continuing conflict with Britain.

The Continental System. Although Napoleon defeated the major powers on the continent, he was unable to bring Britain to its knees. In 1805, he readied a fleet to invade Britain. But Admiral Nelson dashed Napoleon's plans by sinking most of the French fleet at Cape Trafalgar, near Spain. Napoleon then decided to blockade British ports and thereby cut off its vital trade.

Under the blockade, which was called the Continental System, Napoleon ordered all European nations to stop trade with Britain. The British responded swiftly. They declared that any ship bound for France had to stop first at a British port and pay a tax. Napoleon countered with a threat to seize any ship paying the British tax.

Unfortunately for France, the Continental System backfired. Britain did lose trade, but France suffered more. The powerful British navy was able to cut off overseas imports to France and the rest of the continent.* This weakened the French economy. It also increased opposition to Napoleon among neutral nations who blamed him for their loss of trade.

Stirrings of Nationalism

Opposition to Napoleon also grew among the conquered and allied peoples of Europe, who were developing a sense of *nationalism*,

---

*American ships were among those stopped from trading with Europe. In addition, the British seized American sailors, forcing them to serve on British warships. These disputes were partly responsible for the War of 1812 between Britain and the United States.

■ By 1812, Napoleon controlled nearly all of Europe. The Netherlands and parts of Italy had been annexed by France. Some areas, shown in blue on this map, were satellites of France; other areas were allies. What nations were beyond Napoleon's influence in 1812?

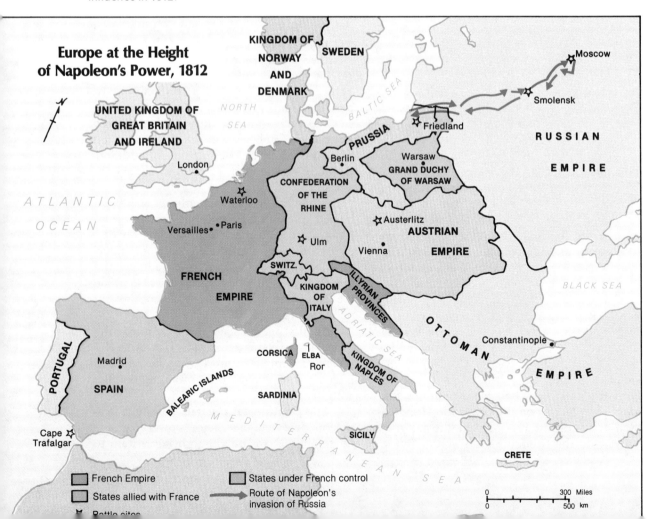

or pride and devotion to one's own country. They resented paying taxes to France and sending soldiers to serve in Napoleon's armies. They wanted to restore their own governments, customs, and traditions. As nationalist feelings grew, revolts broke out all over Europe.

Trouble came first in Spain with an uprising against Napoleon's brother. Spaniards were loyal to their former king and to the Catholic Church. They despised the French, whom they considered atheists and invaders. Bands of patriotic Spaniards ambushed French troops in hit-and-run attacks that became known as *guerrilla warfare*. ("Guerrilla" is a Spanish word meaning "little war.") In 1808, Britain sent troops to help the Spanish and the Portuguese, who also fought against French rule. By 1812, Spanish and Portuguese nationalists had ousted the French from their nations. Each nation then set up a limited monarchy with a written constitution.

In Prussia, nationalist leaders reorganized the government to make it more efficient. They urged the king to create greater loyalty among the middle and lower classes by giving them more political freedom. Prussia also quietly rebuilt its army. The new army rewarded talent and hard work. By 1811, Prussia had an army capable of renewing the struggle against France. It only needed an opportunity to strike. The opportunity arose in 1812 when Napoleon undertook an ill-fated invasion of Russia.

The Emperor's Downfall

In 1807, Czar Alexander I of Russia agreed to abide by the Continental System, but the trade blockade hurt the Russian economy. When Alexander resumed trade with Britain in 1812, Napoleon decided to invade Russia. Napoleon assembled an army of over 500,000 soldiers, and in May 1812, he led this Grand Army into Russia.

Napoleon planned to defeat the Russians in a quick, decisive battle. To his surprise, the Russians refused to stand and fight. Instead, they retreated, burning their crops and homes as they went. They forced Napoleon to lead his army deeper into Rus-

sia. The Russians finally engaged the French near Moscow, 500 miles (800 km) inside Russia. The French won, but when Napoleon entered Moscow, he found the Russian capital in flames. Napoleon soon realized he could not feed and house his army in Moscow. Thus, in October 1812, he ordered a retreat.

During the retreat, the bitterly cold Russian winter turned the French victory into a disastrous defeat. Thousands of Napoleon's soldiers starved or froze to death. The Russian army attacked the stragglers. Fewer than 100,000 escaped from Russia.

A powerful alliance made up of Britain, Austria, Russia, and Prussia pounced on the weakened French army as it limped out of Russia. Napoleon rushed home to raise a new army, but his efforts failed. In March 1814, the allies captured Paris. Napoleon abdicated and went into exile on the island of Elba, off the coast of Italy. The allies installed the brother of the executed Louis XVI as Louis XVIII.

Although the monarchy was restored, the new king did not revive the Old Regime. In 1814, Louis XVIII issued a constitution that provided for equality under the law for all citizens, an elected legislature, and religious freedom. He also kept the Napoleonic Code.

When Louis XVIII became king, many émigrés returned to France and demanded revenge on supporters of the French Revolution. Napoleon took advantage of the resulting disturbances to return to Paris. In March 1815, he again proclaimed himself emperor. Discontented soldiers rallied to his side. For 100 days, he worked to rebuild the French army. But the European allies acted swiftly. In June 1815, a joint British and Prussian army led by the Duke of Wellington defeated the French at Waterloo. Napoleon was exiled to the island of St. Helena in the Atlantic, where he died in 1821.

Legacy of the French Revolution and Napoleon

The era of the French Revolution and Napoleon had a lasting impact on France and the rest of Europe. In France, the revolution ended feudalism, with its special privileges for clergy and nobles. Although the monarchy was eventually restored in France, a written constitution limited the monarch's authority. In the years ahead, French citizens would continue to struggle for the ideals of "liberty, equality, and fraternity."

Under Napoleon, the revolutionary ideals of political and social justice spread throughout Europe. Through his wars and alliances, Napoleon altered European political boundaries. Both the French Revolution and Napoleon contributed to the growing spirit of nationalism in Europe.

Finally, 23 years of warfare had drained French resources. By 1815, France was no longer the strongest and richest nation in Europe. Great Britain had forged ahead in commerce and industry as you will read in Chapter 5.

SECTION REVIEW

1. Locate: Ulm, Austerlitz, Berlin, Cape Trafalgar, Moscow, Elba, Waterloo.
2. Identify: Confederation of the Rhine, Continental System.
3. Define: nationalism.
4. What reforms did Napoleon introduce in Europe?
5. What effect did the Continental System have on France?
6. What event led to Napoleon's invasion of Russia?

IN PERSPECTIVE

In the late 1780s, Louis XVI faced a severe economic crisis. When all efforts at reform failed, the king summoned a meeting of the Estates General. The French Revolution began when representatives from the three estates declared themselves the National Assembly. Between 1789 and 1794, the French Revolution became increasingly radical.

French nobles who opposed the revolution emigrated to other European countries and encouraged foreign rulers to declare war on France. French armies defended the revolution at home and spread its ideas abroad. During the Reign of Terror, thousands of French were executed for supposed disloyalty to the revolution. By 1795, reaction to excesses of the Reign of Terror led to the establishment of the Directory. However, Napoleon Bonaparte overthrew the Directory in 1799 and eventually crowned himself emperor.

Napoleon consolidated many reforms of the revolution. He also led French armies to victory all over Europe. Controlling his empire proved difficult, however. Nationalist movements and the ongoing struggle with Britain drained French resources. In 1812, Napoleon undertook a disastrous invasion of Russia. In 1814, Napoleon's enemies invaded France, and the emperor abdicated. The revolutionary era ended when the monarchy was restored in France.

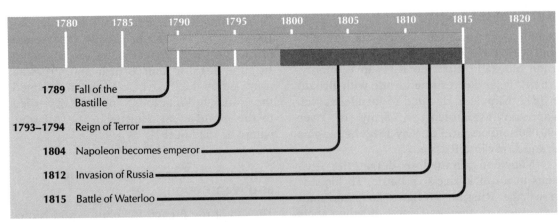

1780   1785   1790   1795   1800   1805   1810   1815   1820

1789 Fall of the Bastille

1793–1794 Reign of Terror

1804 Napoleon becomes emperor

1812 Invasion of Russia

1815 Battle of Waterloo

■ **Era of the French Revolution**   ■ **Napoleon in power**

Arrange the events in each of the following groups in the order in which they occurred.

1. (a) Paris mob attacks the Bastille.
   (b) Louis XVI is executed.
   (c) The Estates General meets.
2. (a) The National Assembly issues the Declaration of the Rights of Man.
   (b) Foreign invaders issue the Brunswick Manifesto.
   (c) Deputies at the Estates General take the Tennis Court Oath.
3. (a) France is ruled by the Directory.
   (b) National Assembly writes the first French constitution.
   (c) Thousands die during the Reign of Terror.
4. (a) Allied armies defeat Napoleon at Waterloo.
   (b) Napoleon invades Russia.
   (c) Napoleon overthrows the Directory.

Chapter Checkup

1. (a) Describe the economic crisis France faced in the 1780s. (b) How did Louis XVI and his ministers try to solve the crisis? (c) How did the existence of the Old Regime hamper their efforts?
2. Describe the major reforms introduced by the National Assembly.
3. Explain how each of the following responded to developments in France between 1789 and 1791: (a) French nobles; (b) Louis XVI; (c) other European monarchs.
4. (a) How did war in 1792 help unite the French people? (b) Why did the war lead to an uprising in Paris? (c) What was the result of the uprising?
5. (a) What actions by the National Convention show that it was more radical than the National Assembly? (b) How did other European monarchs react to the Convention's actions?
6. (a) What steps did the Committee of Public Safety take against counterrevolutionaries? (b) How did it defend France against foreign invaders?
7. (a) How did Napoleon gain popularity? (b) Why was he able to overthrow the Directory so easily? (c) How did he become emperor?
8. (a) Describe Napoleon's reforms in France. (b) Which reforms reflected the ideals of the revolution? (c) How did ideals of the revolution spread to other parts of Europe?

For Further Thought

1. *Analyzing* Describe how each of the following developments led the French Revolution on a more radical course: (a) the fall of the Bastille; (b) Louis XVI's attempted flight from France; (c) the threat of foreign invasion.
2. *Analyzing a Quotation* Robespierre justified the Reign of Terror in these words, "To establish and consolidate democracy, to achieve the peaceful rule of constitutional laws, we must first finish the war of liberty against tyranny. . . . We must annihilate the enemies of the republic at home and abroad, or else we shall perish." (a) Who did the revolutionaries consider the "enemies of the republic at home"? (b) Do you agree with Robespierre that the Reign of Terror was necessary to save the revolution? Explain.
3. *Expressing an Opinion* In your opinion, which of the changes that occurred during the French Revolution had the greatest impact on the lives of French citizens? Why?
4. *Relating Past to Present* (a) How did the French Revolution contribute to the growth of nationalism in Europe? (b) Do you think nationalism is a major force today? Explain.

Developing Basic Skills

1. *Graph Reading* Study the graphs on page 24. Then answer the following questions: (a) What percentage of the population made up the First and Second Estates? (b) What percentage of the land did these two estates own? (c) What percentage of the population made up the Third Estate? (d) What percentage of the land did it own? (e) How did the distribution of land contribute to the problems of the Old Regime?
2. *Analyzing a Primary Source* Reread the Declaration of the Rights of Man on page 28. Then answer the following questions: (a) What Enlightenment ideas appear in the document? (b) How is it similar to the American Declaration of Independence? (c) How can you use this document to learn about the French Revolution?
3. *Map Reading* Study the map on page 38. Then answer the following questions: (a) What lands did Napoleon rule directly? (b) What lands did he control by other means? (c) What problems do you think Napoleon faced in ruling his empire?

See page 203 for suggested readings.

3 Revolutions and Reaction

(1815–1848)

Street fighting in Paris, 1848.

In the fall of 1814, nine kings, dozens of princes, and hundreds of diplomats converged on Vienna, the capital of the Austrian Empire. For ten months, these imposing figures attended the Congress of Vienna, an international peace conference. "There is literally a royal mob here," wrote one visitor to Vienna. "I have worn [my hat] out in taking it off to sovereigns whom I meet at the corner of every street."

After more than 20 years of war, Europe was at peace. Napoleon was in exile on Elba, and Louis XVIII was on the throne of France. The peace was temporarily shattered in March 1815, when Napoleon returned to Paris from Elba. But by June, word reached Vienna of the final victory over Napoleon at Waterloo.

During the Congress of Vienna, the Austrian emperor bore the burden of entertaining his eminent guests. He organized elaborate banquets, hunting parties, and firework displays. In the evenings, the dignitaries dressed for fancy balls that continued far into the night. "The Congress dances," one observer noted, "but accomplishes nothing." However, the festivities served a purpose. They diverted the attention of the less powerful diplomats while the leaders of the great powers negotiated important issues. They wanted to turn the clock back to 1789 and rebuild the balance of power in Europe.

Representatives of Austria, Britain, Russia, and Prussia finally hammered out a treaty. However, the new international order created by the Congress of Vienna could not erase the ideas of political and social justice that the Enlightenment and the French Revolution had planted throughout Europe. The actions of the Congress of Vienna set the stage for unrest and revolt in many countries during the first half of the 1800s.

1 Restoring Peace

When delegates to the Congress of Vienna gathered in 1814, Europe was in chaos. In the preceding 20 years, some monarchs had been overthrown, and many nations had been invaded by revolutionary armies. People in many parts of Europe demanded written constitutions to limit the power of the monarchs that remained in power. The national leaders who met at Vienna were determined to restore the traditions that had existed before the French Revolution. However, they faced new forces that threatened to undermine those traditions.

Old and New Forces

During the 1800s, the philosophies of liberalism and conservatism influenced the way many people thought about government and society. To people at the time, *liberalism* was a philosophy that supported guarantees for individual freedom, political change, and social reform. *Conservatism* supported the traditional political and social order and resisted changes that threatened that way of life.

Liberals accepted the ideas of the Enlightenment and the French Revolution. They supported freedom of speech, press, and religion. To safeguard these rights, they called for written constitutions. As heirs to the Enlightenment, liberals stressed reason, progress, and education. They believed that governments should be reformed so that educated, responsible citizens, like themselves, could participate. Few liberals thought that poor and uneducated people should take part in government.

The ideas of conservatives were expressed by Edmund Burke, an English statesman, in *Reflections on the Revolution in France*. Burke condemned the French Revolution because it brought about radical changes that destroyed traditional institutions such as the monarchy and the nobility. While most conservatives accepted the idea of gradual change, they emphasized re-spect for custom and tradition. They believed that only the wisest, most talented people should run the government. To many conservative nobles, this meant that they alone should hold positions of power.

In the early 1800s, conservatives were in firm control of governments throughout Europe. However, support for liberalism was growing, especially among educated members of the middle class.

Another powerful force shaping Europe in the 1800s was nationalism. As the spirit of nationalism spread, it came to mean more than love of country. It also meant pride in a common cultural heritage regardless of political boundaries. Nationalism became both a positive and a negative force in the 1800s. For example, nationalism could unite people behind a common cause, such as political independence. Yet extreme nationalism sometimes led one group of people to persecute another group who had different cultural traditions.

Liberals and conservatives reacted differently to nationalism. Liberals often supported nationalist leaders who wanted to free their countries from foreign control. Conservatives feared nationalism, in part because it threatened to upset the traditional political order.

The Congress of Vienna

Conservatives dominated the Congress of Vienna. The most influential leaders were *Czar* Alexander I of Russia; King Frederick William III of Prussia; Lord Castlereagh, the British Foreign Minister; and Prince Klemens von Metternich, the Austrian Foreign Minister. The French delegate, Charles Maurice de Talleyrand, also played a major role at the Congress.

Metternich presided over the Congress. He was guided by two general principles: legitimacy and balance of power. By *legitimacy,* he meant restoring to power the royal families that had lost their thrones when

Napoleon conquered Europe. The Congress of Vienna recognized Louis XVIII as the legitimate king of France. It also restored royal families in Spain, Portugal, and Sardinia.

To rebuild the balance of power in Europe and prevent future French aggression, the Congress reduced France to its 1790 frontiers and strengthened the countries on the borders of France. To the north of France, the Dutch and Austrian Netherlands were united into a single country, called the Netherlands, which was ruled by the Dutch king. To the east, 39 German states were loosely joined into the German Confederation, headed by Austria. The Congress recognized Switzerland as an independent nation. In addition, it strengthened the kingdom of Sardinia in northern Italy by giving it Piedmont and Genoa. (See the map on page 45.)

The Congress also made other territorial changes. In return for giving up the Austrian Netherlands, Austria received Lombardy and Venetia in Italy. With these lands, Austria became the strongest power in northern Italy. In southern Italy, the Congress established a Spanish Bourbon as ruler of the kingdom of the Two Sicilies.

In Eastern Europe, the fate of Poland became a thorny issue. Early in the Congress, Czar Alexander had pointed to Poland on a map and announced, "This belongs to me." The king of Prussia then claimed the German state of Saxony. Russia and Prussia supported each other's demands. Metternich, Castlereagh, and Talleyrand objected to these demands because they feared the expansion of Russian power. Eventually, Russia and Prussia settled for smaller portions of the land they wanted, but both still increased their territory.

The Congress of Vienna granted Britain handsome rewards for its long struggle against Napoleon. Great Britain acquired Malta, Ceylon, and islands in the East and West Indies, as well as part of Guiana in South America. It also received the Cape Colony in South Africa.

Delegates to the Congress of Vienna redrew the map of Europe after Napoleon's downfall. Seated at the far left is the Duke of Wellington, who defeated Napoleon at the battle of Waterloo. The Austrian statesman Metternich, standing at left, is introducing Wellington to the other delegates. At right, with his arm resting on the table, is the chief French delegate Talleyrand.

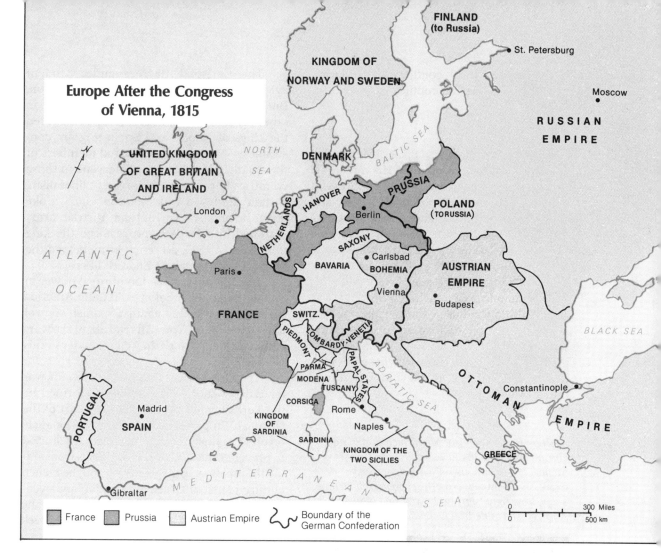

■ This map shows the political boundaries of Europe after the Congress of Vienna. Nations that had fought against Napoleon won new territory, and France lost territory it had conquered. However, the Congress did not treat France as a defeated nation, largely because of the work of the French delegate Talleyrand.

Delegates to the Congress generally ignored feelings of nationalism when they rearranged boundaries. The Congress did not consult the people living in the areas they handed over to Austria, Spain, Russia, Prussia, or Britain.

The Concert of Europe

To protect the peace settlement reached at Vienna, Britain, Austria, Prussia, and Russia formed the Quadruple Alliance in November 1815. Three years later, France was admitted to the alliance. These great powers held periodic meetings to deal with any threat to the peace and stability of Europe.

Although Czar Alexander signed the Quadruple Alliance, he had grander visions. The Czar proposed a Holy Alliance that would bind all rulers to govern according to *Christian* principles. Castlereagh dismissed the idea as a "piece of sublime mysticism and nonsense." Nevertheless, many European rulers eventually joined the Holy Alliance.

The two alliances encouraged nations to act together to preserve the peace. The system of meeting to settle international problems became known as the Concert of Europe. During most of the 1800s, the Concert of Europe enforced the settlement arranged at Vienna. It preserved the balance of power

45

and prevented local conflicts from flaring into a major European conflict.

The Metternich System

For more than 30 years, Prince Metternich dominated European politics. His main goal was to defend the work of the Congress of Vienna. Metternich opposed liberalism and nationalism, and he defended the *status quo*, that is, the existing state of affairs. His policies were known as the Metternich System.

Despite Metternich's efforts, there soon were challenges to the status quo. Students in German universities agitated for liberal reform and unification of the German people. Metternich responded by persuading representatives from the German states to pass the Carlsbad Decrees in 1819. These laws imposed press censorship and suppressed freedom of speech.

Austrian foreign minister Metternich dominated European politics for 30 years after the Congress of Vienna. His enormous self-confidence was expressed in these words: "I say to myself 20 times a day, how right I am and how wrong others are. And yet," he added, "it is so easy to be right."

The Carlsbad Decrees ended student agitation in Germany for nearly a generation. But challenges to the status quo arose in other areas. In 1820, liberal reformers forced the kings of Naples and Spain to grant constitutions. Metternich pressured members of the Quadruple Alliance to intervene in those countries to prevent the spread of liberalism. Britain opposed intervention and broke from the alliance. In 1821, an Austrian army marched into Naples and restored the king to power. In 1823, a French army helped the king of Spain suppress Spanish liberals.

Despite the restoration of royal power in Spain, the Spanish colonies in Latin America successfully revolted against Spanish control during the 1820s. You will read about the wars of independence in Latin America later in this chapter.

The Greeks also fought a successful war for independence. Greece had been ruled by the Turks for nearly 400 years as part of the Ottoman Empire. In 1821, Greek nationalists revolted against Turkish rule. Metternich tried to prevent other European countries from aiding the rebellion. But the British and the French admired ancient Greek civilization and eventually rallied to the Greek cause. In 1829, the Ottoman Empire was forced to recognize Greek independence.

SECTION REVIEW

1. Identify: Edmund Burke, German Confederation, Concert of Europe, Carlsbad Decrees.
2. Define: liberalism, conservatism, legitimacy, status quo.
3. (a) What political ideas did liberals support? (b) What political ideas did conservatives support?
4. (a) Which nations had the most influence at the Congress of Vienna? (b) What leaders represented each of those nations?
5. How did liberals and conservatives react to nationalism?
6. How did the Congress of Vienna try to prevent future French aggression?
7. What challenges to the Metternich System were successful in the 1820s?

2 A New Era of Revolution in France

The success of the Greek revolt gave new hope to many liberals and nationalists. The ideals of the French Revolution also continued to inspire demands for reform, especially in France. Middle class liberals and workers in France joined forces in 1830 and 1848 to upset the status quo created at the Congress of Vienna.

The July Revolution

As you read, the Congress of Vienna had recognized Louis XVIII as king of France. During his reign, Louis sought a compromise between conservatives and liberals. Although he claimed to rule by divine right, Louis realized he could not restore an absolute monarchy. Therefore, he accepted the constitution drawn up in 1814. The constitution guaranteed individual rights and provided for an elected legislature.

Louis's efforts at compromise satisfied few people, however. Liberals criticized the 1814 constitution because it limited the right to vote to wealthy people. Extreme conservatives, led by the king's brother, wanted a return to the Old Regime. On Louis's death in 1824, his brother inherited the throne as Charles X.

A tactless, stubborn man, Charles set about increasing royal power. He warned that the constitution "cannot possibly prevent me from having my way." Supported by the clergy and the nobles, Charles pressured the legislature to pass a law to pay nobles for the lands they had lost during the French Revolution. However, when the legislature refused to approve laws that restricted individual freedom, Charles dissolved it and called for a new election.

The elections of July 1830 surprised the king because voters chose liberal legislators who opposed his policies. Unable to control the newly elected legislature, Charles issued the July Ordinances. These laws dissolved the legislature, ended freedom of the press, and put new restrictions on the right to vote.

French newspapers urged citizens to resist the king's arbitrary rule. On July 28, riots broke out in Paris. Workers, university students, and middle class liberals built barricades in the streets. When soldiers refused to fire on the rebels and began to join them, Charles X abdicated and fled to England.

The July Revolution, as it was called, ended quickly. Many people had hoped to create a republic. But the middle class leaders of the revolution feared that if France became a republic, foreign powers might intervene. Therefore, they established a constitutional monarchy. They chose Louis Philippe, a cousin of Charles X, as king.

The Bourgeois Monarchy

Under Louis Philippe, the 1814 constitution was amended to give more members of the middle class the right to vote. Because the middle class, or bourgeoisie, controlled the legislature and supported the king, Louis Philippe was called the "bourgeois monarch." In keeping with this image, Louis Philippe was the first European monarch to adopt middle class dress. Wearing a top hat, frock coat, and trousers, he often walked through the streets of Paris, greeting citizens.

Although France prospered during most of Louis Philippe's reign, many French people were discontent with his government. The king's policies favored the wealthy, and many citizens felt betrayed by the July Revolution because they had not won the right to vote. Republicans and some liberals organized secret societies to work for an end to the monarchy.

Socialist demands. Changing social and economic conditions also contributed to tensions in France. In the early 1800s, businesspeople set up factories in the cities. As a result, many workers crowded into the cities looking for jobs. Because of poor conditions in the factories and low pay, many working class people listened eagerly to reformers who promised improvements.

In July 1830, workers and middle class liberals set up barricades in the streets of Paris. The streets echoed with the cry: "Down with the Bourbons." Street barricades made it difficult for government troops to move. As this picture shows, people showered troops with furniture, flowerpots, washtubs, and shovels.

One reformer was Louis Blanc. He believed in an economic and political theory called *socialism*. Under socialism, society as a whole rather than private individuals would own all property and operate all businesses. Blanc argued that a socialist government representing society as a whole would be able to protect the interests of the working class and guarantee all of them jobs.

Louis Philippe rejected the demands for reform from socialists as well as those from liberals and republicans. "There will be no reform," he said in 1847, "I do not wish it."

The revolution of 1848. On February 22, 1848, François Guizot (gee ZOH), the king's chief minister, cancelled a huge public banquet in Paris because he feared it would lead to demonstrations and disorder. Hearing that the banquet was cancelled, thousands of workers poured into the streets shouting: "Down with Guizot." To restore order, Louis Philippe dismissed his chief minister, but

demonstrations continued over the next few days. When troops opened fire and killed some demonstrators, the people of Paris erected barricades as they had in 1830.

The revolution of 1848 ended quickly. When crowds marched on the king's palace, Louis Philippe abdicated and fled in disguise to England. The mob swarmed into the palace. Finding the table set for lunch, they sat down to enjoy the royal meal. Meanwhile, leaders of the revolution proclaimed the Second Republic.

The Second Republic

While Paris was in turmoil, the revolutionaries quickly set up a provisional, or temporary, government, which included the socialist leader Louis Blanc. In response to socialist demands, the government created national workshops that would provide jobs for unemployed workers. Nearly 120,000 workers flocked to Paris to register at the national workshops. Because jobs could not be found for all of them, many received government aid in the form of relief payments.

To pay for the national workshops, the government imposed a heavy tax on property. The increased taxes angered the middle class as well as peasants who owned land. They blamed the socialists. Consequently, when elections were held for a National Assembly, moderate delegates who represented middle class interests won a majority.

In June 1848, the National Assembly abolished the national workshops. Paris workers immediately revolted. During the days that followed, clashes between workers and troops left more than 10,000 people killed or wounded. After the revolt was crushed, the National Assembly issued a new constitution. It guaranteed liberty and established an elected legislature and president. In addition, it provided for *universal male suffrage*—that is, all adult men were given the right to vote. However, the fighting left bitter memories and sharp divisions between the middle class and workers.

The first elections under the new constitution were held in December 1848. By an overwhelming majority, voters chose Louis Napoleon, nephew of Napoleon Bonaparte, to be president of the Second Republic. Few people knew much about Louis Napoleon, but they associated his name with order, security, and the glorious victories of French armies.

As president, Louis Napoleon tried to please everyone. He promised jobs to workers, encouraged trade, defended property rights, and supported the Roman Catholic Church. He became so popular that he met little resistance when he set up a virtual dictatorship in December 1851. A year later, he assumed the title Napoleon III, Emperor of the French. Like his uncle, he won approval for this move in a popular vote. Thus, the short-lived Second Republic ended with the creation of the Second Empire.

SECTION REVIEW

1. Identify: July Ordinances, Louis Blanc, Second Republic.
2. Define: socialism, universal male suffrage.
3. Why did the French revolt against Charles X?
4. Why was Louis Philippe known as the bourgeois monarch?
5. What was the purpose of the national workshops?
6. Why did the French support Louis Napoleon?

3 Revolts in Other Parts of Europe

A wave of revolutions swept across Europe in 1830 and 1848. Inspired by events in France, liberals and nationalists in many parts of Europe fought against the old order restored by the Congress of Vienna. As Metternich observed, "When France sneezes, Europe catches cold."

The Revolutions of 1830

At the Congress of Vienna, the Dutch and Austrian Netherlands had been united under the Dutch king. However, the Belgians, who lived in the south of the new country, despised the arrangement. They spoke a different language from the Dutch, and they were largely Roman Catholic, whereas most of the Dutch were Protestants.

These cultural and religious differences sparked a nationalist movement among the Belgians who wanted independence from the Netherlands. In August 1830, riots erupted in Brussels. The Belgians defeated a Dutch army and won the support of Britain and France for their cause. Although Austria, Prussia, and Russia at first opposed Belgian independence, they eventually signed a treaty establishing Belgium as an independent nation.

The July Revolution in France and the nationalist revolt in Belgium succeeded in part because each had the support of a strong middle class. Elsewhere, however, the revolutions of 1830 failed.

For example, Polish nationalists tried to win their independence from Russia in 1830. But the Poles were divided themselves. Moreover, Britain and France did not provide help, as the Poles had hoped. A Russian army crushed the rebels, executed many leaders, and imposed a harsh rule on Poland.

Revolts also flared in Italy and Germany. Austria quickly sent troops to suppress nationalists in Italy, and Metternich persuaded the German states to renew the Carlsbad Decrees, which silenced the unrest in Germany. "The dam has broken in Europe," wrote Metternich in 1830. However, he managed to hold back the flood of liberalism and nationalism until 1848.

Revolts in the Austrian Empire

In March 1848, news of the overthrow of Louis Philippe in France led to an uprising in Vienna. University students joined by workers and middle class liberals poured into the streets. They demanded an end to feudalism, a constitution, and the removal of Metternich. Frightened by the demonstrations, the Austrian emperor promised reform. To show his good faith, he dismissed Metternich.

During the uprising in Vienna, revolts erupted among various nationalities in other parts of the Austrian Empire. In Hungary, the Magyars, led by the fiery nationalist Louis Kossuth (kah SOOTH), demanded a constitution and a separate Hungarian government. In Bohemia, the Czechs issued similar demands. In northern Italy, nationalists in Lombardy and Venetia also revolted against Austria. They were supported by the kingdom of Sardinia and other Italian states.

Overwhelmed by these events, the Austrian government granted the demands of the Magyars and the Czechs and withdrew its armies from northern Italy. Within three months, however, the tide of revolution turned. Germans who lived in Bohemia resented being under Czech control, and they helped an Austrian army occupy Prague. By June 1848, Austria had regained control of Bohemia. In October, government troops bombarded Vienna and crushed the revolution there.

The reconquest of Hungary took longer. To weaken the Magyar cause, the Austrian government took advantage of the cultural differences between the Magyars and the Croatians, a Slavic people who lived in Hungary. The Austrians supplied arms to a Croatian army, which stormed Budapest in September 1848. The Magyars successfully repelled the attack under the leadership of Kossuth. In the spring of 1849, Kossuth proclaimed Hungary a republic.

The Russian czar was anxious to see order restored in Eastern Europe, however, so he offered to help Austria. In August 1849, a Russian army invaded Hungary and suppressed the Magyar revolt.

Uprisings in Italy

The revolts in Lombardy and Venetia against the Austrians were among several uprisings in Italy in 1848. In January, revolutionaries in Sicily had overthrown their king. In other Italian states, people forced their rulers to grant liberal constitutions.

Italian nationalists in Rome tried to win the pope's support for a united Italy. However, the pope refused to give his support because he did not want to offend Austria, the main Catholic nation in Europe. Rebels then took over the city, and the pope fled into exile. Led by Giuseppe Mazzini, nationalists established the Roman Republic in February 1849.

By this time, however, the Austrians had restored order in Vienna and had begun to reestablish their control in northern Italy. Furthermore, Louis Napoleon, who wanted to win favor with the pope, sent French troops to Rome. French troops occupied the city and restored the pope to power.

Although the Italian uprisings were crushed, liberals and nationalists preserved their dreams of a unified Italy. In the years ahead, they looked to the kingdom of Sardinia for leadership because only Sardinia had managed to keep the liberal constitution won in 1848.

The German States

The revolution of 1848 in France inspired German liberals to demand reform. In many German states, rulers promised constitutions and other reforms. However, events took a different course in Prussia.

Prussia. In March 1848, a demonstration in Berlin turned into a riot when police opened fire on the crowd. Workers and middle class liberals set up barricades. When told of the revolt, the Prussian king Frederick William IV was amazed. "It cannot be," he said, "my people love me." To avoid further bloodshed, he withdrew his troops from the city and promised reform.

The Prussians elected a National Assembly to draft a constitution, but a split soon developed between moderates of the middle class and radical workers. Moreover, the king was encouraged by the Austrian success in suppressing revolts. In November, Frederick William dissolved the National Assembly and sent troops back to Berlin. Once he was in full control, the king issued his own constitution for Prussia. The constitution provided for universal male suffrage and an elected legislature.

Attempt to unify Germany. In 1848, German nationalists tried to unite the people of Germany. In May, delegates from the German states met in Frankfurt as a national parliament. They agreed to work peacefully for German unity.

Carl Schurz: Memories of the Revolution of 1848

Carl Schurz was a student at the German University of Bonn when the revolutions of 1848 altered the course of his life. Until this time, Schurz's goal had been to become a professor of history. But in the revolutionary spirit of the times, the 19-year-old student embraced the cause of democratic reform. He became a student leader and ardently supported demands for German unity and a constitution. Later in life, Schurz recalled his early involvement in the events of 1848:

"One morning toward the end of February 1848, I sat quietly in my attic chamber, working hard at the tragedy of *Ulrich von Hutten,* when suddenly a friend rushed breathlessly into the room, exclaiming: 'What, you sitting here! Do you not know what has happened?'

'No, what?'

'The French have driven away Louis Philippe and proclaimed the Republic.'

"I threw down my pen—and that was the end of *Ulrich von Hutten.* I never touched the manuscript again. We tore down the stairs, into the street, to the market-square, the accustomed meeting-place for all the student societies after their midday dinner. Although it was still forenoon, the market was already crowded with young men talking excitedly. ... In these conversations ... certain ideas and catchwords worked themselves to the surface, which expressed more or less the feelings of the people. Now had arrived in Germany the day for the establishment of 'German Unity' and the founding of a great, powerful national German Empire."

Schurz fought bravely in the revolutionary army. He defended one fortress until its surrender and barely escaped a firing squad by clambering through an unused sewer. Although he found a safe refuge in Switzerland, Schurz risked his freedom to return to Germany when he learned that an old friend, a professor whom he greatly admired, had been imprisoned for life. Schurz became a hero of the revolution of 1848 by spiriting the professor safely out of Germany.

Even as an exile, Schurz did not give up his political ideals. He championed the cause of German unity in speeches in France and England. Then, like many other exiles from the political upheavals of 1848, Schurz set sail for the United States. Schurz dedicated himself to his adopted homeland and eventually was elected to the United States Senate.

In April 1849, the parliament issued a constitution for Germany. It then offered the crown of a united Germany to Frederick William IV. To their dismay, the Prussian king refused the crown because it was offered by the people and not by the German princes. He then sent an army to disband the Frankfurt Parliament, thereby ending this early attempt at unification.

Impact of the Revolutions of 1830 and 1848

Some political conditions changed as a result of the revolutions of 1830 and 1848. Greece and Belgium won their independence. Furthermore, in France and Prussia, all adult men were given the right to vote.

For the most part, however, the revolutions of 1830 and 1848 failed. Many revolutionary movements suffered from a lack of unity and clear policies. By 1848, deep divisions had emerged between middle class liberals who wanted moderate reforms and workers who demanded radical changes. In addition, conservatives were strong enough in most of Europe to defeat the rebels.

During the 1850s, conservative governments tried to suppress revolutionary ideas. Faced with political persecution, some liberals fled their homelands and found refuge in North America. But as you will read in the next unit, liberalism, nationalism, and socialism would continue to shape events in Europe in the late 1800s.

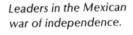

Leaders in the Mexican war of independence.

SECTION REVIEW

1. Locate: Poland, Vienna, Lombardy, Venetia, Budapest.
2. Identify: Louis Kossuth, Guiseppe Mazzini.
3. Where did revolutions occur in 1830?
4. What was the result of the revolution of 1848 in Rome?
5. How did Frederick William IV react to the offer of the crown of a united Germany?

4 The Wars of Independence

Like the 13 colonies in North America, colonies elsewhere in the Americas had many grievances against their European rulers. In the late 1700s, dissatisfaction increased, especially when the colonists read the works of Enlightenment writers such as Locke, Voltaire, and Rousseau. The success of the American and French revolutions encouraged the peoples of Latin America* in their own struggles for independence. In Mexico, Central and South America, and the West Indies, colonists began trying to gain control over their own affairs.

Sources of Discontent

During the 1500s, Spain had established a colonial empire in the Americas. Over the next 300 years, a rigid social structure emerged in the Spanish Empire. This social structure caused much discontent. At the top of colonial society was a small, privileged class of peninsulares. *Peninsulares* were officials who had been sent from Spain to rule the colonies. (The term peninsular referred to the Iberian Peninsula on which Spain and Portugal are located.) Only peninsulares could hold high offices in government or in the Catholic Church, a powerful force in the colonies. The Spanish king often granted peninsulares huge estates in the colonies, enabling them to become extremely wealthy.

Below the peninsulares were the *creoles* (KREE ohls), descendants of Spanish settlers who were born in the Americas. In theory, creoles were equal to the peninsulares, but in practice they were barred from the highest official positions. Nevertheless, many creoles became wealthy land or mine owners, and others were active in commerce and industry.

After the creoles came the *mestizos* (mehs TEE zohs), people of mixed European and Indian heritage. Mestizos held many different jobs in the colonial economy, from day laborers and farmers to lawyers. During the 1600s and 1700s, the mestizo population grew rapidly. At the lowest level of colonial society were Indians and African slaves. African slaves were brought to the Americas to work on the plantations and in the mines.

Except for the peninsulares, each group had reason to resent colonial rule. Creoles objected to colonial rule because it gave European-born peninsulares superior social, political, and economic positions. Furthermore, many creoles had been educated in Europe, where they had absorbed Enlightenment ideas about liberty. On their return home, they helped spread these ideas. Eventually, the Spanish banned the writings of Rousseau and Voltaire in their American colonies because they considered the ideas of these philosophers a threat to their rule.

Mestizos disliked colonial rule because they were treated as third-class citizens and were scorned by the Spanish and the creoles. In theory, Indians were free, but many were forced to work for Europeans. Both Indians and African slaves were ready to fight to gain freedom.

Early Revolts

During the late 1700s and early 1800s, uprisings occurred in several areas of Latin America. In 1781, the Indian leader Tupac Amaru II led a revolt against Spanish rule in Peru. The Indian army was poorly armed, and it was rapidly defeated by the Spanish troops. In the 1780s, nearly 20,000 mestizos and Indians marched on Bogotá, in what is today Colombia, to protest excessive taxes imposed by Spain. The Spanish eventually crushed this revolt and executed the rebel leaders.

As you read at the beginning of the chapter, Francisco Miranda, a creole leader, tried unsuccessfully to organize an uprising against Spanish rule in 1806. Miranda returned to Venezuela in 1810. This time, he

---

* Latin America is the term used to describe the part of the Western Hemisphere south of the United States, where the Latin languages Spanish, French, and Portuguese are spoken.

had the support of the people of Caracas. With other rebel leaders, he ousted the Spanish and set up the first Venezuelan Republic. However, jealousies among the revolutionary leaders enabled the Spanish to regain control of the colony. They captured Miranda and sent him to Spain, where he died in 1816. Although the revolution led by Miranda failed, the Spanish colonies would soon wage successful wars for independence.

Independence for Haiti

While Spanish subjects in the Americas were plotting against their colonial rulers, a successful uprising took place in the French

Toussaint L'Ouverture led the people of Haiti in a successful revolution against French rule. Although Toussaint was taken prisoner by the French, he warned before his death: "In overthrowing me, the French have only felled the tree of black liberty in Saint Domingue [Haiti]. It will shoot up again for it is deeply rooted and its roots are many."

West Indies. The French ruled Haiti, the western half of the island of Hispaniola. In the 1700s, a few French families owned huge sugar plantations worked by nearly one half million African slaves. Overseers brutally mistreated the slaves.

When the French Revolution broke out in 1789, the people of Haiti quickly adopted the ideals of "liberty, equality, and fraternity" proclaimed by the revolutionaries in Paris. When their hopes for freedom were disappointed, thousands of slaves revolted in 1791. They murdered their masters and destroyed many plantations. For the next 13 years, Haiti was the scene of violent struggles as former slaves fought the French for freedom.

The leading figure in this struggle was Toussaint L'Ouverture (too SAN loo vehr TYOOR). By 1801, Toussaint had driven the French from Haiti and conquered the Spanish-held eastern half of Hispaniola. He declared the entire island free from foreign control. In France, Napoleon was outraged by the loss of Haiti, which had been the source of valuable profits from the sugar trade. He decided to restore French rule in Haiti. He sent his brother-in-law, General Charles Leclerc, and 20,000 soldiers to carry out his plan.

The French soldiers suffered heavy casualties at the hands of the Haitians. Moreover, an unanticipated enemy—yellow fever—killed hundreds of French troops each week. Leclerc finally tricked Toussaint by agreeing to peace and then luring him to a dinner party at which the Haitian leader was taken prisoner. Later, Toussaint was sent to France, where he died in prison in 1803.

Two other Haitian leaders, Jean Jacques Dessalines and Henri Christophe, took up Toussaint's struggle. The fighting took a terrible toll. Finally, on January 1, 1804, Dessalines declared Haiti independent, making it the first independent nation in Latin America.

Elsewhere in Latin America, people watched events in Haiti with mixed feelings. Creole landowners, for example, were horrified by the slave revolt. But they were also encouraged by seeing that a strong European power could be defeated by local revolutionaries.

The Revolutionary Spirit Spreads

Spanish colonists were inspired by the revolutionary ideals spreading across Europe. During the early 1800s, events in Europe set off a series of successful revolts in Latin America.

In 1808, Napoleon conquered Spain and ousted the Spanish king Ferdinand VII. He then put his brother Joseph Bonaparte on the Spanish throne. The Spanish colonies in Latin America refused to recognize Joseph Bonaparte as king and began setting up their own governments.

After Napoleon's defeat in 1815, the European powers restored Ferdinand VII to his throne. Ferdinand set out to reestablish control over Spanish colonies in Latin America. However, by 1815, several revolutionary leaders had emerged in Latin America. They resisted the return of Spanish rule.

Simón Bolívar. Perhaps the best known revolutionary leader was Simón Bolívar, often called "the Liberator" for his role in the Latin American wars of independence. Bolívar was born to a wealthy creole family in Caracas, Venezuela. He was educated in Spain and traveled in Europe during the French Revolution. Deeply moved by revolutionary ideals, Bolívar became a firm believer in Latin American independence. He once vowed: "I will never allow my hands to be idle nor my soul to rest until I have broken the shackles which chain us to Spain."

Bolívar also visited the United States and studied the republican form of government there. In 1810, he returned to Venezuela and fought alongside Miranda. Over the next decade, Bolívar continued to lead rebel armies in a seesaw battle against Spain.

In August 1819, Bolívar led an army on a daring march from Venezuela, over the ice-capped Andes, into Colombia. In Colombia, he won a stunning victory over the Spanish. In December, he became president of the independent Republic of Great Colombia, which included what is today Venezuela, Colombia, Ecuador, and Panama. (See the map on page 57.)

Simón Bolívar led the fight for freedom from Spanish rule in much of South America. Like other revolutionary leaders, he was inspired by the ideas of the Enlightenment. True to these ideas, Bolívar freed his slaves and spent his personal fortune to finance wars for independence.

José de San Martín. While Bolívar was leading revolutionary forces in Colombia, another creole, José de San Martín, helped organize a rebel army in Argentina. In 1812, San Martín had returned from Europe, where he had been educated, to join Argentina's struggle for independence. Argentina won its freedom in 1816.

A few years later, San Martín and General Bernardo O'Higgins of Chile endured

55

terrible hardships when they led their troops across the southern Andes into Chile. The Spanish, who never dreamed such a march was possible, were caught off guard and were forced to withdraw from Chile. By 1818, Chile had declared its independence. In the early 1820s, San Martín joined forces with Bolívar to help liberate Peru and Ecuador from Spanish rule.

Independence for Mexico and Central America

During the early 1800s, the people of Mexico also fought to win independence from Spain. In 1810, Miguel Hidalgo (hih DAL goh), a creole priest, organized a large army of Indians who were dissatisfied with Spanish rule. Hidalgo captured several Mexican provinces. He then established a government that reflected the ideals of the French Revolution. For example, he abolished slavery and returned land to the Indians. However, in 1811, Hidalgo was captured by troops that were loyal to Spain, and he was executed.

Another creole priest, José Morelos, took up the cause of Mexican independence. Like Hidalgo, Morelos was successful at first. He announced his goal of liberal reforms, including equal rights for all races and redistribution of land to poor peasants. Morelos' program angered the peninsulares and creoles. They helped Spanish troops suppress the revolt. In 1815, Morelos was captured and shot.

The Mexican war of independence dragged on. Eventually, both liberal and conservative groups united against Spain. In 1821, Agustín de Iturbide, a conservative who had once fought for Spain, declared Mexico an independent state. Because Spain had few remaining supporters, it was forced to recognize Mexican independence.

Iturbide proclaimed himself Emperor of Mexico, but his unpopular rule was short-lived. In 1823, he was forced to abdicate, and a convention met to draw up a constitution. The constitution established Mexico as a republic with a president and a two-house congress.

Emboldened by Mexico's example, creoles in Central America declared their independence from Spain in 1821. Two years later, they created the United Provinces of Central America, including what is today Nicaragua, Costa Rica, El Salvador, Honduras, and Guatemala. (See the map on page 57.)

Brazil Gains Independence

Creoles also led the struggle for independence in Brazil. However, Brazil won its independence more easily than its neighbors in Spanish America had. In 1808, when Napoleon invaded Portugal, the Portuguese royal family fled to safety in Brazil. After the defeat of Napoleon, the Portuguese king returned home. But he left his son Prince Pedro in charge of Brazil. The creoles asked Prince Pedro to end Portuguese rule by declaring Brazil independent. They offered to make him ruler of the new nation.

Pedro, who had lived in Brazil since he was 10, accepted the offer. In 1822, he was proclaimed Pedro I, Emperor of Brazil. However, he agreed to accept a constitution that provided for freedom of the press and religion as well as an elected legislature.

By 1825, most colonies in Latin America had thrown off European rule. (See the map on page 57.) Ahead, the newly independent nations faced the difficult task of establishing stable governments.

SECTION REVIEW

1. Locate: Peru, Bogotá, Colombia, Haiti, Caracas, Venezuela, Chile, United Provinces of Central America.

2. Identify: Tupac Amaru II, Francisco Miranda, Toussaint L'Ouverture, Simón Bolívar, José de San Martín, Miguel Hidalgo, José Morelos, Prince Pedro.

3. Define: peninsulare, creole, mestizo.

4. (a) What European country ruled Haiti? (b) Which group of people in Haiti revolted against foreign rule?

5. How did Napoleon's conquest of Spain affect the Spanish colonies in America?

6. What reforms did Morelos want to introduce in Mexico?

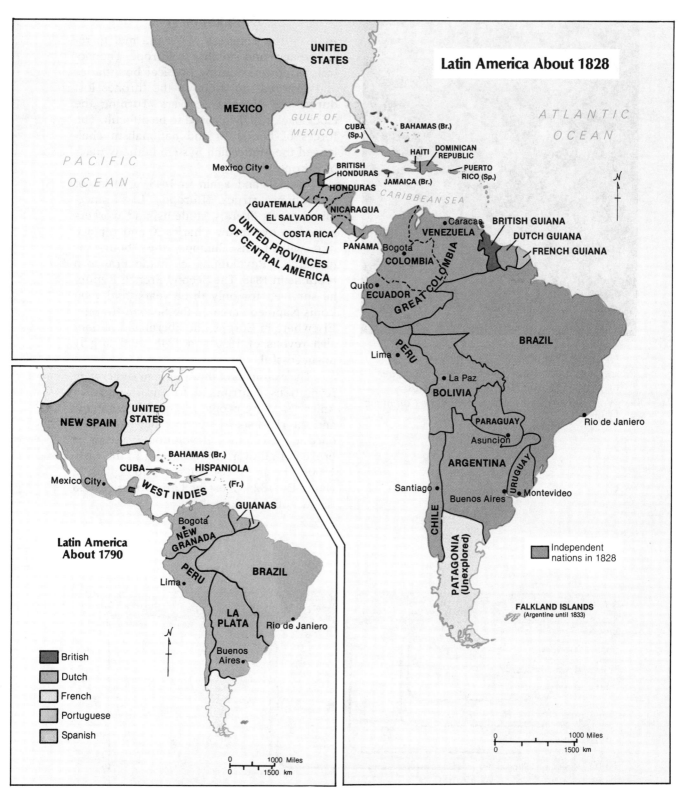

Latin America About 1828

UNITED STATES

MEXICO

PACIFIC OCEAN

GULF OF MEXICO

ATLANTIC OCEAN

Mexico City •

CUBA (Sp.)

BAHAMAS (Br.)

HAITI

DOMINICAN REPUBLIC

PUERTO RICO (Sp.)

BRITISH HONDURAS

HONDURAS

JAMAICA (Br.)

CARIBBEAN SEA

GUATEMALA

EL SALVADOR

NICARAGUA

COSTA RICA

PANAMA

UNITED PROVINCES OF CENTRAL AMERICA

Caracas •

VENEZUELA

BRITISH GUIANA

DUTCH GUIANA

FRENCH GUIANA

Bogota •

COLOMBIA

Quito •

ECUADOR

GREAT COLOMBIA

BRAZIL

Lima •

PERU

La Paz •

BOLIVIA

PARAGUAY

Rio de Janiero •

Asuncion •

ARGENTINA

URUGUAY

Santiago •

Buenos Aires •

Montevideo •

CHILE

PATAGONIA (Unexplored)

☐ Independent nations in 1828

FALKLAND ISLANDS (Argentine until 1833)

0   1000 Miles
0   1500 km

Latin America About 1790

NEW SPAIN

UNITED STATES

Mexico City •

CUBA

BAHAMAS (Br.)

HISPANIOLA

(Fr.)

WEST INDIES

GUIANAS

Bogotá •

NEW GRANADA

PERU

Lima •

BRAZIL

Rio de Janiero •

LA PLATA

Buenos Aires •

■ British
☐ Dutch
☐ French
☐ Portuguese
☐ Spanish

0   1000 Miles
0   1500 km

■ Between 1804 and 1828, most of Latin America won independence from European rule. Which of the nations that won independence in this period were part of the Spanish territory of La Plata in 1790?

French artist Honoré Daumier painted scenes of social protest. In The Uprising, *shown here, he expresses sympathy for poor city workers. Workers like these supported the Paris Commune in 1871.*

IN PERSPECTIVE

In 1814, the Congress of Vienna met to restore peace and stability to Europe. The victorious powers redrew political boundaries and restored monarchs to the thrones lost during the Napoleonic wars. Turning the clock back to 1789 proved to be difficult. The forces of liberalism and nationalism challenged the Metternich System in many parts of Europe.

In 1830 and again in 1848, a series of revolutions struck Europe. In France, middle class liberals, students, and workers united to overthrow Charles X and replace him with Louis Philippe, the "bourgeois monarch." Revolutionaries made France a republic in 1848. The Second French Republic survived for only three years, and then Louis Napoleon created the Second Empire. Elsewhere in Europe, the liberal and nationalist revolts of 1830 and 1848 were largely unsuccessful.

The examples of the American and French revolutions contributed to unrest in Latin America. Many people resented foreign rule and the rigid social stucture that had developed in the colonies. Revolutionary struggles broke out all over Latin America in the early 1800s. The first successful revolt took place in Haiti. By 1825, most of Latin America had thrown off colonial rule.

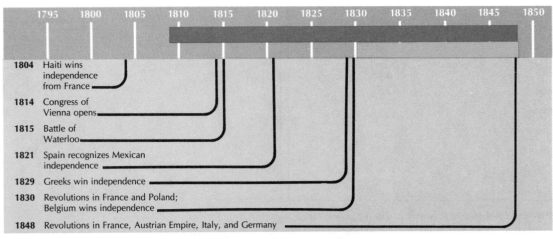

1795 1800 1805 1810 1815 1820 1825 1830 1835 1840 1845 1850

1804 Haiti wins independence from France

1814 Congress of Vienna opens

1815 Battle of Waterloo

1821 Spain recognizes Mexican independence

1829 Greeks win independence

1830 Revolutions in France and Poland; Belgium wins independence

1848 Revolutions in France, Austrian Empire, Italy, and Germany

■ **Metternich as Austrian foreign minister** ■ **Louis Philippe rules France**

Recalling Facts

Decide if the following statements are true or false. If a statement is false, rewrite the statement to make it true.

1. During the 1800s, liberals wanted written constitutions.
2. The Congress of Vienna was dominated by conservatives.
3. Metternich encouraged nationalist revolts.
4. The Carlsbad Decrees gave German students the right to vote.
5. Greece won independence from Austria in 1829.
6. French liberals supported the July Ordinances.
7. Louis Philippe was a constitutional monarch.
8. French socialists opposed the creation of national workshops in 1848.
9. Russia helped Poland win independence in 1830.
10. José de San Martín led revolutionary forces in Colombia.

Chapter Checkup

1. Describe the main concerns of each of the following groups in the early 1800s: (a) liberals; (b) conservatives; (c) nationalists.
2. (a) Describe the early challenges to the Metternich System. (b) How did Metternich respond to each challenge?
3. (a) What groups supported the July Revolution in France? (b) Why did revolutionary leaders decide to establish a constitutional monarchy instead of a republic?
4. (a) Describe the revolution of 1848 in France. (b) What was the outcome of that revolution? (c) What effect did the revolution in France have on the rest of Europe?
5. (a) How were the revolutions of 1830 in Belgium and Poland similar? (b) How were they different?
6. (a) What factors contributed to the revolutions of 1848 in the Austrian Empire? (b) What actions did the Austrian government eventually take in response to the revolutionaries?
7. (a) How did Brazil gain its independence? (b) How was Brazil's road to independence different from those of other Latin American nations?

For Further Thought

1. *Synthesizing* (a) Why did diplomats at the Congress of Vienna want to restore the old order in Europe? (b) Why did they find it so difficult to turn the clock back? (c) Under what circumstances might they have succeeded?
2. *Expressing an Opinion* (a) Why did Metternich want the Quadruple Alliance to intervene in Italy and Spain in 1820? (b) In your opinion, did the Quadruple Alliance have a legitimate reason to intervene? Explain.
3. *Analyzing* Louis Philippe's title was "king of the French by the will of the people." Earlier French kings had been called "king by the grace of God." (a) Do you think Louis Philippe's title was accurate? Why or why not? (b) How does the change in title reflect developments in France since 1789?

Developing Basic Skills

1. *Map Reading* Compare the maps on pages 38 and 45. Then answer the following questions: (a) How did the borders of France change between 1812 and 1815? (b) How does the map on page 45 show that the great powers wanted to limit French power? (c) What nation or nations gained new territory in Europe in 1815?
2. *Researching* Choose one of the leaders at the Congress of Vienna. Research his personal background in order to answer the following questions: (a) What was the person's official title in 1814? (b) How did he gain power in his own country? (c) What were his ideas about government? (d) In your opinion, how did his background and position influence these ideas?
3. *Comparing* Make a chart with two rows and two columns. Title the rows Italy and Germany and the two columns Attempts at Unification and Result. Use what you read about the revolutions of 1848 in Italy and Germany to complete the chart. Then answer the following questions: (a) How were the attempts at unification similar in Italy and Germany? (b) How were they different? (c) Explain what factors made unification in each area difficult.

See page 203 for suggested readings.

Unit Two

Dawn of the Industrial Age

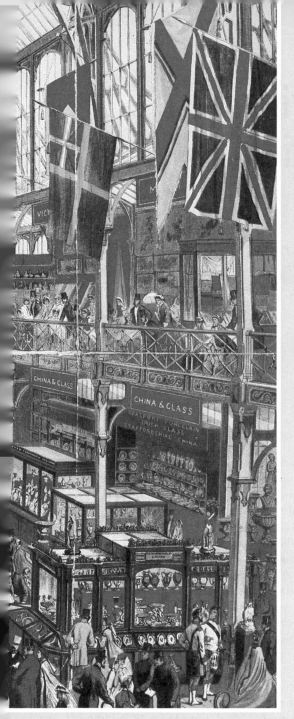

Unit Overview In 1851, huge crowds flocked to London to see the first international industrial exhibition. The Crystal Palace, an imposing structure of glass and cast iron, was built to house this "Great Exhibition of the Works of Industries of All Nations." In this illustration, visitors to the Crystal Palace stroll among the 1,500 exhibits. The crowds marveled at such inventions as the sewing machine and McCormick's reaper. They also admired handicrafts from Austria and furs from Russia.

The Great Exhibition of 1851 celebrated the Industrial Revolution that was transforming Europe and the United States. The Scientific Revolution and the political revolutions that you read about in Unit One helped set the stage for the Industrial Revolution. With the dawn of the Industrial Age, goods began to be mass-produced in factories by machines. Within the brief span of 200 years, the Industrial Revolution would change the world more than any development in the previous 5,000 years.

The Industrial Age was also a time of significant political, social, and intellectual change. The forces of nationalism unleashed by the French Revolution changed the political map of Europe. At the same time, impressive advances in science and technology made people confident that they could solve the problems confronting society.

4 The Triumph of Nationalism

(1848–1914)

Arrival of King Victor Emmanuel in Parma, Italy, May 1860.

Trouble flared in Milan, the capital of Lombardy, over, of all things, Austrian cigars. Cigars were a major source of revenue for the Austrians who ruled Lombardy. To protest foreign control of their province, the residents of Milan refused to smoke cigars.

On January 3, 1848, Austrian authorities responded to this defiance by issuing cigars to their soldiers and telling them to smoke the cigars in the streets of Milan. That afternoon, enraged Italians attacked the cigar-smoking soldiers with angry words, flying fists, and rocks. The Austrian troops answered with drawn swords. By the end of the day, Milan's hospitals were filled with injured and dying Italian patriots. The tense city edged toward rebellion. Overnight, the cigar became a symbol of Italian *nationalism*.

In the next month, news of uprisings in France reached Milan, making the mood of Italian patriots even uglier. The moment to throw off the yoke of Austrian rule and create a democratic Italy seemed at hand. On March 17, a large crowd gathered outside the Austrian government headquarters. Nervous at the sight, Austrian soldiers fired a blank volley to disperse the crowd. Shouting "Viva Italia" ("Long live Italy"), a boy of sixteen fired his pistol at the troops. The mob rushed forward, quickly overpowering the guards.

The Austrians were able to crush the uprising in Milan, but their victory was short-lived. The citizens of Milan were driven by nationalism, one of the most powerful forces during the 1800s. Between 1848 and 1914, nationalism played a key role in events in Central and Eastern Europe. In some areas, it led to the unification of national groups. In other areas, nationalism threatened the stability of large, diverse empires.

1 The Unification of Italy

In 1815, Prince Metternich of Austria called Italy "a geographic expression." But to many people living on the Italian peninsula, it was much more than that. They looked back to the glorious days of the Roman Empire and to the days when Italian city-states were at the center of the Renaissance. Nationalists yearned for a united Italy and a return to past glories.

Nationalism in Italy

Italian nationalism had roots in the French Revolution. Many Italians had been influenced by the ideals of the revolution: liberty, equality, and fraternity. Furthermore, Napoleon Bonaparte had combined small Italian states into larger kingdoms. (See the map on page 38.) This gave Italians a taste of unity.

After the Congress of Vienna, however, most of Italy was under foreign rule. Austria ruled Venetia and Lombardy directly, and Austrian princes ruled in Parma, Lucca, Modena, and Tuscany. The Congress of Vienna had set up the Spanish Bourbon family as rulers of the kingdom of the Two Sicilies.

Italian nationalists struggled for independence and unity throughout the 1830s and 1840s. In 1831, one nationalist leader, Giuseppe Mazzini (mah ZEE nee), founded a secret society called Young Italy to work for unification. Mazzini wanted Italy to be a republic. "I give my name to Young Italy," he proclaimed, "and swear to dedicate myself to [making] Italy one free ... republican nation."

Other nationalists favored a unified Italy led by the kingdom of Sardinia.* Count Camillo Cavour led this group. He edited a newspaper called *Il Risorgimento* (ree SOHR jee MEHN toh), meaning the resurgence or revival. Eventually, the entire movement for Italian unity was called the Risorgimento.

---

* As you can see from the map on page 65, the kingdom of Sardinia included the island of Sardinia plus Piedmont, Nice, and Savoy on the mainland. The capital, Turin, was located in Piedmont.

Nationalist attempts to rid Italy of foreign rule in 1848 failed, as you read in Chapter 3. However, Sardinia emerged from the revolutions of 1848 as leader of the struggle for unification. Furthermore, Victor Emmanuel II, who became king of Sardinia in 1849, was a staunch supporter of Risorgimento.

The First Steps

Victor Emmanuel gave the cause of Italian unification an enormous boost when he named Count Cavour his prime minister in 1852. Cavour, a longtime supporter of Italian unity, was a skillful politician. He wanted Sardinia to be a model for Italian unification. Therefore, he instituted road- and canal-building projects, land reforms, and new tariff policies. This resulted in rapid economic growth. Sardinia soon won recognition as an emerging power among both Italian nationalists and European leaders.

The Crimean War. Cavour also believed that tough, practical international diplomacy was essential to unification. He saw the Crimean War, which broke out in 1854, as a chance to win the allies he needed to drive Austria out of Italy.

France and Britain had declared war on Russia to prevent Russia from gaining too much influence over the weak Ottoman Empire. Sardinia entered this war on the side of France and Britain, who emerged victorious in 1856. Sardinia's participation had two important results. First, Sardinia participated in the peace conference. Cavour used the conference as a stage from which to publicize the demand for Italian unification. Second, Cavour won the support of Napoleon III of France in his effort to end Austrian influence in Italy.

War with Austria. In 1858, Cavour met secretly with Napoleon III to plot a strategy against Austria. Their plan was to trick Austria into declaring war on Sardinia. Then France would send troops to help the Sardinians. In return, Sardinia agreed to give Savoy and Nice to France.

The following year the plan went into action. By encouraging nationalist revolts in the Austrian provinces of Lombardy and Venetia, Cavour provoked Austria into declaring war. As promised, the French sent troops. Following bloody battles at Magenta and Solferino, the French and Sardinians drove Austria from Lombardy.

At this point, Napoleon III suddenly withdrew his support because he thought a completely unified Italy might be a threat to France. Therefore, he negotiated a separate peace treaty with Austria. According to this treaty, Sardinia won Lombardy, but Venetia remained under Austrian control. The status of other states in northern Italy remained unchanged. Soon, however, the people of these states took action themselves. Several states held plebiscites, or popular votes, demanding unification with Sardinia. In this way, Tuscany, Modena, Parma, and the papal province of Romagna joined Sardinia.

Unification Completed

Meanwhile, in southern Italy, the nationalist movement was growing under the leadership of Giuseppe Garibaldi, a dashing military commander. Garibaldi, who had belonged to Young Italy, wanted nothing less than a completely unified Italy with a republican form of government.

In 1860, with the unofficial approval of Sardinia, Garibaldi formed a volunteer army of over 1,000 "Red Shirts," so-named for the color of their uniforms. Their objective was

Garibaldi and his Red Shirts helped free Sicily and all of southern Italy from foreign control. On May 11, 1860, Garibaldi and his forces landed in western Sicily. As they marched inland, recruits flocked to the cause. Four days after landing, Garibaldi's Red Shirts won the battle at Calatafimi, pictured here. Within two weeks, Garibaldi had taken the city of Palermo and set up a provisional government in Sicily.

to attack the kingdom of the Two Sicilies and drive out the Bourbon rulers. "To arms," Garibaldi urged Italian patriots. "Let me put an end, once and for all, to the miseries of so many centuries. Prove to the world that it is no lie that Roman generations inhabited this land."

Garibaldi and his Red Shirts landed on the island of Sicily and conquered it in a daring, brief military campaign. Then they sailed to the mainland, where once again they were victorious. The Bourbon forces fled before the Red Shirts, and Garibaldi triumphantly entered Naples.

Next, Garibaldi turned his attention toward Rome and the Papal States, which were under French protection. At this point, Cavour stepped in. He was afraid an attack on Rome would offend Italians as well as the French government. Cavour sent a Sardinian army to Naples to block Garibaldi. Cavour convinced Garibaldi to turn over Sicily and Naples to Victor Emmanuel. By the end of 1860, Sardinia had annexed Sicily, Naples, and two outlying papal provinces.

In March 1861, a parliament representing all of Italy except Venetia and Rome and its surrounding lands met in Turin. The parliament proclaimed the kingdom of Italy with Victor Emmanuel as king. Three months later, just as the unification of Italy neared completion, Cavour died.

In 1866, Italy joined Prussia in a brief war against Austria. When Prussia won, Italy acquired Venetia from Austria. Four years later, Prussia and France went to war, and France was forced to withdraw its troops from Rome. Italian troops entered the city in September 1870, and the people of Rome voted for annexation to the kingdom of Italy. Nine years after the death of Cavour, his dream of unifying the entire Italian peninsula had at last come true.

Problems of a Unified Italy

Unfortunately, unification created problems for Italy. Pope Pius IX was angry at losing control of Rome and the Papal States. He withdrew into the Vatican and urged Italian Catholics not to cooperate with their new

The Unification of Italy, 1858–1870

Kingdom of Sardinia, 1858
Added to Sardinia, 1859 and 1860
Added to Italy, 1866
Added to Italy, 1870

■ *Italy was united between 1858 and 1870. By 1860, most Italian states had united with Sardinia. In 1861, they declared themselves the kingdom of Italy. What area was added to Italy in 1866? In 1870?*

government. This action strained relations between the Catholic Church and the Italian state. It also put pressure on those people who wanted to be loyal both to Italy and the Catholic Church.

Unification increased antagonism between people living in the north and the south. Southern Italians resented the fact that Sardinians dominated the government. Economic differences contributed to the differences between north and south. While the north began to industrialize, the south remained rural and poor.

65

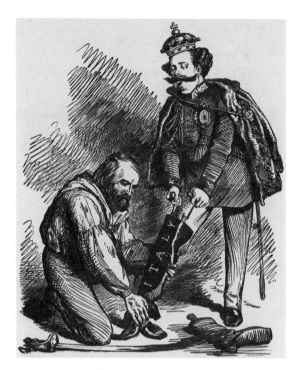

This cartoon illustrates Garibaldi's contribution to Italian unification. Garibaldi is fitting the boot of Italy onto the foot of Victor Emmanuel, advising him: "If it won't go on Sire, try a little more powder."

Ardent republicans such as Garibaldi disliked the government of the new nation. Although Italy had a constitution that limited the power of the king and an elected parliament, only a few men had the right to vote. Of 20 million people, only about 600,000—fewer than 1 in 30—could vote.

Some Italian nationalists were unhappy with unification because they thought it was not complete. They agitated for the addition of Trentino, Trieste, and Dalmatia, still controlled by Austria, as well as for Savoy and Nice, which France ruled. Nationalists called these areas, "Italia irredenta," which means "Italy still unredeemed." The "Italia irredenta," like the other problems of unified Italy, would contribute to unrest and instability in the future.

SECTION REVIEW

1. Locate: Venetia, Lombardy, kingdom of the Two Sicilies, kingdom of Sardinia, Savoy, Nice.
2. Identify: Young Italy, Count Camillo Cavour, Risorgimento, Victor Emmanuel, Giuseppe Garibaldi, Red Shirts, "Italia irredenta."
3. How did the French Revolution affect Italian nationalism?
4. Why did Sardinia become involved in the Crimean War?
5. (a) How did Sardinia gain Lombardy? (b) How did it gain other states in northern Italy?
6. List three problems Italy faced after unification.

2 The Unification of Germany

Like the Italians, the Germans were divided into many separate states in 1815. The German Confederation, created by the Congress of Vienna, included 39 states. The confederation was a loose grouping of independent nations. It did not come close to satisfying Germans who wanted a unified nation. Attempts by nationalists and liberals to unite Germany in 1848 failed, as you read in Chapter 3. During the following years, there continued to be serious obstacles to German unity.

Obstacles to Unity

The presence of Austria in the German Confederation was one of the most serious obstacles to German unity. Austria opposed attempts to unify Germany, fearing it would lose influence among the German states, especially those that bordered Austria in the south. In addition, Austria feared competition if a powerful German nation were created in Central Europe. For the same reason, other countries, especially France and Russia, did not want to see the German states united.

Many smaller German states also opposed unification. They feared that Prussia would control a unified Germany because Prussia was the most powerful state in the confederation. Catholic states in southern Germany were especially concerned about domination by Protestant Prussia. Furthermore, individual German states wanted to protect their own customs and traditions. They did not want to be absorbed into a large nation.

Prussian Leadership

During the 1850s, Prussia emerged as the leader in the effort to unify Germany. Prussia had many advantages over other German states. Since the early 1700s, absolute rulers had made Prussia a strong and powerful state with a large disciplined army.

In the 1800s, the king and Junkers, or aristocratic landowners, controlled the Prussian government. Most government officials and army officers were Junkers. The constitution approved by the king in 1850 contained a provision for a parliament. But the Prussian parliament was dominated by wealthy Junkers, although a new class of industrial capitalists was gaining political influence.

The Industrial Revolution added greatly to Prussian economic strength. The Ruhr Valley in western Prussia contained the largest coal deposits in Europe. During the 1850s, this coal fueled the start of a prosperous Prussian iron and steel industry. Iron and steel production contributed to economic growth and allowed the government to construct an efficient system of railroads. In planning the railroads, the government worked closely with the military.

Government reforms in the first half of the 1800s helped strengthen the Prussian state. Although the constitution left power in the hands of the king and the Junkers, its very existence gave the Prussians a reputation for being somewhat progressive. The abolition of serfdom and the creation of a system of public education added to this reputation. However, these reforms did not mean that Prussia was either liberal or democratic. In fact, it was an authoritarian state that rigorously supported *militarism*, the glorification of the military and a readiness for war.

King William I, who came to the throne in 1861, wanted to make sure Prussia would remain both authoritarian and militaristic. To help him, the king appointed Count Otto von Bismarck as prime minister and minister of foreign affairs.

Bismarck's "Blood and Iron"

Bismarck came from a conservative Junker family. A former military officer, he believed firmly in royal power. Although Bismarck had served in the Prussian parliament, he had no respect for representative government or for liberals. "Germany does not look to Prussia's liberalism," he said, "but to her power."

Bismarck and William I shared the goal of uniting Germany under Prussian control. They wanted a unified Germany to be the most powerful nation in Europe. These goals, Bismarck insisted, would be achieved "not with speeches and majority decisions . . . but with blood and iron."

By "blood and iron," Bismarck meant warfare and the military. Once in office, he began to carry out the king's plan to expand the army. However, the lower house of parliament had to approve the budget to pay for the expansion, and it refused. Bismarck would not let parliament stand in his way. He simply claimed that the government did not need parliament's approval. According to the constitution, Bismarck was wrong, but he ignored the constitution and collected taxes to pay military expenses anyway.

In this matter as in all others, Bismarck followed a policy of "Realpolitik," a German word meaning realism. He took whatever political action he thought necessary, whether or not it was legal or ethical. He freely applied the policy of Realpolitik in the process of creating a united Germany.

First Steps

Bismarck's first step toward unification was to weaken Austria. Ironically, he began his campaign against Austria by forming a military alliance with it.

War over Schleswig-Holstein. In 1864, Prussia and Austria joined forces to seize the provinces of Schleswig and Holstein, which were ruled by the king of Denmark. (See the map on page 69.) Despite fierce resistance from the Danish army, the Austrians and Prussians quickly overran the provinces. According to the treaty that ended the war, Austria would administer Holstein, and Prussia would administer Schleswig.

Bismarck was pleased with the outcome of the war. First, it expanded Prussian influence. Second, the division of the spoils of war soon created trouble between Prussia and Austria. This gave Bismarck an excuse to go to war with Austria.

War with Austria. Before going to war with Austria, Bismarck wanted to make certain that other nations would not support Austria. He made vague promises of ceding territory to France to make sure the French stayed out of any conflict. The Russians also promised neutrality after Bismarck reminded them that Prussia had helped suppress an anti-Russian uprising in Poland in 1863. By promising Venetia to Italy if Austria were defeated, he won Italian support.

In 1866, Bismarck used a dispute over Holstein to provoke Austria into war. Prussian troops marched into Holstein, and Austria declared war. Austrian forces were no match for the highly disciplined Prussian army under brilliant military leadership. The Prussians moved troops rapidly by railroad. They also used new rapid-firing weapons such as a needle gun that fired five rounds per minute. In just seven weeks, the war was over. Observers were stunned at the speed with which the Prussians defeated the Austrians in the Seven Weeks' War.

Bismarck did nothing to humiliate Austria after the Seven Weeks' War. "We had to avoid leaving behind in her any . . . desire for revenge," he wrote later. He followed a fairly lenient policy. Austria lost Venetia to Italy and was forced out of the German Confederation, which was then disbanded. Several states, including Schleswig and Holstein, were annexed by Prussia. One year later, the 21 German states north of the Main River joined a North German Confederation led by Prussia. (See the map on page 69.)

The Franco-Prussian War

After the war with Austria, only the Catholic states of southern Germany remained outside Prussian control. Suspicion of Prussia was strong in these states. They valued their independence and did not want to be dominated by a Protestant nation. But people in the southern states also feared control by France. Bismarck decided to play on these fears. He convinced the southern German states to form a military alliance with Prussia for protection against France. Such a military alliance, he hoped, would eventually lead to political unity. Moreover, he believed that war with France would guarantee this result.

France also seemed to want war. France had suffered several disastrous foreign adventures, and Napoleon III faced growing domestic problems. Napoleon was alarmed at the growing power of Prussia and hoped that a successful war would save his failing regime.

A minor dispute over who would assume the throne of Spain led to war between Prussia and France. In 1868, the Spanish government had offered the throne to Leopold of Hohenzollern, a cousin of William I. This angered the French, who did not want to see a Hohenzollern as king of Spain. A French ambassador visited William I at his vacation retreat at Ems and demanded that the Prussian king promise that no Hohenzollern would ever accept the Spanish throne. William refused. Then he sent a telegram to Bismarck describing the meeting.

The crafty Bismarck saw his chance. He edited the Ems telegram so that it seemed that the Prussian king and the French ambassador had been rude to one another. Then Bismarck released the telegram to the

The Unification of
Germany, 1865–1871

Prussia, 1865	
Annexed by Prussia, 1866	
States joined with Prussia to form North German Confederation, 1867	
Added to form German Empire, 1871	
Boundary of German Empire, 1871	

■ *Over a six-year period, Bismarck created a united Germany. He made skillful use of diplomacy and warfare to accomplish this task.*

press. People in both France and Prussia felt their nations had been insulted, and they clamored for war. On July 15, 1870, France declared war.

Once again, the Prussians could not be stopped. In September, they defeated the French army and took Napoleon III prisoner. By January 1871, all French resistance was crushed. The French had to sign a treaty giving up Alsace and part of Lorraine.

On January 18, 1871, at Versailles, William I was proclaimed kaiser, or emperor, of Germany. The new German Empire included all the members of the North German Confederation, the southern German states, and Alsace-Lorraine. German unification was complete, but the Germans had created a lasting enemy in France.

SECTION REVIEW

1. Locate: Schleswig, Holstein, Main River, Ems, Alsace, Lorraine.
2. Identify: William I, Otto von Bismarck, Realpolitik, Seven Weeks' War.
3. Define: militarism.
4. What states opposed the unification of Germany under Prussian leadership?
5. Describe two reasons why Prussia led the effort to unify Germany.
6. What did Bismarck gain by going to war with Denmark?
7. What did Austria lose as a result of its defeat by Prussia in 1866?
8. (a) Why did Bismarck want war with France? (b) Why did Napoleon III want war with Prussia?

3 Consolidating the German Empire

Following the Prussian victory over France, Bismarck assumed the difficult task of binding the German Empire together. Prussian Junkers were uncomfortable in the new German Empire because they feared losing their traditional privileges. Many Catholics distrusted the Protestant Prussians. Liberals and socialists disliked Bismarck's conservatism. Indeed, the forces of disunity were so great that some observers predicted a quick break-up of the German Empire. But these observers underestimated the political skills of Bismarck.

The New German Empire

The new German Empire was called the Second Reich.* The constitution of the Second Reich established a federation, a union of states. The federation included 25 states, each governed by its own hereditary king, prince, archduke, or duke. Each of these rulers appointed representatives to the upper house of a parliament called the Bundesrat (BOON duhs RAHT). The lower house, called the Reichstag (RĪKS tahg), was elected by male citizens over the age of 25.

The constitution appeared to create a representative government, but the appearance was deceiving. The Bundesrat could veto any decision made by the Reichstag. The emperor and his chancellor, or chief minister, controlled enough votes in the Bundesrat to determine its decisions. Thus, political power rested firmly in the hands of the emperor and the chancellor.

From the start, Prussia dominated the Second Reich. William I was king of Prussia as well as emperor, and he appointed Bismarck chancellor. The German Empire closely resembled the authoritarian and militaristic Prussian state. Prussians were appointed to most top positions in the government of the empire. The Prussian tradition of compulsory military service was extended

throughout the empire, with Prussian officers in charge of the army. These developments won the support of Prussian Junkers for the Second Reich.

During the early years of the empire, Bismarck created a smooth-running empire. The legal systems of the different states were made uniform. The coining of money came under the control of one imperial bank, the Reichsbank. In addition, the railroad, mail, and telegraph systems of individual states were coordinated throughout the empire. Bismarck administered with a firm hand, earning the title of the Iron Chancellor.

Conflict Over Religion

Conflict soon developed between the strong central government and Catholics in Germany. Bismarck considered the Catholic Church a threat to government power. Catholics were a large minority in Germany, and their political party, the Center party, was the second strongest party in the Reichstag. In 1872, Bismarck launched an all-out attack on the Catholic Church. He called this attack the "Kulturkampf," meaning "struggle for civilization." Parliament passed laws expelling the Jesuit order from Germany. Members of the clergy were forbidden to criticize the government, and schools run by Catholic orders were closed.

But Bismarck soon realized that the Kulturkampf was a failure. Rather than weakening the Catholic Church, it united Catholics and strengthened the Center party. In 1878, Bismarck showed his political flexibility, and most of the anti-Catholic laws were repealed. Bismarck needed the support of the Center party because he faced a serious challenge from socialists.

Demands for Political and Social Reform

German liberals had initially been unhappy with the government of the Second Reich. They wanted a more democratic government with a truly representative parliament. Many

---

* "Reich" is the German word for empire. This empire was considered the Second Reich because Germans considered the Holy Roman Empire the First Reich.

admired the British constitutional monarchy. However, gradually, many German liberals came to support Bismarck. A major reason for this change was economic prosperity. Once Germany was unified, it experienced a period of rapid industrialization and economic growth that benefited the middle class and the industrial capitalists. Liberal feelings were strongest among these groups. But many liberals were willing to support Bismarck's government in return for economic well-being.

German workers were less enthusiastic about Bismarck and his programs. As in other nations, rapid industrialization in Germany resulted in poor living and working conditions for workers. In the 1870s, many workers supported the German Social Democratic party. The Social Democratic party, founded in 1869, promoted the ideas of Marxist socialism. (See page 105.) But many German Social Democrats were probably more interested in social and economic reform than in the violent revolution that Marx had predicted.

Bismarck hated and feared socialism, and he was determined to destroy it in Germany. In 1878, he pressured the Reichstag to pass laws restricting the Social Democrats. The laws forbade publication of socialist books and pamphlets. They also gave the police the right to break up socialist meetings and imprison socialist leaders. However, this repression only strengthened the socialists.

Bismarck then changed his tactics. He decided to defeat the Social Democratic party by introducing reforms to win the workers' support for the government. During the 1880s, the government introduced accident, health, and old age insurance for German workers. The German worker thus won a basic social security program from one of Europe's most conservative regimes. Despite Bismarck's plan, however, the Social Democrats continued to win election to the Reichstag.

A New Emperor

In 1888, the 29-year-old grandson of William I inherited the German throne as William II. (William II's father had died after a brief reign.) The new emperor believed firmly in the divine right of his family to govern Germany. He shared with Bismarck a belief that a strong Germany rested on a powerful monarchy as well as on a powerful army. At first, he kept the Iron Chancellor as his chief minister. But William II was an impulsive, self-centered man, and he resented Bismarck's domination. The young emperor was determined to be his own chief minister. In 1890, he forced Bismarck to resign after 28 years of service.

William II sought to win the support of all Germans, including the working class. He allowed the anti-socialist laws to lapse and

As a young man, William II admired Bismarck. But after he became kaiser, he often clashed with the Iron Chancellor. This cartoon compares William II's dismissal of Bismarck to a ship's captain putting the pilot ashore after a difficult voyage.

The Krupp Works: The Arsenal of Germany

In 1811, Friedrich Krupp set up a small iron foundry in Essen, a town in the Ruhr Valley. Krupp employed four workers and experimented with making steel. In succeeding generations, the Krupp family expanded its iron works. By 1914, the Krupp works was the largest manufacturer of artillery, steel, and machinery in Germany, and the Krupp name was known throughout the world.

The growth of the Krupp works paralleled the growth of German industry in the 1800s. The Ruhr Valley was an area rich in iron and coal, minerals essential to the manufacture of steel. Alfred Krupp, son of the firm's founder, developed a process of manufacturing giant rolls of steel from which inexpensive seamless tableware could be made. He also discovered how to make seamless wheels for railroad cars.

In the 1840s, Alfred Krupp launched new ventures. He began manufacturing armaments, including muskets, rifles, and cannons. In 1849, the Prussian army tested the Krupp steel cannon. Krupp showed Prussian generals the benefits of his cannon, which was loaded through an opening in the side of the barrel. Krupp's cannon could be loaded more quickly and safely than the commonly used front loader. But Prussian generals distrusted the new steel barrel, and they did not order any Krupp cannons.

In 1860, the new Prussian king, William I, was impressed by the Krupp cannon, and he made the Prussian army Krupp's best customer. William's faith in Krupp was tested when Prussia declared war on Austria in 1866 and again during the Franco-Prussian war of 1870. By 1870, more than 500 Krupp cannons were in the Prussian arsenal. The power of these weapons helped assure Prussian victories.

After 1870, the success of Krupp was tied to the growing strength of the German nation and the rapid expansion of the German economy. From the blast furnaces of the Krupp works in Essen came weapons not only for Germany but also for armies all over the world.

extended the social insurance programs. No longer subject to repression, the Social Democratic party won widespread support and became the single largest party in the Reichstag. While it continued to demand more democracy, it became less revolutionary in outlook.

Under William II's personal, and often erratic, leadership, Germany set a new course in foreign policy. The ambitious ruler proposed to win Germany "a place in the sun" among great world powers such as Britain, France, and Russia. He wanted Germany to be a major commercial, colonial, and military power. He competed for colonies in Asia, Africa, and the Pacific.

Between 1892 and 1913, William II almost doubled the size of the army. He also devoted much attention to building a large navy that would rival the British navy. Both the army and navy benefited from increased German steel production. By 1900, Germany was the second largest steel producer in the world.

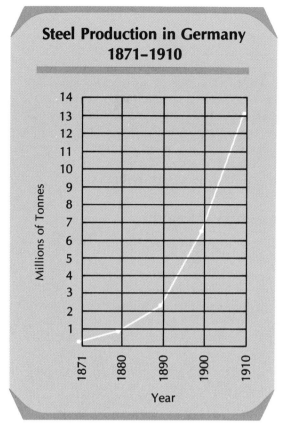

Steel Production in Germany 1871–1910

Millions of Tonnes

Year

Source: B.R. Mitchell, *European Historical Statistics*.

■ *Rising steel production was evidence of rapid economic growth in the German Empire. Compare steel production shown on this graph with German railroad construction shown on the graph on page 93.*

A National Spirit

During the late 1800s, Germans developed a strong sense of national pride. German military victories and economic progress con-tributed to this pride. By the turn of the century, Germany was the leading industrial nation in Europe.

Germans were also proud of their cultural heritage. They took special pride in renowned composers such as Beethoven and Wagner. Another source of national pride was the German educational system, which was considered the best in Europe by 1900. Students from all over the world flocked to German universities, which had a reputation for offering the most advanced scientific and technical education.

In many ways, Prussia still dominated German national life. Prussian respect and admiration for the military was one example of this dominance. As Germany became a major world power, the spirit of militarism increased. One writer summed up German attitudes toward the military in these words:

> After God the Father comes the cavalry offi-cer, then his mount, then nothing, nothing, still nothing, then the infantry officer. Very far behind come the civilians: first the reserve of-ficers and at last. . . . the remainder.

SECTION REVIEW

1. Identify: Second Reich, Bundesrat, Reichstag, William II.
2. Describe three ways in which Prussia domi-nated the Second Reich.
3. Was Bismarck's Kulturkampf successful? Why or why not?
4. What two tactics did Bismarck use in his ef-fort to destroy socialism in Germany?
5. What were William II's foreign policy goals?

4 Repression and Reform in Russia

By the mid-1800s, the Russian Empire sprawled from Europe to the Pacific Ocean. The economy and political system had changed little since the days of Peter the Great. The Russian czars and most aristo-crats wanted to preserve the traditional or-der, but forces of change were at work in Russia as they were in other parts of Europe.

Russia in the Early 1800s

The agricultural economy of the Russian Empire was based on serfdom, as it had been for hundreds of years. Serfdom had been abolished in most of Europe by the mid-1800s, but in Russia forty million serfs lived much as they had during the Middle Ages.

They were permanently attached to the land, and their owners had complete control over them. An owner could sell serfs along with the land, use them as domestic servants, and even send them off to work in factories and take their wages. Runaway serfs could be brutally punished.

The system of serfdom was inefficient. Serfs, who lived in poverty and ignorance, were slow and reluctant workers. At the same time, many landowners were poor managers. As long as they had serfs to do the work, they did not want to introduce new farming techniques. As a result, Russian agriculture suffered.

The Russian Empire was an *autocracy*, that is, a government in which the ruler has unlimited power. The czar was to be obeyed without question. However, it was difficult for the czar to extend autocratic rule over the vast empire, and laws were often enforced with highly repressive measures.

Strengthening the Autocracy

Alexander I, who became czar in 1801, was influenced by Enlightenment thinkers early in his reign. But when he realized that reform would weaken his power, he abandoned Enlightenment ideas. At the Congress of Vienna in 1815, Alexander was a strong defender of the traditional order.

The war against Napoleon had a lasting effect on Russians. Many of the officers who fought in Western Europe were impressed with what they saw there. Upon their return to Russia, some formed secret societies to discuss and spread ideas for reform. When Alexander I died in 1825, a group of army officers staged an uprising, called the Decembrist Revolt because it took place on December 26. The Decembrists demanded a constitutional monarchy. The revolt was quickly crushed, but it left a strong impression on the mind of Alexander I's successor, Nicholas I.

Nicholas I was determined to strengthen the autocracy during his reign. He did everything he could to stamp out opposition to the government. He gave secret police almost unlimited power over Russian life. People suspected of treason could be arrested, imprisoned, and deported without trial. The police censored newspapers and other written material to suppress subversive ideas. Universities were a special target because Nicholas was afraid students would adopt dangerous foreign ideas. The outbreak of the 1848 revolutions in other parts of Europe confirmed the czar's conviction that strict control was necessary in Russia.

A Period of Reform

Despite the efforts of Nicholas I to prevent change in Russia, demands for reform grew. Some Russians reacted against the years of repressive rule. Others began to realize that serfdom was inefficient. As Russia began to industrialize, factory owners could not find enough free workers because so many people were serfs. In addition, the number of serf revolts had increased.

When Russia was defeated in the Crimean War, many Russians blamed the defeat on the weaknesses of serfdom and the autocratic political system. Nicholas I died in the midst of the Crimean War and was succeeded by his son Alexander II. The new czar, like his father, believed firmly in the autocracy, but he thought that some reforms were needed to prevent revolution.

In 1861, Alexander II issued the Emancipation Edict freeing the serfs. The czar declared: "It is better to abolish serfdom from above than to wait until it is abolished from below." Serfs were given personal freedom, but they received no free land as many had hoped they would. Instead, the government paid landowners handsomely for their land. Then it parceled the land out to village communities, called *mirs*. The peasants who lived in the mirs had to pay the government for the land over a period of 49 years. Therefore, peasants were heavily in debt and seldom had enough land to farm efficiently. Consequently, Russian agriculture improved little.

The czar introduced other reforms. He relaxed censorship and restrictions on universities. The jury system was introduced, and regulations governing soldiers were

Before 1861, Russian nobles owned huge estates on which serfs lived and worked in virtual slavery. Nobles often led idle lives. They wasted time and money gambling and attending lavish parties. In this cartoon by French artist Gustave Doré, Russian nobles use bundles of serfs as bets in a card game.

made less harsh. The government also created local elected assemblies called *zemstvos*. Many zemstvos established schools and improved health care. In addition, through the zemstvos, some Russians gained experience in government.

The reforms of Alexander II encouraged revolutionary activity in Russia. During the 1870s, thousands of educated young people left the cities. They went into the countryside to convince peasants to support revolutionary goals. These populists, as they were called, had little success organizing the peasants. A few populists eventually formed political parties to work for revolution. The most radical populists formed a group called the People's Will. Its goal was the assassination of the czar. After several attempts, they finally succeeded in assassinating Alexander II in 1881.

A Return to Repression

Alexander III, who succeeded his father, moved quickly to crush revolutionaries and end reform. He reduced the powers of the zemstvos, restored strict censorship, and directed the secret police to seek out critics of the government.

Because of its vast size, the Russian Empire contained many ethnic minorities, including Ukrainians, Finns, Poles, and Jews. Many of these people opposed Russian rule. Alexander III wanted to strengthen the autocracy through a policy called Russification. The czar tried to force all people in the empire to use the Russian language and to adopt the Russian Orthodox religion.

The Jews were a special target of Russification. They were forbidden to own land and were forced to live in certain areas of the country. Government troops took part in *pogroms*, murderous raids on Jewish communities. This persecution drove hundreds of thousands of Jews out of Russia. Many immigrated to North America.

In 1894, Nicholas II succeeded his father and continued his father's repressive policies. Nicholas II faced new unrest as Russia began to industrialize more rapidly. By 1900, Russia was the fourth largest iron producer in the world, and the number of industrial workers reached two million. Like workers in other countries, Russian workers labored long hours for little pay. Labor unions were illegal in Russia, but labor unrest led to numerous strikes, many of them violent.

The Revolution of 1905

As the new century dawned, Nicholas II sat uneasily on the throne. In addition to labor unrest, the government faced opposition from landless peasants, national minorities, and middle class liberals, who demanded a constitutional government. In addition, assassination of government officials by revolutionaries had become commonplace.

In 1904, war broke out between Russia and Japan. The two nations had been competing for influence in Manchuria and Korea. Nicholas II hoped that a Russian vic-

tory would ease discontent at home. But the Russians were soundly defeated by Japan. This humiliating defeat further increased tensions at home.

On January 22, 1905, a peaceful parade of workers approached the czar's palace in St. Petersburg. The workers wanted to present Nicholas II with a petition for better working conditions, greater personal liberties, and an elected national legislature. Some carried large pictures of the czar as a sign of their loyalty. They believed that only the czar could help improve their lot. But Nicholas saw the parade as a threat to his power. He hurriedly left the palace. But before he left, he ordered the soldiers to fire on the crowd. About 1,000 workers were killed on the day that became known as Bloody Sunday.

After Bloody Sunday, the discontent that had been building for years exploded.

The Russian people's faith in the czar was badly shaken by the events of Bloody Sunday. The massacre of unarmed demonstrators led to further protests and bloodshed in the Revolution of 1905. This painting shows mounted Russian soldiers charging a crowd and scattering them by using whips.

Russia was quickly engulfed in revolutionary turmoil. Riots and strikes swept major industrial centers. Bands of peasants roamed the countryside, pillaging and burning mansions of nobles.

By October 1905, the clamor for more freedom and a democratic government was so loud that the czar reluctantly promised "freedom of person, conscience, assembly, and union." He approved the creation of a national assembly called the Duma. This and other concessions, he hoped, would end the violence. For a time, they did. The Revolution of 1905 came to an end. However, Nicholas' confidence returned, and he never gave the Duma any real power. In 1906, he simply dismissed the first Duma when it would not cooperate with him.

The czar emerged from the Revolution of 1905 with his power largely intact. New Dumas were elected, but they were dominated by supporters of the autocracy. Nevertheless, between 1906 and 1911, the government introduced some reform. For example,

the czar's chief minister, Peter Stolypin (stoh LEE puhn), began a program to help peasants buy their own land. But Stolypin was assassinated in 1911, and the government again became repressive. The problems left unsolved by the Revolution of 1905 remained as seeds for a future revolution.

SECTION REVIEW

1. Identify: Decembrist Revolt, Nicholas I, Alexander II, Alexander III, Russification, Nicholas II, Peter Stolypin.
2. Define: autocracy, mir, zemstvo, pogrom.
3. How was the system of serfdom inefficient?
4. Why did Nicholas I think he had to strengthen the autocracy?
5. What helped convince Alexander II to free the serfs?
6. What effect did the Industrial Revolution have on Russia?
7. How did Nicholas II respond to the Revolution of 1905?

5 Nationalism in Eastern Europe

At the start of the 1800s, much of Eastern Europe was divided between the Austrian Empire and the Ottoman Empire. Nationalism, which helped create unity in Italy and Germany, threatened the unity of the Austrian and Ottoman empires. Each empire contained many different ethnic and religious groups. Between 1848 and 1914, nationalities in Eastern Europe agitated for self-rule or independence from the Austrians and the Ottomans. This situation contributed to tensions within the empires and throughout Europe.

The Austrian Empire

The Austrian Empire included more than 12 different nationalities. The Germans of Austria and the Magyars of Hungary were the two largest groups, but neither made up a majority in the empire. Other major nationalities included Poles, Czechs, Croatians, Slovaks, and Romanians. (See the map on page 78.)

The national groups within the Austrian Empire had a strong sense of pride in their own languages and customs. Most resented domination by the Austrians. As you read earlier, the Hapsburg rulers of Austria successfully crushed the nationalist revolts of 1848. (See page 50.) But this defeat did not end the agitation by nationalist groups for greater control of their own affairs.

Francis Joseph became emperor of Austria in 1848 at the age of 18. Throughout his long reign, which lasted until 1916, he sought ways to keep his diverse empire together. During the 1850s, he tried to end all nationalist agitation. However, setbacks in foreign policy forced him to consider a new policy.

In 1859, Austria lost Lombardy to Italy. In 1866, as a result of its rapid defeat by

Prussia, Austria lost its influence among the German states. (See page 68.) Although Francis Joseph continued to oppose nationalism, he realized that Austrians had to strengthen the empire at home. He decided to compromise with the Magyars.

Creation of the Dual Monarchy

The Magyars had long demanded greater *autonomy*, or self-government, within the Austrian Empire. Even though the Austrians had ignored these demands, the Magyars fought loyally with them in the war with Prussia. The Hungarian leader Francis Deák (DEH ahk) thought the time was right to win concessions from the emperor. Deák wanted Hungary to be recognized as a separate kingdom with its own territory and its own constitution.

■ *Many different nationalities lived in Austria-Hungary, the Russian Empire, and the Ottoman Empire. Some major nationalities are shown on this map. The dotted line is the boundary between Austria and Hungary after 1867.*

Nationalities in Eastern Europe About 1870

In 1867, Francis Joseph agreed to the creation of a dual monarchy. The old Austrian Empire was divided into two parts: the empire of Austria and the kingdom of Hungary.

The Dual Monarchy of Austria-Hungary was united by a single ruler, the Hapsburg emperor, who would be the emperor of Austria and king of Hungary. Austria and Hungary shared ministries of war, finance, and foreign affairs, but in other areas they were independent of each other. Each had its own constitution and its own parliament.

The creation of the Dual Monarchy satisfied the Magyars, but other nationalities in Austria-Hungary remained dissatisfied. Austrians were a minority in Austria, and Magyars were a minority in Hungary. The Austrian government made minor concessions to other nationalities. But the Magyars tried to force everyone in Hungary to give up their own ethnic identity and become Magyars. The Romanians and the Slavs in Hungary felt especially oppressed by Magyar rule. The unrest among the nationalities in Austria-Hungary continued to threaten the unity of the empire and the peace in Europe.

Life in Austria-Hungary

In both Austria and Hungary, a small noble class dominated the political, economic, and social life. Nobles owned huge estates, while peasants had only small plots. For example, in 1895, fewer than 200 noble families owned over half the farmland in Austria-Hungary. At the same time, over one million peasants subsisted on seven acres or less per person.

Democracy made little headway in Austria-Hungary. For the most part, government remained in the hands of the wealthy nobles. Universal male suffrage was introduced in Austria in 1907. However, the elected parliament was paralyzed by division among the nationalities. Debates were sometimes accompanied by violent clashes between deputies, who threw inkwells at one another. In Hungary, voting was limited to 6 percent of the population. This prevented any effective challenge to the Magyar ruling class.

The economy of Austria-Hungary remained mainly agricultural during the 1800s.

Late in the century, Austria began to industrialize slowly, and Hungary followed.

The Ottoman Empire and the Balkans

The Ottoman Empire reached the height of its power in the 1500s, extending from Eastern Europe across Asia Minor into the Middle East and Egypt. But since that time it had steadily declined. Corruption in the wealthy ruling class was common.

The Ottoman Empire contained many nationalities who sought freedom from Ottoman rule. Gradually, portions of the empire had broken away. By 1850, Egypt and Arabia had gained autonomy within the empire, and Algeria was controlled by France. In the Balkans, Greece won independence in 1830, and Serbia and Montenegro gained autonomy.

In 1844, Czar Nicholas I called the Ottoman Empire "the sick man of Europe." Throughout the 1800s, many diplomats expected it to collapse, as one national group after another fought for independence. However, Britain and France worked to prevent a collapse. They considered the Ottoman Empire a block against the expansion of Russia or Austria-Hungary into the Balkan region. Therefore, in 1854, Britain and France entered the Crimean War on the side of the Ottoman Empire. They wanted to prevent the Russians from gaining control of Constantinople and the Dardanelles.

Although Russia was defeated in the Crimean War, the Ottoman Empire continued to decline. Rumania gained autonomy in 1859. In 1875, revolts against the Turks broke out in the Balkans. The Turks moved to suppress the revolts, but the Russians came to the aid of the Slavic peoples in the Balkans. In 1877, the Russians defeated the Turks and forced them to sign the Treaty of San Stefano. It gave the Russians the right to occupy a large, independent Bulgarian state.

Other European powers, fearing increased Russian influence in the Balkans, objected to the treaty. They pressured the Russians to attend an international congress at Berlin in 1878. The Congress of Berlin created a much smaller Bulgarian state, which was to be autonomous within the Ottoman Empire. Serbia, Romania, and Montenegro

As the Ottoman Empire declined in the 1800s, independent states were created in the Balkans.

gained complete independence. Britain received Cyprus from the Ottoman Empire, and Austria-Hungary won the right to administer the areas of Bosnia and Herzegovina. (See the map above.)

The Congress of Berlin recognized new states in the Balkans, which pleased nationalists. However, it also caused much bitterness and left unfulfilled hopes. The Russians thought they had been cheated. Furthermore, the new states did not include all members of a nationality. For example, many Serbs lived in Hungary, while fellow Serbs had an independent nation across the border. The Balkans would continue to be a source of unrest and conflict.

A New International Order

The results of the Congress of Berlin reflected the new international order that had developed in Europe by the late 1800s. The emergence of new nations such as Germany and Italy and the decline of old empires upset the balance of power worked out at the Congress of Vienna in 1815. During the first half of the 1800s, the Austrian Empire under Metternich had been the dominant force in Europe. During the second half, Germany under Bismarck took the lead.

The international order was further affected by the Industrial Revolution, which had fueled economic growth in all parts of Europe, especially in Britain and Germany. Developments in technology led to new military weapons, which increased the capacity for war. Disputes over territory in Europe and the scramble for empires would cause conflict and war.

SECTION REVIEW

1. Locate: Greece, Serbia, Montenegro, Bulgaria, Bosnia and Herzegovina.
2. Identify: Francis Joseph, Francis Deák.
3. Define: autonomy.
4. What two events led the Austrians to agree to the creation of the Dual Monarchy?
5. How were Austria and Hungary independent of each other in the Dual Monarchy?
6. Why did Britain and France want to preserve the Ottoman Empire?

IN PERSPECTIVE

Nationalism was a major force in Europe during the second half of the 1800s. Italian nationalists led a successful struggle for the unification of Italy. Once united, however, Italy still faced economic problems and tensions caused by conflicts between different parts of the nation.

A united Germany had been a goal of German nationalists for many years. Bismarck realized this goal through a series of wars with Denmark, Austria, and France. He tied the German states together into a powerful, prosperous empire.

In Russia, the czars tried to maintain their autocratic rule, but they found that some reform was necessary. The attempt to impose the Russian nationality on the diverse peoples of the empire and repressive political control, however, led to a revolution in 1905. The reforms carried out after the Revolution of 1905 had a limited effect on the problems in the Russian state.

Nationalism also created problems for the rulers of the Austrian and Ottoman empires. The Austrians compromised with the Magyars by creating the Dual Monarchy of Austria-Hungary, but other nationalities within the empire continued to demand greater autonomy. Throughout the 1800s, parts of the Ottoman Empire broke away.

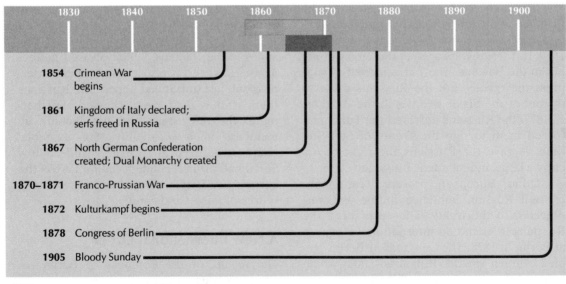

1854	Crimean War begins
1861	Kingdom of Italy declared; serfs freed in Russia
1867	North German Confederation created; Dual Monarchy created
1870–1871	Franco-Prussian War
1872	Kulturkampf begins
1878	Congress of Berlin
1905	Bloody Sunday

■ Unification of Italy   ■ Unification of Germany

Recalling Facts

Review the time line on page 80 and your reading in this chapter. Then choose the letter of the correct time period for each of the following events.

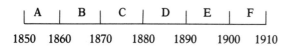

| A | B | C | D | E | F |

1850   1860   1870   1880   1890   1900   1910

1. Bismarck begins the Kulturkampf.
2. Serfs freed in Russia.
3. Crimean War breaks out.
4. Bloody Sunday takes place.
5. Austria-Hungary created.
6. Kingdom of Italy declared.
7. Cavour becomes prime minister of Sardinia.
8. Franco-Prussian War begins.

Chapter Checkup

1. (a) How did the goals of Young Italy and Cavour differ? (b) Which goal was achieved by 1870? (c) What groups were unhappy with the unification that was achieved? Why?

2. (a) What obstacles stood in the way of German unification? (b) How did Bismarck overcome these obstacles?

3. (a) In what ways did the German Empire have a representative government? (b) In what ways did it not have a representative government?

4. (a) How did Bismarck try to strengthen the government of the German Empire? (b) How did William II try to win public support?

5. (a) Describe the system of serfdom in Russia. (b) How did the existence of serfdom affect agriculture? (c) What effect did emancipation have on the serfs?

6. Describe how each of the following tried to strengthen the autocracy in Russia: (a) Nicholas I; (b) Alexander III; (c) Nicholas II.

7. (a) How did nationalism threaten the existence of the Austrian Empire? (b) How did Austria deal with its national minorities? (c) How did Hungary deal with its national minorities?

8. (a) What evidence convinced many diplomats that the Ottoman Empire was going to collapse during the 1800s? (b) How did the empire survive until the end of the century?

For Further Thought

1. *Comparing* Compare the ways in which Italy and Germany were unified. (a) What role did warfare play in the unification of each nation? (b) What role did international diplomacy play? (c) In which nation do you think a strong national leader was more important? Why?

2. *Analyzing* Otto von Bismarck believed that the key to German unity and power was "blood and iron." Which national leaders discussed in this chapter do you think would have agreed with Bismarck's philosophy? Explain.

3. *Relating Past to Present* (a) Do any nations today have problems with national minorities? (b) How are these problems similar to problems faced by the Austrians? (c) How are they different?

Developing Basic Skills

1. *Analyzing Political Cartoons* Political cartoons can be valuable historical evidence. By analyzing political cartoons, you can learn how people at the time viewed public issues. Study the cartoon on page 66 and then answer the following questions: (a) What is the main topic of the cartoon? (b) What political figures are shown? (c) What does the boot represent? (d) Do you think the cartoonist approved of the events taking place in Italy? Explain.

2. *Map Reading* Study the map on page 69 and then answer the following questions: (a) What is the topic of the map? (b) Describe the area of Prussia in 1865. (c) What territory was added to Prussia in 1866? (d) Why do you think Austrian influence was greater among the southern German states than among the northern German states?

3. *Graph Reading* Study the graph on page 73 and then answer the following questions: (a) What information is shown on the graph? (b) How much steel did Germany produce in 1880? (c) How did German steel production change between 1871 and 1910? (d) How do you think steel production in Germany during this period probably affected economic development?

See page 203 for suggested readings.

5 The Industrial Revolution

(1750–1914)

To one British author, Charles Dickens, whose novel *Hard Times* was published in 1854, a typical factory town was "a town of machinery and tall chimneys, out of which interminable serpents of smoke trailed themselves for ever and ever, and never got uncoiled. It had a black canal in it, and a river that ran purple with ill-smelling dye, and vast piles of buildings full of windows where there was a rattling and trembling all day long, and where the piston of the steam engine worked monotonously up and down, like the head of an elephant in a state of melancholy madness."

To Dickens, the people of the town shared the same "melancholy madness." They were "equally like one another. . . . all went in and out at the same hours, with the same sound upon the same pavement, to do the same work and to whom every day was the same as yesterday and tomorrow, and every year the counterpart of last and the next."

The conditions Dickens described were the result of the Industrial Revolution. The Industrial Revolution was neither sudden nor swift. It was a long, slow process in which production shifted from hand tools to machines and in which new sources of power such as steam and electricity replaced human and animal power.

The Industrial Revolution had two distinct stages. During the first stage, from about 1750 to 1850, Great Britain took the lead in shifting to new methods of production. During the second stage, from the mid-1800s to about 1914, the nations of Western Europe and North America developed into modern industrial powers. The Industrial Revolution was to completely transform the patterns of life in these nations.

Detail from St. Lazare Station, *by Claude Monet.*

1 Beginnings of the Industrial Revolution in Britain

By the mid-1700s, new methods of producing goods were being developed in Great Britain and France. Many of these new methods were outgrowths of inventions made during the Enlightenment, a time when people began to apply scientific principles to practical problems. (See page 4.) During the late 1700s, the French Revolution disrupted the political and economic life of France. This was one reason that Britain emerged as the leader of the Industrial Revolution.

The Agricultural Revolution

One key to the beginning of the Industrial Revolution in Britain was a revolution in agriculture that greatly increased the amount and variety of food produced. During the 1700s, farmers began growing new crops, such as potatoes and corn, that had been introduced from the Americas. They also developed new ways of using the land that made it more productive.

Since the Middle Ages, farmers had planted the same crop in a given field year after year. Every third year, they left the field fallow to prevent the soil from wearing out. In the 1730s, Charles Townshend discovered that fields did not have to be left fallow if farmers would rotate the crops they planted in a field. He suggested that farmers grow wheat or barley in a field for one or two years and then plant clover or turnips in the field for one or two years.

Townshend's ideas helped revolutionize agriculture. Crops such as clover and turnips replenished the soil with the nutrients that wheat and barley used. Moreover, clover and turnips provided excellent feed for animals. Thus, farmers could raise cattle and sheep for food. As meat became available at lower cost, people could add more protein to their diet.

The invention of machines also increased food production. Jethro Tull found a method of planting seeds that was better than scattering them randomly. When the seeds were scattered, they would grow wherever they landed, and fields became a tangle of crops and weeds. Tull developed a seed drill that planted the seeds in straight rows. The seed drill reduced the amount of seed used in planting. It also allowed farmers to weed around the straight rows of growing crops.

During the 1700s, iron plows replaced less efficient, wooden plows. In the 1800s, mechanical reapers and threshers began to replace hand methods of harvesting crops. This further increased farm production.

Changing patterns of land ownership in Britain also contributed to the Agricultural Revolution. Since the Middle Ages, farmers had worked small strips of land in scattered fields. They grazed their animals and gathered timber on common, or public, lands. In the 1500s, wealthy landowners began claiming the right to these common lands. The *enclosure movement*, fencing off of public lands by individual landowners, spread rapidly in the 1700s.

The enclosure movement made agriculture more efficient because wealthy landowners farmed larger amounts of land and experimented with new crops. However, it forced many small farmers off land they had worked for years. Some became tenant farmers on land owned by others. Others drifted to the towns in search of work.

The Agricultural Revolution helped set the stage for the Industrial Revolution. Increased food production improved people's diet and health, which contributed to rapid population growth. As the population increased, the demand for manufactured goods, such as clothing, grew. Furthermore, more efficient methods of farming meant that fewer people were needed to work the land. Unemployed farmers, including those forced off the land by the enclosure movement, formed a large new labor force.

Changes in the Textile Industry

While improvements in agriculture released many workers from farming, inventions—especially in the British textile industry—created new demands for laborers. During the 1500s and 1600s, entrepreneurs developed a system of having work done in the countryside, known as the *domestic system*. Rural families were supplied with raw wool and cotton. In their own cottages, family members cleaned and spun the wool or cotton into thread. They then used hand looms to weave the thread into cloth.

The domestic system could not keep up with a steadily rising demand for cloth, especially cotton cloth. In the 1700s, practical-minded individuals developed ways to improve the manufacture of cloth. Each invention triggered others, revolutionizing the whole textile industry.

Mechanical inventions. In 1733, the clockmaker John Kay invented the flying shuttle, which replaced the hand-held shuttle used in weaving. This invention greatly speeded up the weaving process. Weavers were soon using thread faster than spinners could produce it.

In 1764, James Hargreaves, a carpenter, developed a way to speed up spinning. He attached several spindles to a single spinning wheel. Using this spinning jenny, as it was called, a person could spin several threads at once. In 1769, Richard Arkwright devised a machine that could hold up to 100 spindles. Arkwright's invention was too heavy to be operated by hand, so he used water power to turn it. Thus, the machine was called the water frame. Ten years later, Samuel Crompton developed the spinning mule, which used features of Hargreaves' spinning jenny and Arkwright's water frame. Once again, the production of cotton thread was increased.

With more thread now available, the need arose for faster looms. In 1785, Edward Cartwright built a loom in which the weaving action was powered by water. Using this power loom, a worker could produce 200 times more cloth in a day than had previously been possible.

In 1793, the American Eli Whitney gave the British cotton industry a further boost. Before cotton fibers could be spun into cloth, workers had to remove sticky seeds, an extremely slow process. Whitney invented the cotton gin, a machine that tore the fibers from the seeds, thus speeding up the process of cleaning cotton fibers. The invention of the cotton gin helped the British cotton industry because it increased the production of raw cotton and made it cheaper. By the 1830s, Britain was importing 127 000 t (tonnes) of raw cotton every year and had become the cotton manufacturing center of the world.

The factory system. The new spinning and weaving machines were expensive. They also had to be set up near rivers, where running water was available to power them.* Inventors such as Arkwright built spinning mills and started hiring hundreds of workers to run the new machines.

---

* Water flowing down a stream or river turned a water wheel that produced power to run the machines.

The Industrial Revolution began in the textile industry. By the early 1800s, large spinning mills like this one were operating all over England. Steam-powered looms required constant tending. Notice the worker at right who is cleaning debris from under the threads. The air inside the mills was kept hot and humid because threads broke less often under such conditions.

Coal fueled the early Industrial Revolution. In this 1814 print, a coal miner stands in front of a steam engine that is pulling a load of coal. The print is the first English picture of a steam-powered vehicle. Despite the use of steam engines, work in the coal mines remained largely dependent on the backbreaking labor of men, women, and children.

The early textile mills were examples of the factory system, which gradually replaced the domestic system of production. The *factory system* brought workers and machines together in one place to manufacture goods. Everyone had to work a set number of hours each day, and workers were paid daily or weekly wages.

Development of the Steam Engine

Many early inventions in the textile industry were powered by running water, but soon steam became the major source of energy. The idea of a steam-powered engine had existed for a long time. In 1698, Thomas Savery constructed a steam-driven pump to remove water from flooded coal mines. Unfortunately, Savery's pump often exploded because of the intense pressure of the steam.

In the early 1700s, Thomas Newcomen developed a safer steam-powered pump. But Newcomen's engine broke down frequently and required a lot of coal to fuel it. Finally, in the 1760s, James Watt, who had repaired several Newcomen engines, developed ways

of improving the engine. Watt's steam engine got four times more power than Newcomen's engine from the same amount of coal.

The British found many uses for steam power. Steam engines were used in the growing textile industry. They also became important in coal mining.

Development of the Iron and Coal Industries

Producing and operating the new machines, including the steam engine, required large quantities of iron and coal. Fortunately, Britain had extensive deposits of both. During the Industrial Revolution, the iron and coal industries benefited from improved production techniques.

Iron was produced by a smelting process. Iron ore, which contains only small amounts of iron, was heated to high temperatures to burn off impurities. Then the molten iron was poured off. Charcoal, a fuel made by partially burning hard woods, was used to heat the ore. But hard woods were becoming scarce in Britain. Ironworkers experimented with using coal instead of charcoal. However, coal had many gases that mixed with the molten iron, making the iron hard to work. In the early 1700s, Abraham Darby helped solve this problem. He developed a way to use coke, or coal with the gases burned off, in place of charcoal.

Iron making was further improved in the 1780s, when Henry Cort developed a puddling process in which molten iron was stirred with a long rod to allow impurities to burn off. Iron produced in this manner was stronger than iron produced in other ways and less likely to crack under pressure. Cort also developed a technique to run molten iron through rollers to produce sheets of iron.

Improved production methods enabled Britain to quadruple iron production between 1788 and 1806. In addition, the demand for coal, both for making iron and for powering steam engines, triggered a boom in coal mining.

In the 1850s, the iron industry received another boost when Henry Bessemer developed a procedure that made the production of steel, an alloy of iron and other materials, cheaper and easier. In the *Bessemer process*, blasts of cold air were blown through heated iron to remove impurities. The result was stronger, more workable steel. As steel became readily available, it triggered the growth of other industries.

Advances in Transportation and Communication

Industry requires a good transportation system to bring raw materials to factories and distribute finished goods. In the 1700s, the need for rapid, inexpensive transportation led to a boom in canal building in Britain. In 1759, the Duke of Bridgewater built a canal to connect his coal mines and his factories. Soon, canals were being built all over the country.

The 1700s were also a time of road building in Britain. The Scottish engineer John McAdam invented a road surface made of crushed stone. This surface made roads usable in all weather. By the 1800s, road travel in England had become almost as fast as it had been in Roman times.

The need for good transportation led to the development of the railroad industry. For years, mine carts had been pulled along iron rails by workers or donkeys. In 1829, George Stephenson, a mining engineer, developed the Rocket, the first steam-powered locomotive. The Rocket could barrel along iron rails at 36 miles per hour (58 km/h), an astounding speed at the time.

Between 1840 and 1850, the British built over 5,000 miles (8,000 km) of railway tracks. As steel rails replaced iron rails, trains reached speeds of 60 miles per hour (96 km/h). Railroads brought raw materials, factories, and markets closer together than ever before. They also increased the demand for coal and steel.

In the 1800s, Britain led the way in railroad building and shipbuilding. However, it was an American engineer, Robert Fulton, who developed a way to use steam power for ships. In 1807, Fulton successfully tested the *Clermont*, a paddle-wheeled steamship, on the Hudson River. Other inventors improved the steamship. By 1850, steamships regularly crossed the oceans.

The railroad and the steamship improved communications within nations and across the world. Britain introduced an inexpensive postal system, which further improved communication. In 1837, Samuel F.B. Morse, an American, devised the telegraph, which sent messages by electrical impulses. Messages that once would have taken days to arrive now took minutes or seconds. In 1851, the first underwater telegraph cable was installed under the English Channel. It made rapid communication between Britain and the continent possible.

Why Britain Led the Industrial Revolution

Britain enjoyed many advantages that helped it take an early lead in the Industrial Revolution. As you have read, with the Agri-

The Industrial Revolution in Great Britain: Reading Thematic Maps

Maps provide much useful information about how geography can influence historical events and developments. Many of the maps you have studied in this text have shown topographical features, such as rivers and oceans, as well as political boundaries. Some have also given information about military advances.

However, there are other kinds of maps that give valuable information about population, natural resources, rainfall, and crop production. Maps that provide this kind of specialized information are called thematic maps. Practice reading thematic maps by studying the map at right. Then follow these steps.

1. **Decide what is shown on the map.** On a thematic map, the legend tells you what the symbols mean. Answer the following questions about the map: (a) What is the topic of the map? (b) What do the areas shaded orange represent? (c) What do the purple squares represent? (d) What other information is given on the map?

2. **Read the information on the map.** Answer the following questions about the map: (a) Name two cities on the map with populations of 300,000 or over. (b) Name two cities with populations of 100,000 to 300,000. (c) Which cities with populations over 300,000 were located near iron and coal resources? (d) Which large cities were probably ports?

3. **Draw conclusions about a historical event or development.** (a) What relationship does the map show between areas with coal and iron resources and those with large cities? (b) What areas of Britain were probably the most industrialized? Explain. (c) What areas were probably the least industrialized? Explain.

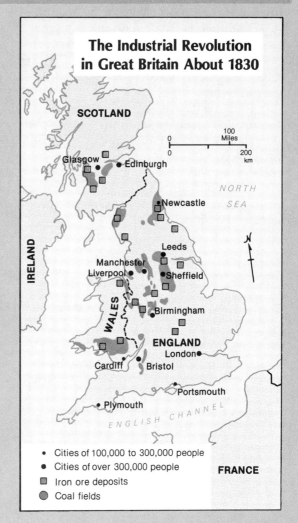

The Industrial Revolution in Great Britain About 1830

- Cities of 100,000 to 300,000 people
- Cities of over 300,000 people
- Iron ore deposits
- Coal fields

cultural Revolution came increased food production, freeing many laborers to work in industry. Moreover, Britain had plentiful iron and coal resources, and it developed an excellent transportation system to speed the flow of goods.

Britain was also the leading commercial power in Europe. Since the 1500s and 1600s, British merchants had made huge profits from the international trade in tobacco, sugar, tea, and slaves. As a result, British entrepreneurs had the financial resources to invest in industries such as textiles, mines, railroads, and shipbuilding. Britain also had a large colonial empire that supplied raw materials to its factories. In addition, people in

87

the colonies bought finished goods produced by British industry.

The British government adopted policies that encouraged industrial growth. It lifted restrictions on trade, giving manufacturers and merchants opportunities to make large profits. It encouraged road- and canal-building schemes and maintained a strong navy to protect British merchant ships all over the world.

The intellectual and social climate in Britain also encouraged industrialization. Although a clear class structure existed in British society, individuals could improve their social standing. The British accepted the idea that poor people did not have to stay poor forever but through talent and hard work could improve themselves.

SECTION REVIEW

1. Identify: Charles Townshend, John Kay, James Hargreaves, Richard Arkwright, Edward Cartwright, James Watt, Abraham Darby, George Stephenson, Samuel Morse.
2. Define: enclosure movement, domestic system, factory system, Bessemer process.
3. List two factors that led to the Agricultural Revolution in Britain.
4. Choose one invention and describe how it affected the production of textiles.
5. How did the factory system differ from the domestic system?
6. Describe how each of the following improvements was important to the iron industry: (a) puddling process; (b) Bessemer process.

2 The Rise of Modern Industry

After the 1850s, the pace of industrialization quickened, and the Industrial Revolution entered its second stage. Between 1850 and 1914, industry grew rapidly in the nations of Western Europe, including Belgium, France, and Germany. At the same time, the United States began to industrialize and soon rivaled Britain in many fields. Japan also joined the ranks of industrialized nations, as you will read in Chapter 8.

The Spread of Industrialization

During the second half of the 1800s, other nations began to challenge British leadership in the Industrial Revolution. Belgium was one of the first nations on the continent to industrialize. Like Britain, Belgium had large deposits of coal and iron. Belgium also had a long manufacturing tradition, especially in textiles. Thus, it had a skilled labor force willing to work in industry. Moreover, Belgian entrepreneurs had the capital needed to invest in factories and machinery.

France, too, built a strong textile industry with a number of inventions. In the early 1800s, Joseph Marie Jacquard developed the first power loom that could be used to weave complex patterns. The Jacquard loom had a punched card system that controlled the intricate pattern.* Textiles produced on Jacquard looms commanded high prices among the fashion-conscious upper classes in Europe.

The French government encouraged the textile industry at home by imposing high tariffs on cloth imported from other nations. Because imported cloth was thus more expensive, people bought French textiles. The French government also supported projects to improve transportation, especially the building of railroads.

Across the Atlantic, the United States had considerable natural resources. Aided by large investments of capital from Europe, Americans began to exploit these resources. Railroad building fostered rapid economic growth in the United States. In 1869, the first railroad spanned the United States. In the 1870s, American iron and steel production was

---

* The punched cards used in early computers were based on Jacquard's idea.

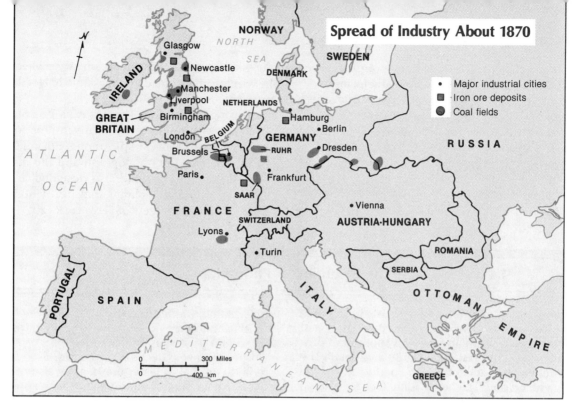

Spread of Industry About 1870

- Major industrial cities
- Iron ore deposits
- Coal fields

■ *During the second half of the 1800s, the Industrial Revolution spread beyond Britain to other European countries. Iron and coal were essential to the growth of industry on the continent, as they had been in Britain. Some of the major iron deposits and coal fields are shown on this map. Which industrial cities in Germany, Belgium, and France were located near these resources?*

well on the way to outstripping that of Britain. In the next decade, the United States surpassed Britain as the leading industrial nation.

In the 1850s and 1860s, German industry suffered from a lack of political unity among the German states. After Germany achieved national unity, it rivaled the United States and Britain as a leading industrial power, as you read in Chapter 4.

The nations of southern and eastern Europe remained largely agricultural during the 1800s. In Spain, Italy, Austria, and Russia, governments did little to encourage industrial growth.

Advances in Science and Technology

During the early Industrial Revolution, most inventors were people looking for ways to repair tools or improve machinery. After 1850, however, people turned to science not only to solve problems of manufacturing but also

to discover new products to manufacture. Scientific research soon resulted in many inventions as well as extraordinary advances in technology. Knowledge of new technology spread quickly from one nation to another.

The results of scientific research brought sweeping changes to various industries. For example, the English chemist William Perkins discovered a brilliant dye that could be made cheaply from coal. German chemists also discovered ways to make dyes cheaply. The textile industry quickly adopted the new dyes to replace more costly natural dyes such as indigo. Other discoveries led to the development and widespread use of chemical fertilizers, which radically increased food production.

The work of physicists also stimulated new technology. In 1800, Alessandro Volta, an Italian physicist, used his knowledge of electricity to build one of the first electric batteries. The work of Michael Faraday, an English scientist, led to the construction of electric generators, which eventually replaced steam engines in many factories.

Discoveries in the field of electricity also improved communications. In 1866, the first underwater telegraph cable across the Atlantic Ocean was successfully installed. Ten years later, Alexander Graham Bell invented the telephone. By the end of the century, Italian physicist Guglielmo Marconi had developed a way to send electric signals without wire or cable. His invention was called the wireless in England and the radio in North America.

During this period, Thomas Alva Edison produced a stunning array of inventions in his New Jersey workshop. Among Edison's inventions were the phonograph and the incandescent light bulb. He also designed an electric generating plant that provided power to light the streets of New York City.

The Invention of Photography

On a summer afternoon in 1839, people crowded into an auditorium in Paris. They had gathered to learn about a new method of producing pictures of great clarity and detail. The method had recently been perfected by the painter Louis Daguerre (duh GEHR), shown here. These pictures, soon called daguerreotypes, were early photographs.

The audience listened intently while Daguerre's process was described. Daguerre had placed a polished silver plate coated with light-sensitive silver iodide in the camera and exposed it to light for several minutes. When the plate was removed from the camera, it appeared to be blank. But when it was treated with mercury fumes, an image appeared on the surface. The plate was then washed to remove the chemicals and coated with everyday table salt to keep the image from fading.

Many people in the audience were excited about the new invention. "[I] ran straight off to buy iodine," reported one listener. "I hated to see the sun go down, for it forced me to put off my experiments until the next day. A few days later, cameras were focused on buildings everywhere. Everyone wanted to take the view from his window, and anyone who got at the first attempt a silhouette of rooftops against the sky was in luck ... the technique was so novel and seemed so marvelous that even the poorest result gave indescribable joy."

News of Daguerre's technique traveled swiftly. But there was one drawback to this early form of photography. It was hard to produce more than one print of a daguerreotype. A British inventor, William Fox Talbot, discovered a way to produce paper negatives that allowed photographers to make as many prints as they wanted. Talbot's method, which was also announced in 1839, became the basis for modern photography.

In the following decades, inventors discovered how to make clearer prints. They also reduced the amount of time needed for exposure and experimented with ways to produce color prints.

The use of photography spread rapidly during the last half of the nineteenth century. During the American Civil War, Mathew Brady photographed battle scenes and developed prints in a horse-drawn darkroom. Newspapers and magazines began publishing photographs of events, recording them for future generations.

Thomas Edison called his research laboratory in Menlo Park, New Jersey, the "invention factory." There, he invented the incandescent light, storage battery, sound-synchronized motion pictures, mimeograph machine, and ore separator. This photograph of Edison was taken after he had just worked 72 hours straight improving the wax cylinder phonograph on the table.

A Revolution in Transportation

Dramatic advances were made in transportation in the late 1800s. Perhaps the most significant advance was the development of the internal combustion engine. The internal combustion engine had a number of advantages over the steam engine. For example, it could be started and stopped more easily.

In 1886, the German scientist Gottlieb Daimler devised an internal combustion engine that was fueled by gasoline and could power a small vehicle. Daimler used his engine to build one of the first automobiles. A few years later, another German engineer, Rudolf Diesel, developed an internal combustion engine that could power larger vehicles such as trucks, ships, and locomotives. This diesel engine, as it became known, used petroleum oil for fuel.

The development of the internal combustion engine would eventually revolutionize the transportation industry. By the 1920s, automobiles were a familiar sight in North America and Europe. The growth of this industry triggered booms in industries necessary to the production of automobiles, including petroleum, steel, and rubber.

New Methods of Production

New machines and technology improved worker productivity, the amount of goods a worker could turn out in a specific time. Early in the Industrial Revolution, Eli Whitney introduced the idea of *interchangeable parts*, identical component parts that can be used in place of one another in manufacturing.

Whitney owned a factory in which guns were made. Before Whitney, parts for guns were handmade, and each similar part was slightly different. Whitney manufactured large numbers of identical parts. When guns were made of these parts, a broken part could be easily replaced. The use of interchangeable parts spread to other industries, where it improved efficiency.

Another improvement in production was the assembly line, introduced by Henry Ford in 1914. On an *assembly line*, the complex job of assembling many parts into a finished product was broken down into a series of small tasks. Each worker performed only one or two tasks. Ford, who owned an automobile factory in Highland Park, Michigan, used an assembly line to speed up production. Workers stood along a conveyor belt. As the auto body moved past, they each added their part to it.

The efficiency of the assembly line allowed manufacturers to reduce costs and lower prices. As more people were able to afford goods such as automobiles, the demand for these products rose. To meet the demand, manufacturers introduced *mass production*, turning out large quantities of identical goods.

Financing Industrial Growth

As machinery grew more complex and more expensive, new ways of financing industry developed. During the 1800s, the corporation slowly became the dominant form of business organization in industry. A *corporation* is a business owned by many investors, each of whom has bought a share in the corporation. Investors have limited liability for the debts of the corporation. They risk only the amount of their investment.

After 1870, giant corporations often bought up many small companies. Often, a corporation would establish a *monopoly*, or total control over the market for a particular product. In the United States, the Standard Oil Company, organized by John D. Rockefeller, acquired a virtual monopoly in the oil industry.

To gain this position, Standard Oil bought into the many industries connected with oil production. It owned railroads, barrel companies, pipelines, and refineries. This form of business, in which a corporation controls the industries that contribute to its final product, is known as *vertical integration*. In both Europe and North America, large corporations used vertical integration as a means of eliminating competition.

Banks played a prominent role in financing industry. People deposited money in banks. Banks, in turn, invested this money in businesses, which grew as a result. The House of Rothschild in Paris was one of the world's leading investment banks. During the 1840s, it helped finance the building of the French railway system.

By the late 1800s, industrial growth had resulted in a complex international econ-

The Flight at Kitty Hawk

For as long as people have watched the birds, they have dreamed of finding a way to fly. Orville and Wilbur Wright, two bicycle repairmen from Dayton, Ohio, became interested in flying experiments in the late 1800s. They built and flew a glider in 1900, developing a method for guiding its flight. After testing the glider successfully on the sand dunes near Kitty Hawk, North Carolina, they began work on the next step: attaching a motor to the craft.

The Wrights built a wind tunnel in which to test wing shapes. Because existing gasoline engines were too heavy for flight, they built one of their own. It had 4 cylinders and produced 8952 W. They attached the engine to a pair of 2.4 m wooden propellers and mounted it on their craft, which they named *Flyer*. The Wright brothers took the *Flyer* to Kitty Hawk for a test flight. Ten years later, Orville Wright recalled the event:

Orville Wright

During the night of December 16, 1903, a strong cold wind blew from the north. When we arose on the morning of the 17th, the puddles of water which had been standing about camp since the recent rains were covered with ice.... We thought that by facing the flyer into a strong wind, there ought to be no trouble in launching it from the level ground about camp. We realized the difficulties of flying in so high a wind, but estimated that the added dangers in flight would be partly compensated for by the slower speed in landing....

After running the motor a few minutes to heat it up, I released the wire that held the machine to the track, and the machine started forward into the wind. Wilbur ran at the side of the machine, holding the wing to balance it on the track.... Wilbur was able to stay with it till it lifted from the track after a 12.2 m run....

The course of the flight up and down was exceedingly erratic, partly due to the irregularity of the air and partly to lack of experience in handling this machine.... A sudden dart when a little over 30.5 m from the end of the track, or a little over 36.6 m from the point at which it rose into the air, ended the flight.... This flight lasted only 12 seconds, but it was nevertheless the first in the history of the world in which a machine carrying a man had raised itself by its own power into the air in full flight, had sailed forward without reduction of speed, and had finally landed at a point as high as that from which it started.

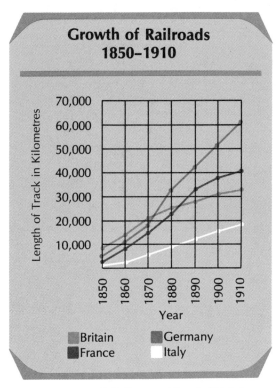

Growth of Railroads 1850–1910

Length of Track in Kilometres

70,000
60,000
50,000
40,000
30,000
20,000
10,000

1850 1860 1870 1880 1890 1900 1910

Year

■ Britain ■ Germany
■ France ▢ Italy

Source: B.R. Mitchell, *European Historical Statistics*.

■ *The building of railroads stimulated industrial growth in many countries. Because large amounts of iron and coal were needed to build railroads, the iron and coal industries grew. Once completed, railroads carried vital resources to factories and finished products to market.*

omy. Trade expanded to meet the demands for raw materials and markets. Goods, services, and money flowed across the world. Regions distant from each other became dependent on one another as suppliers or consumers of goods. Investors in one country often organized companies in another. Many corporations and banks in Europe and North America sought new opportunities in overseas business ventures such as building railroads in Asia and Africa. As a result, governments became increasingly involved in protecting the international markets and investments of their citizens.

SECTION REVIEW

1. Identify: Alessandro Volta, Michael Faraday, Alexander Graham Bell, Guglielmo Marconi, Thomas Edison, Gottlieb Daimler.
2. Define: interchangeable parts, assembly line, mass production, corporation, monopoly, vertical integration.
3. (a) Which European nations industrialized rapidly after 1850? (b) Which European nations remained largely agricultural?
4. Give one example of how scientific research affected industry.
5. Describe one result of the development of the assembly line.

3 Effects of Industrialization

Before 1800, most people in Europe and North America farmed the land. They lived and worked in the country or in small towns. They owned their own tools and were generally self-employed. The Industrial Revolution radically changed these patterns of life. By 1900, between one third and one half of the people in the industrialized countries of Western Europe and North America lived in cities. Most were employed in industry rather than agriculture. Furthermore, more workers had become wage earners, and fewer were self-employed workers and artisans.

The Population Explosion

The beginning of the Industrial Revolution was marked by a population explosion that was to have far-reaching effects. Between 1750 and 1914, the population of Europe grew from one hundred and forty million people to four hundred and sixty-three million.

The Agricultural Revolution improved the diets of many people, so the people were healthier. The Industrial Revolution also contributed to the population growth. Medical discoveries and public sanitation reduced the numbers of deaths caused by

Populations of Six European Nations, 1750–1910

(in thousands)

	1750	1800	1850	1880	1910
Belgium	2,150	2,960	4,426	5,520	7,422
Britain	10,012	14,997	27,201	34,623	44,915
France	24,600	27,800	35,630	37,450	39,528
Germany	12,770	17,200	35,310	45,093	64,568
Italy	13,150	16,900	*	28,211	34,377
Russia	*	31,000	60,000	85,200	142,500

*Not available

Source: Witt Bowden, et. al., *An Economic History of Europe Since 1750.*

■ The population of European nations grew dramatically between 1750 and 1910, as you can see from this table. Between which years did the population of Germany increase the most?

disease. Furthermore, in the 1800s, European nations fought no major wars. Industry provided jobs as well as goods for the growing population.

Problems of Growing Cities

Until the 1800s, cities, which were often located along land or water trade routes, served mainly as marketplaces. But the Industrial Revolution changed the nature of cities. Cities seemed to spring up almost overnight as people flocked to mill and factory sites. When people poured into these fast-growing cities in search of jobs, living conditions rapidly grew worse.

The city of Manchester, England, provides an example of what often happened during the Industrial Revolution. In 1750, Manchester was a fairly quiet market town with 16,000 residents. Manchester proved to be an attractive site for industry because there were iron and coal deposits nearby. Textile manufacturers built factories there. By 1855, Manchester was the center of the British cotton industry, and its population had grown to 455,000.

The rapid growth of Manchester brought severe problems. Thousands of factory workers crowded into poorly built houses. A family of six or ten might live in a single dark, airless room. The city had an inadequate water system and almost no sanitation system. Overcrowded city slums became the breeding grounds for disease. Sewage was simply flung into open trenches along the streets. In many cities, pigs roaming the streets were the only "garbage collectors." Manchester was not even chartered as a city so it could not tax citizens to raise money for improving living conditions. Nor could it pass laws to ensure that housing met minimum standards of safety or sanitation.

Living conditions in rural areas had often been difficult, but in the country, people usually could count on help from their neighbors. During the early Industrial Revolution, one writer described the plight of city people who sat "in their little cells; divided by partitions of brick and board, they sit strangers. . . . They do not work together, but scramble against each other."

Working in a Factory

Most of the new city residents found themselves working in factories, where working conditions were as miserable as living conditions outside the factory. The supply of unskilled workers was large, so wages were very low. Often a whole family worked to survive. Women and children—some of whom started to work at age five—were in great demand because they worked for even lower wages than men.

Work days lasted from 12 to 16 hours, or from sunrise to sunset. Men, women, and children worked six days a week. There were no paid holidays, vacations, or sick leaves. Factories were often unhealthy, dangerous places to work. Fumes from machines combined with poor ventilation made the air foul. The loud, monotonous noise of machines assaulted the ear. Lighting was poor, and machines were not equipped with safety devices, so accidents occurred frequently. A worker injured on the job received no compensation. If an injured worker could no longer do the job, he or she was thrown out of work.

A New Social Structure

The Industrial Revolution transformed the social structure of Europe. Before industrialization, the wealthy, landowning aristocracy occupied the highest social position. Below the aristocracy was a relatively small middle class, which included merchants, lawyers, and the clergy. Next came skilled workers such as shoemakers, potters, and silversmiths. Finally, the vast majority of the people were small farmers or farm workers.

During the 1800s, the middle class expanded and challenged the landowning aristocracy in wealth and power. The wealthiest and most powerful members of the new middle class were factory and mine owners, bankers, financiers, and merchants. The middle class also included managers and the

The French artist Gustave Doré made this engraving, called Over London By Rail, *in 1872. The artist conveys the bleak, overpowering sameness of a London working class neighborhood. In the smoke-filled industrial cities of Europe, most working class families lived in just one room. Crowded conditions, open sewers, polluted rivers, and filthy streets bred crime and disease.*

The Industrial Revolution forced many women to seek jobs outside the home. Employers often exploited women workers by paying them lower wages than men. In this printing shop, The Victoria Press in London, women work as compositors, setting type for books and newspapers.

owners of small businesses. They were joined by professional people such as doctors and lawyers. Farther down the scale, artisans and business clerks also entered the ranks of the middle class.

Wealthy members of the middle class tried to adopt the customs of aristocrats. They bought magnificent country estates, which they decorated luxuriously. They took up aristocratic sports such as horseracing and sailing. Other members of the middle class lived comfortably but on a less lavish scale. Most middle class families were very conscious of their social position. They were constantly striving to live what they considered to be polite, respectable lives.

The Industrial Revolution produced a new social class of industrial workers. Largely unskilled, they occupied the lowest rank in society. Industrial workers were very much aware that they belonged to a separate social class. They saw themselves as people with little political or economic power. By mid-century, workers began banding together to change their working and living conditions, as you will read.

Changing Roles for Women

Traditionally, most women had either helped farm the land or worked in the home earning money through the domestic system. Some women also worked as servants in the homes of the wealthy. The Agricultural Revolution and new farm machinery reduced the need for both men and women on the farms. As the Industrial Revolution got underway, the factory system replaced the domestic system.

To help support their families in the industrial economy, many women went to work in the factories or the mines. Often, the entire family worked in the same place. In mines, for example, men often dug the coal, women dragged coal trucks through low tunnels, and children sorted coal.

Working in a factory added greatly to a woman's responsibilities. She worked outside her home for 12 to 16 hours a day. Yet, she still had to cook, clean, and sew for her family. A woman's role was made even more difficult by the squalid living conditions in the factory towns and cities.

By the late 1800s, however, other developments affected the role of women in industrialized nations. As you will read in the next section, the standard of living and wages of workers began to improve. Thus, it became possible for many working class families to live on the income of only one person. As a result, a new pattern of family life emerged. Husbands tended to be the sole wage earners, and women remained at home.

At the same time, the demand for domestic servants in the cities was growing. Middle class families could afford to hire domestic servants to work as cooks, maids, and nurses for children. Many women, especially single women, left their homes to take these jobs. In Britain in the late 1800s, about one third of all women working outside the home were employed as domestic servants.

Few middle class women worked outside their homes because the social attitudes of the time encouraged women to marry and stay at home to raise their children. During the 1800s, a comfortable home became the ideal of many families as popular songs about "Home, sweet home" and mottoes such as "East, west, home's best" demonstrate.

SECTION REVIEW

1. Give two reasons why the population of Europe increased in the 1800s.
2. What problems did factory workers face in industrial cities such as Manchester?
3. Why were factories often dangerous places in which to work?
4. How did the makeup of the middle class change during the Industrial Revolution?
5. Why did women take jobs in factories early in the Industrial Revolution?
---

4 Responses to the Industrial Revolution

During the early Industrial Revolution, many members of the middle class were indifferent to the suffering of workers. Factory owners, for example, had little sympathy for workers. They had invested their entire capital in risky undertakings, and they wanted to ensure survival of their businesses. As industrialization continued, however, some people began to call for reforms to improve conditions for workers.

Demands for Change in Britain

Because the Industrial Revolution began in Britain, workers there were the first to feel its effects. They suffered from low wages, dangerous working conditions, and frequent unemployment. They protested against conditions in the new industrial system, sometimes violently.

Between 1811 and 1816, workers in many parts of Britain smashed the machines that they considered the cause of their suffering. In 1819, a demonstration in Manchester was attended by about 80,000 workers who demanded economic and political reforms. Nervous soldiers fired on the orderly crowd, killing 11 men and women and wounding about 400. Initially, the British Parliament had little sympathy for the workers, and it applauded the actions of the soldiers. However, worker discontent continued to erupt in violence both in Britain and on the continent.*

Parliament investigates. Eventually, in 1831, Parliament began a series of investigations of factory and mine conditions. Middle class liberals opposed reforms that would regulate working conditions. They believed the government should not interfere in business. However, conservatives sometimes attacked the conditions in factories and mines. As aristocratic landowners, they despised the way industrialization was changing life. The findings of investigators confirmed workers' complaints and shocked many middle class people.

One cotton mill worker told investigators that the workday of his entire family lasted "from six in the morning till half-past eight at night." His children were worn out at the end of the long day. He and his wife "cried often when we have given them the little food we had to give them; we had to shake them, [or] they would have fallen asleep with the food in their mouths many a time."

---
* As you read in Chapter 3, workers in Paris helped overthrow the French monarchy in the revolutions of 1830 and 1848.

97

Child labor was one of the worst abuses of the early Industrial Revolution. Many parents needed what little money their children could earn. As a result, they put their sons and daughters to work as soon as they could walk. Here, a young girl changes empty bobbins in a textile mill.

A 17-year-old girl described her work in a coal mine. She spent her days on her hands and knees hauling carts loaded with coal through narrow mine shafts. She dragged the carts "a mile [1.6 km] or more underground and back. I never went to day-school," reported the girl, "I go to Sunday-school, but I cannot read or write; I go to the pit at five o'clock in the morning and come out at five in the evening."

While Parliament pursued its official investigations, the cause of reform received a boost from a few reform-minded journalists and writers. They described in vivid detail the deplorable conditions they saw in the factories and mines. Journalists awakened thousands of middle class readers to the appalling poverty among workers. Novelists also helped create a climate for reform. Charles Dickens, for example, attacked the evils of child labor in his novels *Oliver Twist* and *David Copperfield.*

Reforms begin. Prodded by its own findings and the growing public concern, Parliament took action. It passed the Factory Act of 1833, which limited the working day for children. Between the ages of 9 and 13, boys and girls could work no more than 8 hours a day. For children aged 14 to 18, the limit was 12 hours a day.

In 1842, Parliament passed the Mines Act. This law barred employers from hiring women to work in mines and made 13 the minimum age for hiring boys. A few years later, the Ten Hours Act limited the work-day for women and children under 18 years of age to 10 hours. Finally, in 1874, the 10-hour day was extended to all workers.

Rise of Labor Unions

Early in the Industrial Revolution, factory workers began forming associations to gain better wages, hours, and working conditions. These early worker associations later developed into labor unions.

Labor unions developed first in Britain, and from the start they met with strong opposition. The government saw labor unions as dangerous organizations. Moreover, employers argued that the shorter hours and higher wages demanded by unions would add to the cost of goods, reduce profits, and hurt business. Parliament passed the Combination Acts in 1799 and 1800 to outlaw labor unions. On the continent, similar laws were passed. A French banker summed up the attitude of many employers and government officials to worker efforts to win better treatment: "The workers must realize that their only salvation lies in patient resignation to their lot."

Yet workers refused to accept "their lot." In Britain, they struggled to have the Combination Laws repealed. They won this battle in the 1820s, although workers were still barred from striking or picketing. In the following decades, skilled workers in Britain formed trade unions based on a craft or trade such as cabinetmaking and hatmaking. Because the workers had skills that were valuable to employers, the trade unions were able to bargain with employers.

Slowly, local trade unions formed larger associations to support both political and economic goals. They struggled for the right to vote, the 10-hour workday, and the right to strike. By 1868, over 100,000 workers belonged to trade unions. In the 1870s, British unions won the right to strike and picket peacefully.

The success of the trade unions encouraged unskilled workers to form their own unions in the 1880s. They organized on the basis of their industries, forming unions of coal miners and dock workers. By 1889, London dock workers were organized well enough to mount a strike in support of their demands for higher wages. The London dock strike effectively shut down one of the world's busiest ports. From this point on, the strike was a common tool of labor unions. By the end of the century, union membership was growing rapidly in Britain, the rest of Western Europe, and the United States.

Gains for Workers

Between 1870 and 1914, the lot of industrial workers improved dramatically. Wages rose significantly. In Britain and France, wages nearly doubled in the last half of the 1800s, and workers could buy twice as much as they had before. In addition, thanks to more efficient methods of production, goods such as clothing were often cheaper than before.

Gradually, employers came to believe that workers would be more productive in a safe, healthy environment. They installed proper ventilation in factories, equipped machines with safety devices, and switched to new electric lighting. When some employers refused to make improvements, governments passed laws to ensure better conditions. Britain, Germany, and France led the way in establishing factory codes that set up minimum standards for safety and sanitary conditions.

Governments took other steps to satisfy the demands of workers. In the new industrial society, workers frequently faced financial disaster because of unemployment, accident, sickness, or old age. To protect workers from such disasters, governments in many industrial nations passed laws setting up insurance funds. These funds would help workers who could not earn a living because of sickness or accident. Some governments also established old age pension funds as well as systems of unemployment insurance for workers who lost their jobs as a result of business failure or economic slowdown.

By 1914, workers enjoyed a better standard of living than workers had 100 years earlier. They could also look forward to a better future for their children. By then, free public schools had been set up in all the industrial nations. Moreover, living conditions in cities had improved.

Improving City Life

As you have read, living conditions in early industrial cities were deplorable. As cities continued to grow, the need for reform became urgent. In Britain and France, city governments began programs to provide adequate water and sewage systems. City governments also passed building codes that set up minimum standards for housing.

Between 1850 and 1870, the city of Paris was almost completely rebuilt. Narrow, crooked streets were replaced by straight, wide boulevards. New and better houses were constructed, and large parks were opened for people to spend their leisure time. In London, a reform-minded member of Parliament, Sir Robert Peel, helped establish the first police force in that city. Londoners referred to members of the new police force as Bobbies or Peelers.

Cities became safer with the installation of gas, and later electric, lights that lit the

Fire posed a hazard to city dwellers. Some cities had voluntary bucket brigades. But steam-powered water pumps introduced in the late 1800s proved to be far more effective. Fire hydrants were set up along city streets. Professional firefighters gradually replaced volunteers. This 1866 print shows a horse-drawn wagon with a steam pump rushing to a New York fire.

streets at night. Use of electric power also led to improvements in transportation. In the 1890s, many European cities adopted an American invention, the electric streetcar. Electric streetcars were much cheaper and cleaner than horse-drawn streetcars. The new streetcars encouraged growth, enabling people to live on the outskirts of the city and travel to work. Cities such as London, Boston, New York, Paris, and Berlin also built subway systems.

By the 1900s, cities had become increasingly attractive places to live. Pockets of poverty and slums still existed, but in general even the poor had money to spend on the products of the new industrial society.

SECTION REVIEW

1. Identify: Factory Act of 1833, Mines Act.
2. (a) What was the attitude of the British government toward labor unions in the early 1800s? (b) How did this attitude change by the 1880s?
3. (a) What type of labor union developed first? (b) Why were these unions able to bargain successfully?
4. List three ways in which the lives of workers had improved by the late 1800s.
5. How did city governments improve living conditions?

IN PERSPECTIVE

The Industrial Revolution began in Great Britain in the mid-1700s. A series of inventions revolutionized the textile industry by introducing machines to do work once done by hand. Machines and workers were soon brought together in the factory system.

As the Industrial Revolution unfolded, new sources of power were found. The steam engine and later the internal combustion engine were invented. Inventions often triggered the rise of new industries.

Between 1850 and 1914, the nations of Western Europe and the United States industrialized. During this period, scientific research led to the development of many new technologies. The factory system became more efficient as new methods of production were introduced. Powerful corporations and banks acquired an influential place in industrial economies because they raised the money needed to finance new industries.

Industrialization contributed to population growth, the rise of large cities, and the development of a new social structure. Early in the Industrial Revolution, workers lived under terrible conditions, working long hours for low pay. However, the demands for change from reformers and labor unions eventually brought about improvements.

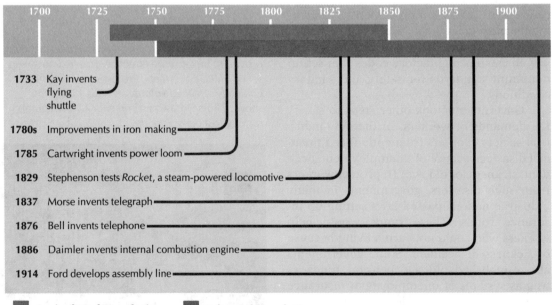

1733 Kay invents flying shuttle

1780s Improvements in iron making

1785 Cartwright invents power loom

1829 Stephenson tests *Rocket*, a steam-powered locomotive

1837 Morse invents telegraph

1876 Bell invents telephone

1886 Daimler invents internal combustion engine

1914 Ford develops assembly line

■ Agricultural Revolution   ■ Industrial Revolution

Match each inventor listed in Column 1 with the appropriate invention listed in Column 2.

Column 1

1. Henry Bessemer
2. Jethro Tull
3. Thomas Alva Edison
4. Eli Whitney
5. Robert Fulton
6. James Watt
7. John Kay
8. Guglielmo Marconi
9. George Stephenson
10. Samuel Morse

Column 2

a. paddle-wheeled steamship
b. flying shuttle
c. radio
d. phonograph
e. steam engine
f. telegraph
g. steam-powered locomotive
h. new process of making steel
i. cotton gin
j. seed drill

Chapter Checkup

1. (a) Describe the Agricultural Revolution in Britain. (b) How did the Agricultural Revolution help make the Industrial Revolution possible?

2. (a) How did inventions revolutionize the textile industry? (b) How did new technology trigger the rise of new industries?

3. (a) Why did Britain take the lead in the Industrial Revolution? (b) Why was Belgium one of the first nations on the continent to industrialize?

4. (a) What improvements were made in communications during the Industrial Revolution? (b) What improvements were made in transportation? (c) How did these improvements contribute to a further growth in industry?

5. (a) What new methods of production were developed during the Industrial Revolution? (b) How did these methods affect the production of goods?

6. Describe how the Industrial Revolution affected each of the following: (a) population; (b) cities; (c) the way people worked; (d) the social structure in European countries.

7. (a) What groups in Britain supported reform to improve conditions for workers? (b) What groups opposed reform? (c) What types of reforms did governments institute? (d) What other factors contributed to improved conditions for workers?

For Further Thought

1. *Comparing* (a) How were women's roles during the 1800s similar to women's roles before industrialization? (b) How were they different?

2. *Expressing an Opinion* Do you think the positive results of the Industrial Revolution outweighed the negative results? Give reasons to support your answer.

3. *Relating Past to Present* (a) How is the way of life that developed in industrial nations during the 1800s similar to life in Canada today? (b) How is it different?

4. *Understanding Economic Ideas* (a) What role did corporations play in the Industrial Revolution? (b) Why do you think corporations replaced individual entrepreneurs?

5. *Synthesizing* One historian has suggested that the Industrial Revolution was "the greatest transformation in human history since the remote times when men invented agriculture, . . . writing, the city and the state." What evidence can you use to support this idea?

Developing Basic Skills

1. *Graph Reading* Study the graph on page 93 and then answer the following questions (a) What is the topic of the graph? (b) How many kilometres of railroad track did Britain have in 1850? (c) How many kilometres of track did Germany have in 1900? (d) Which nation had the most track in 1910? (e) Why do you think Italy had the fewest kilometres of railroad track in 1910?

2. *Ranking* Make a list of what you consider the five most important inventions of the Industrial Revolution. Rank them in order of importance. Then explain why you ranked them in this order.

3. *Researching* Read about the life of one of the inventors discussed in this chapter. Then write a report in which you explain why you think he became an inventor.

See page 203 for suggested readings.

6 Currents of Thought

(1800-1914)

Detail from Hove
Beach, *by John
Constable.*

"I started from my sleep with horror; a cold dew covered my forehead, my teeth chattered, and every limb became convulsed; when, by the dim and yellow light of the moon, as it forced its way through the window shutters, I beheld the wretch—the miserable monster whom I had created. He held up the curtain of the bed; and his opened eyes, if eyes they may be called, were fixed on me. His jaws opened, and he muttered some inarticulated sounds while a grin wrinkled his cheeks. He might have spoken, but I did not hear; one hand stretched out, seemingly to detain me . . . ."

This scene is from the novel *Frankenstein,* written by Mary Shelley in 1818. It describes a nightmarish encounter between a young scientist, Frankenstein, and the grotesque monster he created. *Frankenstein* weaves together two of the major influences on thought during the 1800s: a growing interest in science and the belief that imagination and emotion were as important as reason. In the newly industrialized societies of Europe and the United States, many people had great faith in science. Scientific research, they thought, could solve the problems facing society.

The Industrial Revolution and the profound changes it caused were reflected in the work of many philosophers and artists during the 1800s. Philosophers sought to explain the changes they saw, often proposing solutions to problems created by early industrialization. Early in the century, some artists rejected industrial society and sought comfort in a simpler, more rural way of life. By mid-century, however, many writers and painters had come to accept industrialized society, and they portrayed it realistically. The feelings of nationalism unleashed by the French Revolution and Napoleon's conquests also influenced currents of thought in Europe during the 1800s.

1 New Ideas About Organizing Society

The Industrial Revolution brought about wide-ranging social changes, as you read in Chapter 5. It changed the way people worked, the way businesses were organized, and where people lived. As philosophers became aware of the problems created by industrialization, they began to consider ways of dealing with those problems. Some proposed new ways of organizing society. Some built on the work of earlier philosophers such as the physiocrats, who had foreseen some of the important developments of the 1800s.

Laissez Faire Economics

During the Enlightenment, the physiocrats had formulated natural laws that they thought explained the economy. (See page 4.) They believed that if these natural laws were allowed to operate, everyone would benefit. Consequently, the physiocrats opposed any attempt by government to interfere with the natural laws of economics. The economic system described by the physiocrats is called *laissez faire* (LEHS ay FEHR), meaning let people do as they choose.

The ideas of the physiocrats were summarized in the late 1700s by the Scottish professor Adam Smith in his book *The Wealth of Nations*. Smith contended that if individuals were allowed to act in their own self-interest, society as a whole would benefit. He argued that profits made by industrialists paid the salaries of workers and contributed to the wealth of the nation. Therefore, Smith continued, the government should not try to restrict the actions of industrialists.

In England, Thomas Malthus and David Ricardo also supported laissez faire economics. In his *Essay on Population*, Malthus stated that the human population grew much faster than food production. Only forces such as disease, natural disaster, and famine kept the population from outdistancing food supplies. Malthus believed that this was a law of nature and that interfering with the process would make conditions worse. He argued that if the government tried to correct social problems, the population would increase more rapidly. This would put even greater strains on the food supply. It would also increase the number of workers competing for a limited number of jobs. Wages would then go down, and workers would be even more miserable.

David Ricardo agreed with Malthus' analysis. His ideas gave rise to what was called the Iron Law of Wages. According to the Iron Law of Wages, population and wages go through inevitable cycles. High wages encourage workers to have more children, ultimately leading to a surplus of workers and lower wages. Lower wages meant workers would have fewer children. Thus, there would be a shortage of workers and employers would have to pay higher wages. Once wages went up, the cycle would begin again.

Malthus and Ricardo presented a gloomy picture of economics. They claimed that the economic cycle condemned workers to recurring periods of low wages and misery. Thus, economics as they described it came to be called the "dismal science."

Laissez faire theories remained influential throughout the 1800s. Industrialists supported these theories because they wanted to run their businesses as they saw fit. They warned that attempts to interfere by labor unions or governments would violate the natural laws of economics and create even more misery.

Calls for Reform

Not all observers of the effects of early industrialization accepted the conclusion that poverty was natural or inevitable. Some, such as English philosophers Jeremy Bentham and John Stuart Mill, thought efforts should be made to improve living and working conditions.

Like the laissez faire economists, Jeremy Bentham believed that it would be best if the government did not become involved

The teeming streets of early industrial cities revealed some of the problems caused by rapid population growth. This print by Gustave Doré shows the crowds and chaos of London streets in the 1800s. Many reformers looked for ways to improve living conditions in cities.

in the way people ran their businesses. However, he argued that the government should intervene if the actions of a few individuals brought misery to many.

John Stuart Mill supported active reform to correct the problems created by industrialization. He thought workers should act through labor unions or other organizations to improve working conditions. He believed that the government should take action, when necessary, to protect workers. Mill also thought both men and women should have the right to vote and the right to a good education.

Both Bentham and Mill supported the capitalist system, in which private investors own and control the means of production.* They thought industry should remain in pri-

_____

* The means of production include land, machines, and factories, which are used to produce food and manufactured goods.

vate hands, and they advocated government action only to correct abuses of the system. Another group of reformers, the socialists, challenged the whole idea of capitalism.

Socialists argued that the capitalist system rewarded only the industrialists and not the workers whose labor supported it. Many socialists thought that the capitalist system should be replaced by a system in which the workers owned and controlled the means of production. Others favored a system of government ownership. But all believed that the means of production should be operated for the benefit of all the people.

Utopian Socialists

A group of early socialists called utopian socialists dreamed of reorganizing industry so that a new kind of society could grow out of it. This would be a utopia, or an ideal society. This utopia would have no poverty. Workers would truly share in the fruits of their labor, and all people would be treated fairly.

One of the early utopian socialists was Robert Owen. As a ten-year-old textile worker in Manchester, England, he personally experienced industrial abuses. But by age 23, Owen had become a successful cotton manufacturer himself, and he had time to think about how industry should best operate. He believed that people would work better if they lived in a healthy environment.

In 1800, Owen established an industrial community in New Lanark, Scotland, to test his ideas. Owen did not give the textile workers at New Lanark control of the factory, but he did improve their living and working conditions. He paid high wages, built comfortable and sanitary housing, provided schools, and set up stores where goods were sold at low prices.

Owen's experiment succeeded. The textile mill was profitable, and the workers prospered. From 1805 to 1825, New Lanark became a showplace for Owen's ideas, and thousands of visitors came to marvel at it.

In France, Charles Fourier (foo ree AY) was shocked by the conditions he saw in factories. Like Owen, Fourier believed that poverty would end if workers were given the chance to work together in their own best interests.

Fourier drew up plans to establish small model communities of 500 to 2,000 people. In each of these communities, called phalansteries, people would do the jobs for which they were best suited and would share the profits. Several phalansteries modeled after Fourier's plans were set up in France. Two were established in the United States—one at Brook Farm in Massachusetts and a second near Red Bank, New Jersey. All these experiments failed, but many ideas of the utopian socialists lived on.

In the mid-1800s, Louis Blanc, a French journalist, proposed that workers set up cooperative workshops with financial support from the government. As you read in Chapter 3, national workshops were set up briefly in France during the revolution of 1848 when Blanc was a member of the government. Blanc's guiding principle was "from each according to ability, to each according to need."

Karl Marx and Scientific Socialism

Two German philosophers, Karl Marx and Friedrich Engels, were formulating a different type of socialism. Karl Marx was a journalist who had been exiled from Germany for his political and religious views. Marx moved to Paris. There he met Friedrich Engels, whose father owned a textile mill in Manchester, England. Their meeting marked the beginning of a lifelong friendship and working partnership.

Both men were horrified by the working conditions in factories. They blamed the system of industrial capitalism for the terrible conditions. In 1848, Marx and Engels published their theories in *The Communist Manifesto*. In this work, they described a form of complete socialism in which there would be public ownership of all land and all other means of production. Today, such a system is called *communism*.

Marx's theories. Marx thought utopian socialists were impractical dreamers whose ideas would never work. He claimed that his theories of socialism were based on a scientific study of history, and he called his theories "scientific socialism."

Marx believed that history followed scientific laws just as nature did. He claimed the course of history was determined by economics. Marx concluded that the way goods are produced shapes the social and political structure of a society. The people who control the means of production have all the power and wealth and thus control society.

According to Marx, throughout history societies had been divided into two classes—the "haves" and the "have nots." As examples, he cited the masters and slaves of ancient Greece, the patricians and plebeians of ancient Rome, and the lords and serfs of the Middle Ages. He contended that the "haves" and "have nots" have always struggled with each other.

In industrialized societies, the bourgeoisie were the "haves" and the *proletariat,*

In this print, German artist Käthe Kollwitz pictures the bleak lives of workers. The miserable conditions of the early Industrial Revolution led to worker protests and demands that governments correct abuses. Socialists, such as Karl Marx, blamed the entire capitalist system for the abuses. Marx believed that workers would overthrow capitalism in an international revolution.

or working class, were the "have nots." Just as earlier ruling classes had been replaced, Marx argued, the bourgeoisie led by industrial capitalists, would be replaced. He predicted that the proletariat would rise up to take control of the means of production. Once this revolution was won, the proletariat would destroy the capitalists and rid themselves of the ruling class. Then a classless society would emerge, and everyone would share wealth and power.

Weaknesses of Marxism. Marx thought a revolution by the proletariat was inevitable—that is, it had to happen. But history did not follow the course Marx predicted, for a number of reasons. For example, Marx thought that capitalism would drag more and more people into poverty until, in desperation, they rebelled. But this did not happen. As you read, the standard of living rose in industrialized countries during the late 1800s.

Furthermore, many abuses common early in the Industrial Revolution disappeared. Governments initiated reforms that improved working conditions, public health, and public education. Labor unions gradually won higher wages and shorter working hours. Health and accident insurance, unemployment insurance, and paid vacations also improved the lives of workers. As workers made gains under the capitalist system, they were not eager to overthrow it.

In addition, Marx had not understood the attitude of workers toward their countries. He believed that all workers, regardless of nationality, would unite against their common enemy, the capitalists. However, most workers had strong feelings of nationalism. They did not see themselves as members of an international community of workers, striving to establish a socialist state.

Nevertheless, Marx's idea of a classless society in which all would share equally appealed to many people. During the late 1800s and early 1900s, socialist parties were formed in many countries to work toward the goals Marx described. These parties have had a significant impact on historical developments throughout the world.

SECTION REVIEW

1. Identify: Adam Smith, Iron Law of Wages, utopian socialists.
2. Define: laissez faire, communism, proletariat.
3. Why was economics, as described by Thomas Malthus and David Ricardo, known as the "dismal science"?
4. Under what conditions did Jeremy Bentham and John Stuart Mill think the government should interfere in the way people ran their businesses?
5. Describe Robert Owen's utopian community in New Lanark, Scotland.
6. (a) According to Karl Marx, what two classes were struggling against one another during the 1800s? (b) What did he think the outcome of the struggle would be?

---

2 An Age of Science

During the 1800s, scientific discoveries revolutionized life. Developments in transportation, communication, and manufacturing advanced industry, as you read in the last chapter. Important developments also occurred in biology, chemistry, physics, and the new social sciences—sociology and psychology. Many of these developments improved people's lives and contributed to future advances. Some created great controversy.

Charles Darwin

The work of British biologist Charles Darwin sparked a controversy that has lasted for well over 100 years. In his works *The Origin of the Species* and *The Descent of Man*, Darwin presented a theory of evolution. According to Darwin's theory, all forms of life evolve, or change, over a long period of time. Simpler forms of life evolve into more complex forms, and new forms evolve out of older ones.

Darwin based his theory on the work of earlier scientists and on observations he made during an expedition to South America. Starting in 1831, Darwin had spent five years sailing along the coast of South America and to the Galapagos Islands aboard the *Beagle*. He made a detailed study of the forms of life he saw. Upon his return to England, he began working out a theory of how and why forms of life change over time.

Darwin based his theory in part on Malthus' theory that living things tended to multiply faster than the food supply. Darwin concluded that when food grew scarce living things competed with each other for food. The strongest living things would survive to reproduce, and their offspring would inherit the biological characteristics that had helped them survive. Thus, certain characteristics would survive and others would not. Darwin called this process natural selection or *survival of the fittest* because nature weeded out weak characteristics.

Reaction to Darwin's Theory

When Darwin first published his ideas in 1859, he was greeted with a storm of protest. Darwin proposed that all life had evolved from one original organism. Some scientists accused Darwin of saying that human beings were descended from apes.

A bitter controversy. Religious leaders such as Samuel Wilberforce, a bishop in the Church of England, said Darwin's theory of evolution contradicted the Bible, ignored the human soul, and failed to explain why humans were supreme on earth. Wilberforce claimed that Darwin's theory denied God's role in creation. Many Roman Catholics and fundamentalist Protestants, who believe that the words of the Bible must be interpreted literally, also condemned Darwin's theory.

In time, many religious people concluded that the theory of evolution did not necessarily deny God's role in creation. They believed that God was still the creator of life, but that the Biblical account of creation was a symbolic rather than a literal one. Others continued to believe that Darwin's theory was in error. Scientific study of Darwin's the-

At age 22, Charles Darwin signed on as a member of a British scientific expedition to South America. Its mission was to chart the coastline of South America and study the plant and animal life. The expedition sailed on H.M.S. Beagle, *shown here at anchor off Rio de Janeiro, Brazil. During the voyage, Darwin observed many species of plants and animals he had never seen before. In Brazil, for example, he counted over 60 different varieties of beetles.*

ory of evolution has continued to the present.

Social Darwinism. Some people applied Darwin's ideas to the social, economic, and political issues of the 1800s. For example, the English philosopher Herbert Spencer translated Darwin's biological theory into a social theory. All human life, Spencer argued, is a struggle for existence, and in this struggle only the fittest survive. The theories of people like Spencer are called Social Darwinism.

Many industrialists eagerly adopted Social Darwinism because they saw economic competition as a struggle for survival in which strong competitors drove out weaker ones. They believed their success in business proved they were fit to survive.

Extreme nationalists also used Darwin's ideas. Nations are in a permanent struggle for existence, they argued. Strong nations who defeated weaker nations in war were superior and therefore fit to survive. Rudyard Kipling, a popular writer of the time, summarized the main idea of Social Darwinism in these words: "They should take who have the power. And they should keep who can."

Advances in Biology and Medicine

Darwin had proposed that living things passed their biological characteristics on to their offspring, but scientists did not know how they did this. During the 1870s, German biologist August Weismann studied this question. He based his work on an earlier theory that all living things are made up of tiny cells. As a result of his research, Weismann concluded that there were two kinds of cells: reproductive cells that transmit biological characteristics to the next generation and body cells that die when the living thing dies.

At about the same time, Gregor Mendel, an Austrian monk, was also investigating how living things pass on biological characteristics. By crossing different strains of garden peas, he was able to change their characteristics over successive generations. This result led him to formulate a series of laws to explain how heredity worked. Mendel's work became the basis for the scientific breeding of plants and animals.

The work of other scientists led to significant advances in medicine. The French chemist Louis Pasteur proved that tiny organisms called bacteria caused beer and wine to turn sour. He also found that bacteria could be killed by heat. Pasteur then applied this knowledge to the problem of milk spoilage. He developed a process called pasteurization in which milk was heated enough to kill most bacteria and then cooled to slow the growth of remaining bacteria.

French scientist Louis Pasteur made important breakthroughs in the study of bacteria and immunity. He won great fame when he successfully prevented a nine-year-old boy who had been bitten by a rabid dog from contracting rabies.

The German scientist Robert Koch showed that bacteria cause many diseases. He also found the specific bacteria that cause anthrax, an animal disease, tuberculosis, and cholera. Pasteur then proved that animals can be protected against diseases caused by bacteria. When he injected a weakened strain of anthrax bacteria into sheep, the sheep developed a resistance to anthrax. Later, he used the same method, called vaccination, to prevent the viral disease rabies. As other bacteria were isolated, scientists found ways to immunize people against many diseases.

The English surgeon Joseph Lister applied the findings of Koch and Pasteur to the problem of infection after surgery. Lister developed ways to kill bacteria on surgeons' hands and surgical instruments so bacteria would not be introduced into a patient's body during surgery. As Lister's methods were adopted, deaths due to post operative infection declined dramatically. Such advances in medicine led to an increase in the human life span. (See the graph below.)

Discoveries in Chemistry and Physics

The study of chemistry was revolutionized in the early 1800s by the work of John Dalton, an English schoolteacher. Earlier scientists had suggested that everything is made up of tiny, indivisible particles called atoms. Dalton concluded that all the atoms of a particular element were identical and unlike the atoms of any other element. An element is a substance that cannot be broken down chemically into different substances.

Years later, the Russian chemist Dmitri Mendeleev (MEHN duh LAY uhf) found that the properties of elements are based on their atomic makeup and that elements with similar atomic makeups have similar properties. He then drew up a periodic table in which he listed elements according to their atomic structures. Chemists used Mendeleev's discoveries to predict the properties of combinations of elements. This knowledge led to the development of alloys and synthetics used in industry.

The revolution in chemistry was accompanied by a revolution in physics. The Scottish physicist James Clerk Maxwell predicted that electric and magnetic energy move in waves. In 1895, the German physicist Wilhelm Roentgen discovered energy waves that could penetrate solid matter. He called these waves x-rays. X-rays were soon put to work in the field of medicine.

At about the same time, in France, Henri Becquerel discovered that the element uranium had unusual properties. Marie and Pierre Curie determined that these properties were due to uranium's atomic structure. They found two new elements—radium and polonium—that had similar properties.

In 1910 and 1911, the British scientist Ernest Rutherford conducted experiments based on the work of Joseph J. Thomson. He found that the atom is actually made of separate particles, a nucleus and electrons.

The work of these physicists ushered in the era of modern physics. In the early 1900s, the German-born scientist Albert Einstein used their work to develop new laws of physics. Einstein rejected the idea that matter and energy were separate things. He proposed that energy and matter were interchangeable.

Einstein also argued that since all matter is in constant motion, there is no fixed point from which to measure motion. The motion of one object can be measured only by comparing it to the motion of another. All measurements are therefore relative. This theory is called the theory of relativity. It represented a radical departure from Newtonian physics, which assumed no relative motion.

■ *An increase in the average life expectancy contributed to population growth during the 1800s and early 1900s. The average life expectancy is the average number of years people born in a given year could be expected to live. For example, people born in 1860 lived an average of about 42 years. The average life expectancy today is over 70 years.*

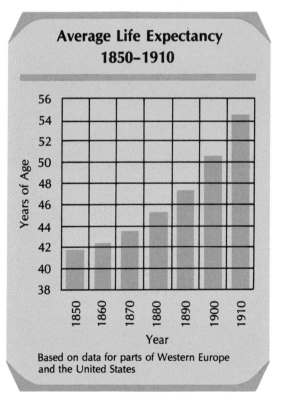

Average Life Expectancy 1850–1910

Years of Age / Year

Based on data for parts of Western Europe and the United States

Source: E.A. Wrigley, *Population and History.*

109

Marie Curie: A Pioneer in the Study of Radioactivity

In the late 1800s, the University of Paris attracted many scientists, including Pierre Curie and Marie Sklodowska. The two were married in 1895, and together they pioneered in a new field of study—radioactivity.

In 1896, a professor at the University of Paris, Henri Becquerel, discovered that uranium emitted something that could darken a photographic plate from a distance. Soon after Becquerel's discovery, Marie Curie began studying pitchblende, the ore in which ura-

nium is found. She found that pitchblende was more radioactive than uranium alone. She concluded that there were other radioactive substances, as yet unknown, in the pitchblende.

Pierre Curie stopped his own research to work with his wife in her study of pitchblende. The Curies worked in the kitchen of their home trying to break the pitchblende down into its basic components. During their research, they boiled over 7.2 t (tonnes) of ore on their cast-iron stove. When the smell became unbearable, they moved their equipment into a small shed in their back yard.

The work was heavy and difficult. Marie wrote, "I came to treat as many as 20 kilograms of matter at a time, which had the effect of filling the shed with great jars. . . . It was killing work to carry the receivers, to pour off the liquids, and to stir, for hours at a stretch, the boiling matter in a smelting basin."

In 1898, the Curies finally met with success. They discovered two new elements in the pitchblende: polonium, which Marie Curie named after her native Poland, and radium, which was a hundred times more radioactive than uranium. In 1903, the Curies and Henri Becquerel received the Nobel Prize in Physics for their work on radioactivity. In 1911, Marie Curie won a second Nobel prize, this time in chemistry, for her study of the chemical properties of radium.

New Fields of Study

Enthusiasm for science during the 1800s prompted a renewed interest in using scientific methods to study human behavior. This led to the development of two new social sciences—*sociology*, the study of society, and *psychology*, the study of behavior. Sociologists study how people act in groups. Psychologists study the behavior of individuals.

The French philosopher Auguste Comte was one of the founders of sociology. Comte argued that society, like nature, operated according to certain laws. He thought that once these laws were discovered, there would be a scientific basis for social organization and action. Comte stressed that sociologists, like other scientists, had to follow strict guidelines in their research. Only if they measured and reported what they found accurately and objectively would they arrive at valid findings.

Russian scientist Ivan Pavlov was an early psychologist. He began his work by studying the behavior of dogs. Pavlov set up an experiment in which he always rang a bell before he gave food to a dog. Food caused the dog to salivate. Eventually, the dog became so used to hearing the bell before eating that it would salivate whenever it heard the bell.

Pavlov concluded that the dog had been "conditioned" to respond in a certain way to the bell even when the original stimulus, the food, was no longer there. Pavlov thought that people also were conditioned to respond automatically to a given stimulus. Therefore, he argued, some human behavior is determined by unconscious responses rather than by conscious thought.

Sigmund Freud of Austria based his work on the idea that an unconscious part of the mind governs much human behavior. He argued that motives for a person's actions are sometimes hidden in the unconscious. Freud developed psychoanalysis, a method

of trying to discover those motives. Freud's ideas and methods still influence the study of psychology.

SECTION REVIEW

1. Identify: Social Darwinism, Gregor Mendel, Louis Pasteur, Wilhelm Roentgen, Marie and Pierre Curie, Auguste Comte, Ivan Pavlov, Sigmund Freud.
2. Define: survival of the fittest, sociology, psychology.
3. (a) Explain Darwin's theory of evolution. (b) Why did some religious leaders of the time object to his theory?
4. How did Pasteur's work with bacteria help make surgery less dangerous?
5. Why did Albert Einstein conclude that all measurements are relative?

Popular Culture at the Turn of the Century

During the late 1800s, the middle and working classes had more leisure time than ever before. People in Europe and the United States discovered new ways to fill their leisure time. Their interests and tastes helped shape the pastimes of future generations.

The growth of public education in the 1800s greatly increased the number of people who could read. Publishers churned out popular novels of romance, mystery, and adventure. Booksellers peddled thousands of copies of "penny dreadfuls," inexpensive magazines that featured bloodcurdling stories. The invention of motion pictures in the early 1900s brought millions of people into theaters for the first time.

Perhaps the fastest growing form of entertainment was sports. During the late 1800s, many sports emerged in the forms that are familiar today. For example, soccer—known to Europeans as football—began as a game played by boys in private schools. Each school had its own rules for the game. At most schools, players kicked the ball with their feet but were not allowed to touch it with their

hands. But at the Rugby School in England, players were allowed to carry the ball in their hands. Rugby football became the basis for football as it is played in the United States today.

In the 1880s, British factory workers began playing soccer, forming their own soccer clubs or teams. These clubs standardized rules so that teams from different places could play one another. By the early 1900s, Britain had over 10,000 soccer teams. In 1901, the British national soccer playoff drew 110,000 spectators. When the top soccer teams played, they charged admission to their games. Soon, athletes were paid for playing, and sports became a business.

Women also took an interest in sports. They joined gymnastic societies and played golf, tennis, and field hockey. Sports influenced women's fashions. Women who rode bicycles daringly raised their skirts above the ankle. Women also exchanged layers of skirts and petticoats for simpler clothes. Gradually, the new sporting fashions were accepted for everyday wear.

3 Reforms in Great Britain

Victoria was queen of a nation that was stable, patriotic, and proud of being a world power. However, by the 1800s, the political power of the British monarch had been limited. The power of Parliament had grown during the 1600s and 1700s, as you read in Chapter 1. Yet, in the early 1800s, Parliament was far from being a democratic body. In addition, the British faced the harsh social and economic conditions that accompanied the early Industrial Revolution. As a result, there were many voices demanding political and social reform.

Early Attempts at Reform

Great Britain, unlike other European nations, had had a parliamentary system of government for hundreds of years. However, in the early 1800s, a small number of people dominated the British Parliament. Members of the House of Lords inherited their positions. Also, only 6 percent of British men could vote for members of the House of Commons. Few middle class men, no rural or urban workers, and no women had voting rights.

Furthermore, election districts, set up originally in 1688, did not reflect population changes. Rural districts with small populations, called "rotten boroughs," were well represented in the House of Commons. But growing industrial centers, such as Birmingham and Manchester, had little representation.

The middle class demanded the vote and greater representation in Parliament. Workers supported these demands. They hoped to eventually win the vote themselves. In 1832, a major political reform bill was passed by Parliament.*

The Reform Bill of 1832 gave industrial areas more representation in Parliament,

---

* Britain had escaped the revolutions that erupted on the continent in 1820 and 1830. But there was scattered violence. Rioting in Bristol in 1832, for example, helped convince the House of Lords to approve the reform bill.

and it extended the *franchise*, or right to vote, to virtually all middle class men. After passage of the bill, 20 percent of adult men were qualified to vote. Since voters were still required to own a certain amount of property, however, neither urban nor rural workers qualified.

Disappointed with the Reform Bill of 1832, reformers continued to demand the vote for workers. In 1838, they drew up a document called the People's Charter. The Chartists, as these reformers were called, demanded the secret ballot and universal male suffrage, or the vote for all adult men. They also thought members of Parliament should receive a salary so poor people could afford to serve. The Chartists had little immediate success, and their movement died out in the 1850s. Nevertheless, most of their demands eventually became law.

Another complaint of urban workers was the Corn Laws. In 1815, Parliament had passed the Corn Laws, which put a tariff, or tax, on imported grain. Landlords and farmers favored the Corn Laws because the tariff kept the price of grain high. However, city dwellers despised the Corn Laws because high prices for grain meant high prices for bread, the staple of the working-class diet.

Demands for repeal of the Corn Laws finally met with success in 1846. Because of crop failures in the early 1840s, the British had to import large amounts of grain. Therefore, Parliament repealed the unpopular Corn Laws. Cheap grain flowed in from outside Britain, and the price of bread went down.

Extending Democracy

In the 1700s, both British political parties had represented wealthy landowners. (See page 14.) As more middle class men won the right to vote in the 1800s, both the Whig party, which became known as the Liberal party, and the Tory party, which became known as the Conservative party, tried to win the support of the new voters. They also responded to continuing demands to extend the franchise. Two capable politicians led the parties in this direction—the Conservative Benjamin Disraeli (dihz RAY lee) and the Liberal William Gladstone.

Benjamin Disraeli thought that the Conservative party should support reforms that would improve the country. He considered

Emmeline Pankhurst and Votes for Women

In the mid-1800s, women in Britain began demanding the right to vote. At first, their demands received little support, although Parliament had extended voting rights to all adult men by 1885. But in the early 1900s, a strong-minded woman, Emmeline Pankhurst, set out "to wake up England to the justice of women's suffrage."

Emmeline Pankhurst and her two daughters, Christabel and Sylvia, founded the Women's Social and Political Union (WSPU) in 1903. The WSPU urged Parliament to give women the right to vote. When the government failed to act, the Pankhursts and their supporters took direct action. WSPU members distributed leaflets and organized marches. Women who demonstrated for the right to vote were called suffragettes. Mounted police often broke up suffragette marches by charging into the crowds of demonstrators.

The WSPU responded with more militant actions. WSPU supporters broke into cabinet meetings. Women chained themselves to the visitors gallery in the House of Commons. They threw stones at cars of government officials, broke street lamps, and painted the slogan "Votes for Women" on sidewalks and walls. In 1908, Emmeline and Christabel Pankhurst were arrested and sent to prison for distributing leaflets urging people to "Rush the House of Commons."

The Pankhursts continued their campaign from prison. They refused to obey prison regulations. When punished with solitary confinement, they went on hunger strikes, risking death by starvation. The government responded to the hunger strikes by ordering prison authorities to force-feed the imprisoned suffragettes.

Many people were horrified by the forced feedings. Because Parliament was afraid of making the hunger strikers into martyrs, it passed the Prisoners Act of 1913. The law allowed hunger strikers to be released from prison, but they could be rearrested at a later date to complete their prison terms. Under this act, suffragettes who participated in prison hunger strikes were released and rearrested several times.

In 1918, British women over 30 years of age were granted the right to vote. Weakened by hunger strikes and many prison terms, Emmeline Pankhurst died in 1928, one week before Parliament passed a bill finally giving all women over 21 years of age the right to vote.

himself "a conservative to preserve all that is good in our constitution and a radical to remove all that is bad." William Gladstone began his career as a Conservative, but he became a staunch Liberal. These two men served alternately as prime minister from the mid-1860s to the early 1880s. Both played a key role in passing political and social reform measures during this period.

In 1866, Gladstone introduced a bill to extend the vote to working men in cities. The bill did not pass, but Disraeli introduced a similar bill the next year. In his opinion, the reform was inevitable, so he hoped the Conservatives could get credit for it and thereby win the votes of urban workers. The Reform Bill of 1867 passed with both Liberal and Conservative support. It nearly doubled the number of eligible voters.

Five years later, Parliament passed a bill introducing the secret ballot. In 1884 and 1885, other reform bills gave the vote to rural working men. Thus, by 1885, most adult men in Britain had the right to vote. In 1911, Parliament passed a bill that ended the right of the House of Lords to veto measures. The House of Lords resisted this bill. But it gave in when the king threatened to appoint new lords who would vote for the bill.

Throughout the late 1800s, the Conservatives and Liberals competed for support from the new working-class voters. Social reforms were passed, but many workers felt that the existing political parties did not do enough on their behalf. In 1900, they founded the Labour party, headed by Ramsay MacDonald.

Other Reforms

Throughout most of the 1800s, social reform accompanied political reform in Britain. During the 1820s, Parliament lifted restrictions on the political activity of Catholics and Protestants who did not belong to the Church of England. Parliament also repealed the ban on the organization of workers, and it reformed the criminal code, reducing the number of crimes punishable by death. The slave trade had been outlawed in 1807, and in 1833 slavery itself was abolished throughout the British Empire.

The Factory Acts of the early 1800s were followed by additional labor and social legislation. By the end of the century, Parliament had passed laws that regulated the number of hours a person worked and protected working women and children. David Lloyd George, a leader of the Liberal party, summed up the need for such laws. "Four spectres haunt the poor," he said, "old age, accident, sickness, and unemployment." He vowed to rid the country of them.

In 1912, Parliament passed a law establishing minimum wages. Parliament also extended workers' compensation to cover more workers in case of sickness or accident on the job. In 1909, it passed an old age pension bill that offered benefits to every British subject "of good character." Labor exchanges were set up to help find jobs for the unemployed. In 1911, the National Insurance Act provided health and unemployment insurance.

By the late 1800s, both Liberals and Conservatives recognized the need for better educated voters. In the 1860s, education was not compulsory, and students usually left school by age 11. The Education Act passed in 1870 allowed local school boards to require attendance. It also extended government aid to more schools. Later acts made education free and compulsory.

SECTION REVIEW

1. Locate: Manchester, Birmingham.
2. Identify: People's Charter, Benjamin Disraeli, William Gladstone, David Lloyd George.
3. Define: franchise.
4. What groups of people won the right to vote by the Reform Bill of 1832?
5. (a) Why did city dwellers oppose the Corn Laws? (b) What effect did the repeal of the Corn Laws have on urban workers?
6. What groups won the right to vote between 1832 and 1885?
7. Describe three social reforms passed by Parliament in the 1800s.

HOURS *AND* WAGES
OF IMMIGRANT
INDUSTRIAL WORKERS

UNLOADING SCRAP IRON

THEY WORK LONG HOURS FOR SMALL WAGES AT THE HARD WORK WE WILL NOT DO. IN SOME OF OUR MILLS THEY WORK 12 HOURS A DAY OR NIGHT FOR 16¢ AN HOUR.

The reform spirit that spread through Europe was also felt in Canada. Similar concerns were expressed about Canadian factory workers, particularly about immigrant workers. Various church groups felt that new Canadians provided cheap labor for the factories and increased profits for the owners. This poster was issued by the Presbyterian Church in the early 1900s.

IN PERSPECTIVE

During the 1800s, philosophers reacted in different ways to the effects of the Industrial Revolution. Laissez faire economists thought that governments should not interfere in the economy because it was ruled by natural laws. Other economists thought reforms were needed. Utopian socialists and Marxist socialists argued that the capitalist economic system needed to be replaced.

While reformers tried to solve the problems of industrialization, scientists carried on research that had long-lasting effects. Charles Darwin's theory of evolution sparked a continuing controversy among scientists and religious leaders. Research about the causes of disease helped improve the lives of people. Discoveries in chemistry and physics laid the groundwork for major developments in the 1900s. The fields of sociology and psychology were born when scientists began to study society and human behavior.

In Britain, the government became more democratic. First middle class men and then working class men won the right to vote. As the right to vote was extended, the British Parliament passed social and economic legislation to protect workers from some of the hardships of industrialization.

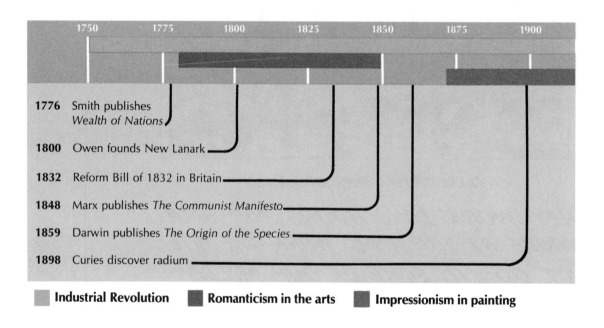

1776	Smith publishes *Wealth of Nations*	
1800	Owen founds New Lanark	
1832	Reform Bill of 1832 in Britain	
1848	Marx publishes *The Communist Manifesto*	
1859	Darwin publishes *The Origin of the Species*	
1898	Curies discover radium	

Industrial Revolution   **Romanticism in the arts**   **Impressionism in painting**

Decide if the following statements are true or false. If a statement is false, rewrite the statement to make it true.

1. Adam Smith thought governments should correct problems created by industrialists.
2. The Iron Law of Wages stated that a surplus of workers would lead to lower wages.
3. Industrialists opposed the ideas of laissez faire economics.
4. Robert Owen's utopian community at New Lanark, Scotland, was successful.
5. Darwin's ideas on evolution were met with much criticism.
6. Gregor Mendel discovered that bacteria caused disease.
7. Ernest Rutherford proved that the atom was the smallest particle of matter.
8. Psychology is the study of behavior.
9. The corn laws were repealed because of the Reform Bill of 1832.
10. The Reform Bill of 1867 extended the vote to urban working men.

1. Explain how the ideas of each of the following people contributed to the laissez faire theory of economics: (a) Adam Smith; (b) Thomas Malthus; (c) David Ricardo.
2. (a) What was the goal of the utopian socialists? (b) Why did Marx think his economic theories were more scientific than the theories of the utopian socialists?
3. What were the weaknesses of Marx's socialist theories?
4. (a) How were Darwin's ideas applied to social, political, and economic issues? (b) How did his ideas contribute to further discoveries in biology?
5. Describe how the work of each of the following scientists helped improve human health: (a) Louis Pasteur; (b) Robert Koch; (c) Joseph Lister.

6. (a) How did the selection of members of the British Parliament become more democratic during the 1800s? (b) Which political parties supported the growth of democracy? Why?

1. *Expressing an Opinion* Adam Smith thought that government had only three duties: "First, the duty of protecting the society from . . . invasion; secondly, . . . the duty of establishing an exact administration of justice; and thirdly, the duty of erecting and maintaining certain public institutions." Do you agree that these are the only duties a government should have? Why?
2. *Relating Past to Present* Which of the scientific discoveries discussed in this chapter do you think has had the most direct effect on your life? Why?
3. *Synthesizing* Review what you learned in Chapter 5 about the development of labor unions in Great Britain. Which of the following people do you think would have approved of this development: Karl Marx, Adam Smith, John Stuart Mill, David Ricardo? Explain.
4. *Expressing an Opinion* Reread the special feature on page 113. Then answer the following questions: (a) What militant actions did the Pankhursts take to win the right to vote for women? (b) Why did they feel such actions were necessary? (c) Do you think their actions were justified? Explain.

1. *Graph Reading* Study the graph on page 109. Then answer the following questions: (a) What is the topic of the graph? (b) What was the average life expectancy in 1850? (c) What was the average life expectancy in 1880? (d) How did the average life expectancy change between 1850 and 1910? (e) What developments help explain this change?

See page 203 for suggested readings.

Unit Three

The Age of Imperialism

Unit Overview Until the 1800s, there was limited contact among the civilizations of Africa, Asia, and Western Europe. When Europeans expanded overseas in the 1500s and 1600s, they conquered the New World but established only a few trading outposts in Africa and Asia. In China, for example, foreigners were restricted to trading at Canton. This painting by an unidentified Chinese artist shows foreign trading posts at Canton about 1800. From left to right, the flags are those of Denmark, Austria, the United States, Sweden, Britain, and the Netherlands.

In the 1800s, a shift in the world balance of power occurred. The scientific, political, and industrial revolutions you read about in Units One and Two greatly strengthened Western European nations and the United States. The Industrial Revolution, for example, gave Europeans power unparalleled in history and enabled them to dominate the world for a time.

During the Age of Imperialism, which began in the late 1800s, the civilizations of different parts of the world were brought into closer contact than ever before. Europeans extended their control over parts of Asia and Africa. In Latin America, the newly independent nations faced the tasks of establishing stable governments and guarding against foreign intervention. But in the 1800s, Europeans and North Americans exercised influence over the new nations.

Chapter 7 Africa in the Age of Imperialism (1700-1914)

Chapter 8 Asia and the West (1650-1920)

A European view of Africa about 1500.

7 Africa in the Age of Imperialism

(1700–1914)

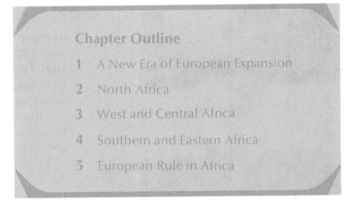

In the late 1800s, Europeans entered a new era of overseas expansion. They explored and rapidly colonized much of the globe. In Africa, European expansion upset traditional patterns of life. In the novel *Things Fall Apart,* Nigerian writer Chinua Achebe (ah CHEE bee) writes about what happened in a village when Europeans arrived. The following excerpt is a conversation between a villager named Okonkwo and his friend.

" 'What has happened to that piece of land in dispute?' asked Okonkwo.

" 'The white man's court has decided that it should belong to Nnama's family, who had given much money to the white man's interpreter and messengers.'

" 'Does the white man understand our customs about land?'

" 'How can he when he does not even speak our tongue? But he says that our customs are bad; and our brothers who have taken up his religion also say that our customs are bad. How do you think we can fight when our brothers have turned against us? The white man is very clever. He came quietly and peaceably with his religion. We were amused at his foolishness and allowed him to stay. Now he has put a knife on things that held us together and we have fallen apart.' "

During the Age of Exploration, Europeans built a few trading posts on the coast of Africa, but for centuries they had little direct influence on the lives of most Africans. In the 1800s, a dramatic change occurred. The Industrial Revolution and the growth of nationalism strengthened European nations. In the 1870s, they were seeking new resources and markets. They found these resources and outlets in many parts of the world, including Africa.

1 A New Era of European Expansion

In the late 1800s, the industrial nations of Europe competed with one another for world empires. Within a few decades, European powers extended their control over much of the world. In this new age of overseas expansion, Africa, which had been largely unknown to Europeans, suddenly became the focus of attention.

Scramble for Africa

Until the 1870s, Europeans had little interest in Africa. In the 1600s and 1700s, the Portuguese and Dutch had established forts and trading posts along the African coast. The British and French had also acquired outposts in Africa. However, they used these posts only for trade, not as bases for conquest.

Between 1870 and 1914, a dramatic change occurred. With the exception of Liberia and Ethiopia, the entire African continent came under European rule. First, King Leopold II of Belgium acquired the Congo, today called Zaire. Then, the French moved into the interior of West Africa, and the British extended their control across much of the continent. Germany, Spain, Portugal, and Italy also entered the race for African territory.

The "scramble for Africa" brought European powers to the brink of war. To settle their disagreements, they held a conference in Berlin. At the Berlin Conference of 1884 to 1885, these European nations drew boundary lines on a map of Africa, dividing up the continent and approving each other's claims to different African lands. (See the map on page 122.) They then proceeded to establish control over these regions.

The Age of Imperialism

The partitioning of Africa is just one example of European expansion in the late 1800s. As you will read in Chapter 8, the nations of Western Europe along with the United States gained influence or won control of land in Asia and Latin America as well. The period from about 1870 to 1914 is often called the Age of Imperialism. *Imperialism* is the domination by a country of the political, economic, or cultural life of another country or region.

European nations exerted their control over other parts of the world in many ways. The most common forms of imperial rule were colonies, spheres of influence, and protectorates. A *colony* is a possession that the imperial power controls directly. A *sphere of influence* is a region in which the imperial power claims exclusive investment or trading privileges. The local government usually controls all other matters. A *protectorate* is a country that has its own government but whose policies are guided by the imperial power.

A variety of motives stimulated European expansion in the Age of Imperialism. Nationalism played a major role in sending Europeans overseas. A nation increased its prestige and power by winning an overseas empire. Political rivalries and military strategy also contributed to imperialism. One nation might seize a territory to prevent a rival from expanding into that region.

The desire to expand economically was also a strong motive. Industrialists urged their governments to acquire new markets for their products. In addition, they wanted to control the supply of raw materials. Individuals, too, sought personal wealth.

Humanitarian and religious concerns often motivated individuals and their governments. Some Europeans wanted to end the slave trade in Africa. Christian missionaries were convinced that the peoples of Africa and Asia would become "civilized" only if they converted to Christianity and adopted European ways. Many Europeans believed in the superiority of the white race. They spoke of the "white man's burden" of carrying the benefits of western civilization to other parts of the world.

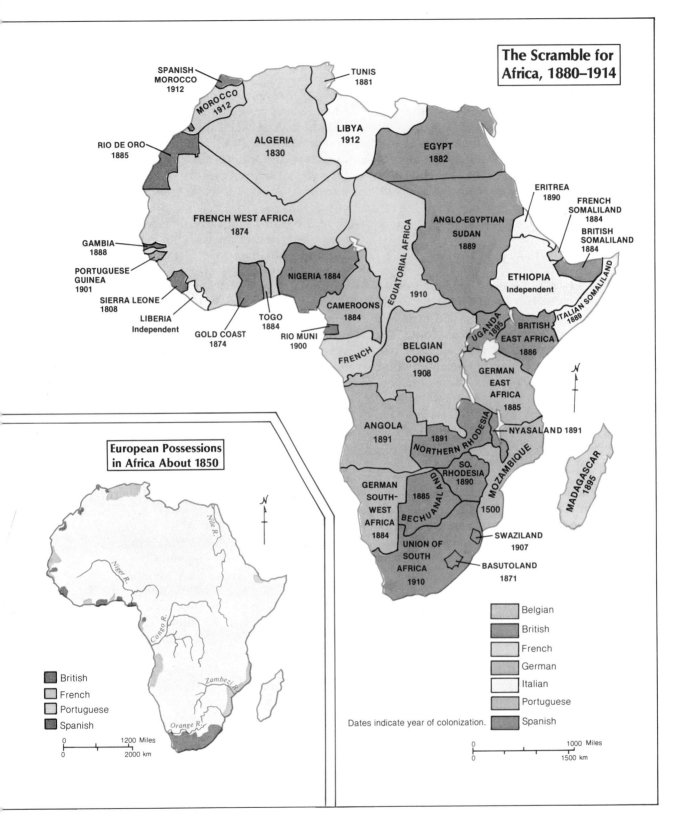

The Scramble for Africa, 1880–1914

SPANISH MOROCCO 1912
TUNIS 1881
MOROCCO 1912
LIBYA 1912
ALGERIA 1830
EGYPT 1882
RIO DE ORO 1885
FRENCH WEST AFRICA 1874
ANGLO-EGYPTIAN SUDAN 1889
ERITREA 1890
FRENCH SOMALILAND 1884
BRITISH SOMALILAND 1884
GAMBIA 1888
PORTUGUESE GUINEA 1901
SIERRA LEONE 1808
LIBERIA Independent
GOLD COAST 1874
TOGO 1884
RIO MUNI 1900
NIGERIA 1884
CAMEROONS 1884
EQUATORIAL AFRICA 1910
FRENCH
ETHIOPIA Independent
ITALIAN SOMALILAND 1889
UGANDA 1895
BRITISH EAST AFRICA 1886
BELGIAN CONGO 1908
GERMAN EAST AFRICA 1885
ANGOLA 1891
1891
NORTHERN RHODESIA
NYASALAND 1891
MOZAMBIQUE
MADAGASCAR 1895
GERMAN SOUTH-WEST AFRICA 1884
1885
BECHUANALAND
SO. RHODESIA 1890
1500
SWAZILAND 1907
UNION OF SOUTH AFRICA 1910
BASUTOLAND 1871

Belgian
British
French
German
Italian
Portuguese
Spanish

Dates indicate year of colonization.

0   1000 Miles
0   1500 km

European Possessions in Africa About 1850

Nile R.
Niger R.
Congo R.
Zambezi R.
Orange R.

British
French
Portuguese
Spanish

0   1200 Miles
0   2000 km

■ *In the late 1800s, European nations scrambled to claim territory in Africa. By 1914, almost the entire continent had been partitioned, as you can see above. Only Ethiopia and Liberia remained independent.*

The philosophy of Social Darwinism was used to justify imperialism. As you read in Chapter 6, Social Darwinists argued that in nature only the strongest survived. They applied this idea to political affairs, arguing that it was natural for strong nations to conquer weaker states.

Exploring the Interior

Until the 1800s, Europeans had very little knowledge of the interior of Africa. African and Arab merchants on the coast knew the best routes into the interior, but few Europeans bothered to ask them for information. Instead, Europeans and Americans financed dozens of expeditions to explore the African continent.

Perhaps the best known explorer was David Livingstone, a British physician and missionary. Livingstone spent many years setting up Christian missions in Central Africa. He wrote detailed reports about the regions he visited. His reports made the British public aware of opportunities in Africa for businesspeople as well as missionaries.

Exploration along African rivers was the first step toward opening the continent to European expansion. In the 1830s, Sir George Goldie charted the Niger River. Dozens of other Europeans explored the various regions of Africa. In the 1870s, Henry Stanley trekked inland from the East African coast to discover the source of the Congo River. He then traveled down the Congo to the Atlantic Ocean.

New Technology

Despite the expeditions into the African interior, disease and resistance by Africans prevented much European expansion beyond the coastal areas before 1870.

As European interest in Africa grew, doctors searched for the causes and treatment of diseases such as malaria and yellow fever, which claimed many European lives in Africa. By the 1880s, they had learned that mosquitoes carried malaria and yellow fever. They also found that quinine, made from the bark of a certain tree, prevented people from catching malaria. Such medical discoveries made it easier for Europeans to move into the interior of Africa.

The development of new weapons gave Europeans a military advantage over Africans. These weapons included rifles and the Maxim gun, the earliest machine gun. Africans armed with weapons such as muskets had little success against Europeans using the new weapons.

SECTION REVIEW

1. Locate: Liberia, Ethiopia, Niger River, Congo River.
2. Identify: Berlin Conference, David Livingstone, George Goldie, Henry Stanley.
3. Define: imperialism, colony, sphere of influence, protectorate.
4. Describe three motives behind European imperialism.
5. What two new technological developments helped Europeans expand into Africa?

---

2 North Africa

The people of North Africa had had contacts with other parts of the world since ancient times. During the Middle Ages, North Africa was an important part of the Islamic Empire, and Islamic culture helped shape the political and social life. In the early 1500s, the Ottoman Turks conquered North Africa. As the Ottoman Empire weakened in the late 1700s, four North African states—Algiers, Tunis, Tripoli, and Egypt—gained virtual independence. A fifth state, Morocco, was outside Ottoman control.

The Egyptian Empire

When Napoleon invaded Egypt in 1798, Egyptians broke away from Ottoman rule. The French invasion sparked a long civil war. Muhammed Ali, who had led Egyptian resistance to the French invasion, seized control of the country in 1805.

Ali ruthlessly suppressed his opponents and embarked on an ambitious program of reform to make Egypt a strong power. He began by introducing more efficient agricultural techniques. He had dykes and irrigation canals built so that arid land could be cultivated. He then sent peasant farmers to grow cash crops on the new lands. *Cash crops* are crops such as cotton, sugar, and tobacco that can be sold for money on the world market. Egypt soon became a major exporter of cotton to industrial nations such as Great Britain.

Income from cash crops helped pay for Ali's other projects. He established schools and sent thousands of Egyptians to study in Europe. He brought European experts to Egypt to help set up textile mills, iron works, and shipyards. He also invited French military officers to reorganize, train, and equip the Egyptian army. With a strong modern army to support him, Ali built an empire. During the 1820s and 1830s, Egyptian armies seized territory along the Red Sea coast and moved up the Nile River into the Sudan.

Growing European Interest in Egypt

Ali's programs were expensive. To finance them, he borrowed money from European banks. Under Ali's successors, Egyptian debts increased. Gradually, European creditors gained political and economic influence in Egypt. They pressured Egyptian leaders to follow policies that favored their financial interests.

The Suez Canal. Europeans had relatively little interest in Egypt until 1859, when the French began building the Suez Canal. Ali had opposed construction of a canal to link the Mediterranean Sea and the Red Sea. He feared that such a canal would increase European interest in Egypt because it would cut thousands of kilometres off the trip from Europe to Asia. However, his successors approved the project.

Between 1859 and 1869, a French company headed by Ferdinand de Lesseps built the Suez Canal. At first, Egyptians controlled the canal. But as British influence in India grew, Britain came to see the Suez Canal as the "lifeline of the British Empire."*

---

* You will read about British rule in India in Chapter 8.

A combination of engineering skill, steam-powered machinery, and a huge investment of money made possible the construction of the Suez Canal. Ferdinand de Lesseps, a successful promoter and engineer, oversaw the project. He predicted that the canal "will open the world to all people." When the 160.9 km canal was completed in 1869, it cut in half the length of the journey between Europe and Asia.

British occupation of Egypt. In the 1870s, Britain acquired partial control over the Suez Canal by buying shares of stock from Egyptian ruler Ismail. Ismail sold the stock because the Egyptian government faced a severe financial crisis. The chaotic state of Egyptian finances eventually provided the British with an excuse to intervene militarily in Egypt. Claiming that it wanted to protect European loans and investments and reorganize the Egyptian treasury, Britain sent troops to occupy Egypt in 1882. The British then made Egypt a protectorate.

Under British control, Egypt paid off its foreign debts and built a dam at Aswan on the upper Nile. The dam improved agricultural production by supplying water for irrigation. However, Egyptian nationalists resented foreign control. They criticized the British for not encouraging education or helping Egyptian industries.

The Fashoda incident. British occupation of Egypt led to an explosive confrontation with France. The British thought their control of Egypt and the Suez Canal would only be assured if they also possessed the headwaters of the Nile in the Sudan. For 16 years, Sudanese nationalists resisted attempts to occupy their land. Finally, in 1898, a combined force of British and Egyptians conquered the Sudan. Meanwhile, a French army had reached the Sudan from bases in West Africa. British and French forces faced each other at Fashoda. For weeks, the two European powers seemed on the brink of war.

In the end, a domestic crisis forced the French to withdraw.* Britain and Egypt then established joint control over the Sudan. The Fashoda incident reminded Europeans of the very real possibility that overseas rivalries could drag them into war.

French and Italian Expansion

While Britain was establishing control over Egypt and the Sudan, France extended its rule over other parts of North Africa. Between 1830 and 1912, France conquered Algiers, Tunis, and Morocco.† By 1861, most of Italy had been united. It began to challenge France in North Africa.

Algeria. In 1830, the French king Charles X launched an expedition against the ruler of Algiers, in part to avenge an insult to a French diplomat. Charles was also in serious political trouble at home. He hoped that a victory in Algeria would divert the attention of the French people. However, although Charles gained a foothold in Algeria, he was toppled by the revolution of 1830. (See page 47.)

During the following decades, the French government encouraged Europeans to settle in Algeria. Colonists took lands, especially along the fertile Mediterranean coast, and established successful farming and business communities.

The Algerians resisted French expansion into their land for 40 years. So many Algerians were killed in the fighting that France became even more eager to attract European settlers to Algeria. In all, almost one million Europeans settled in Algeria during the 1800s.

France took little interest in other North African lands until the 1880s. Then, as Britain moved into Egypt, the French rapidly occupied Tunisia. French expansion along the Mediterranean worried the Italians, whose interest in North Africa was growing.

Ethiopia and Libya. Both France and Italy sought control of the horn of Africa, present-day Somalia and Ethiopia. Aware of the European threat, the Ethiopian emperor Menelik II bought rifles and other new weapons and trained his army to use them. Thus, when the Italians invaded Ethiopia in 1896, they were defeated by strong, well-armed Ethiopian forces.

Italy had to be content with establishing protectorates over Eritrea and part of Somaliland. In 1912, the Italians occupied Tripoli, which they set up as the colony of Libya. By controlling Libya, the Italians prevented further French expansion eastward across North Africa.

---

*In 1894, Captain Alfred Dreyfus, a Jewish officer in the French army, was accused of giving French military secrets to the Germans. Five years after his conviction, he was pardoned.

†Algiers and Tunis are now called Algeria and Tunisia.

Menelik II, Emperor of Ethiopia

During the Age of Imperialism, Ethiopia preserved its independence largely because of the enlightened policies of its emperor Menelik II. Menelik was descended from a dynasty that had ruled Ethiopia since the 1200s. When he came to the throne in 1889, he faced many difficulties. Ethiopia was only loosely united, and local rulers showed little loyalty to the emperor. In addition, both Italy and France were acquiring colonies on the borders of Ethiopia.

Menelik moved quickly to consolidate power. He brought local rulers under his control and built a new capital at Addis Ababa, where he set up a strong central government. He asked European advisors to help him establish a modern system of education, and he promoted talented individuals. Gradually, his policies helped create a sense of national unity among the people of Ethiopia.

Menelik displayed a shrewd diplomatic ability in his dealings with European powers. He warned Britain, France, Italy, Germany, and Russia: "If powers at a distance come forward to partition Africa between them, I do not intend to be an indifferent spectator." Menelik backed up this declaration by skillfully playing off one European power against another. He acquired arms from both Italy and France, who were eager to gain influence with the Ethiopian emperor.

Menelik used his new armed forces in a showdown with Italy. In 1893, Menelik renounced a treaty he had signed with the Italians. Two years later, Italian troops seized several Ethiopian towns. Menelik stalled the Italian advance by calling for negotiations. In the meantime, he allowed inaccurate maps of his country to fall into Italian hands and sent

spies to give the Italians misleading information.

On March 1, 1896, the armies of the two nations met at Adowa. Menelik's forces routed the Italians, who were greatly outnumbered. The painting above, by an Ethiopian artist, shows the Ethiopians in triumph over their enemies. This victory ensured the independence of Ethiopia and the success of Menelik's program of strengthening his nation.

Crisis Over Morocco

Morocco, at the northwestern tip of Africa, remained largely outside European control until the 1880s. Learning from the Egyptian example, the Moroccan ruler avoided building up large debts in Europe. Despite his efforts, European nations used Morocco as a pawn in their political maneuverings.

For years, Britain and France had quarreled over Egypt. In 1904, they finally reached an agreement. France would recognize British interests in Egypt, and Britain would let France establish a sphere of influence in Morocco and not protest any French efforts to take over Morocco directly.

The agreement between Britain and France alarmed the German emperor William II. He thought that improved relations between Britain and France would threaten German power. Thus, in 1905, he visited Morocco and boldly announced that Germany would support an independent Morocco. William II's actions, however, only brought France and Britain closer together. In 1906, an international conference of European powers recognized French influence in Morocco.

SECTION REVIEW

1. Locate: Sudan, Algeria, Tunisia, Morocco, Ethiopia, Somaliland, Libya.
2. Identify: Muhammed Ali, Ferdinand de Lesseps, Menelik II.
3. Define: cash crop.
4. Describe three reforms Muhammad Ali introduced in Egypt.
5. How did Britain gain partial control over the Suez Canal?
6. (a) Describe the Fashoda incident. (b) Why was it significant?
7. What parts of North Africa did the French control by 1912?

3 West and Central Africa

In the late 1400s, Portuguese sailors had explored the west coast of Africa. Over the next 350 years, Portugal and other European nations set up small trading posts and forts along the coast. By the 1600s, these outposts had become the center of a profitable slave trade across the Atlantic to the Americas. Until the 1800s, most European interest in West Africa revolved around this transatlantic slave trade.

The Transatlantic Slave Trade

Slavery had existed in Africa since ancient times, as it had in many parts of the world. In Africa, many slaves were captives taken in war. Others were people who sold themselves into slavery for food and shelter during drought or famine. Sometimes, a society took slaves in order to increase its population. Slaves were often gradually absorbed into their new societies.

The transatlantic slave trade was very different from African slavery. Africans were forced to leave their traditional societies and were transported thousands of kilometres across the Atlantic. In the Americas, they encountered a completely unfamiliar culture. White slave owners looked on black Africans as inferior beings whose only value was their labor.

The transatlantic slave trade involved large numbers of people. Experts now estimate that between 1451 and 1870 about nine and a half million slaves were sent to the Americas. Thousands died during the Middle Passage, as the brutal voyage across the Atlantic was known.

Slaves were captured in the interior of Africa and led in chains to the coast. There, they awaited shipment across the Atlantic, as this drawing shows. In the mid-1700s, about 100,000 Africans were shipped to the Americas each year.

A SLAVE-SHED.

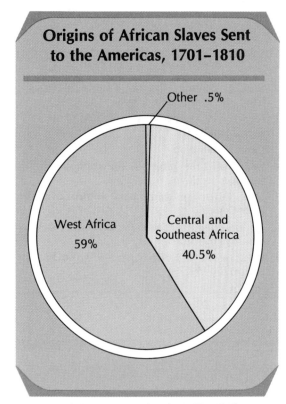

Origins of African Slaves Sent to the Americas, 1701–1810

West Africa
59%

Central and Southeast Africa
40.5%

Other .5%

Source: Philip D. Curtin, *The Atlantic Slave Trade*.

■ *Over a period of three centuries, more than nine million Africans were sent to the Americas as slaves. The majority of these Africans came from West Africa, as this graph shows.*

Europeans relied on African rulers and merchants to bring slaves to trading posts on the coast. The Africans exchanged slaves for guns, ammunition, and manufactured goods. They used the guns to raid villages and capture more slaves. This exchange between Africans and Europeans has often been called the slave-gun cycle.

The demand for slaves caused several changes among West African societies. New states rose whose wealth and power were based on the slave-gun cycle. For example, in the 1700s and early 1800s, rulers of the Dahomey and Ashanti kingdoms used muskets acquired through the slave trade to conquer large areas. Raids to capture slaves created tensions among West African societies.

A Century of Change

In the century before 1870, two developments changed conditions in West Africa. First, European nations abolished the slave trade. Second, there was a revival of Islam in several West African states.

Abolition of the slave trade. During the Enlightenment, some Europeans called for an end to the slave trade and slavery. By the early 1800s, this humanitarian concern was having an effect. Britain outlawed the slave trade in 1807. Britain also convinced other nations at the Congress of Vienna to condemn the slave trade. But Portugal, Spain, and France did not end their slave trade until 1820.*

Soon after Britain abolished the slave trade, it established the West African Patrol, a naval force with orders to prevent slave ships from leaving West African ports. When the patrol captured ships with slaves on board, it carried the Africans to Freetown in the British colony of Sierra Leone. The British had established Freetown in the late 1700s for slaves they freed during the American Revolution. In the 1800s, Sierra Leone became a haven for other freed slaves. Christian missionaries worked among the African settlers there, encouraging them to adopt European ways.

In 1822, a group of free black Americans established another refuge for former slaves in West Africa. The new settlement was called Liberia. In the 1830s and 1840s, hundreds of former slaves in the United States emigrated to Liberia. By 1850, Liberia had become an independent nation.

The abolition of the slave trade undermined the economic strength of the West African states that had supplied slaves to the Europeans. Some states, such as Dahomey, declined rapidly. As the demand for slaves declined, West African societies had to find other items to trade for European manufactured goods. They began to plant cash crops, including cotton and cacao beans, which were introduced from the Americas. As a result, West African economies remained closely tied to European demand for these products.

---

* Although these European nations officially abolished the slave trade, many people still participated in it illegally. Moreover, European nations did not abolish slavery itself until later. Britain abolished slavery in all its territories in the 1830s. Other European nations ended slavery by the 1860s.

Revival of Islam. The most important development in West Africa during this period was the revival of Islam. Arab traders had introduced Islam into West Africa in the 800s. However, generally only rulers and their officials converted to Islam. Most people in West Africa either continued to believe in their traditional religions or mixed Muslim beliefs with their own faiths. Devout Muslims detested the mixing of Islam with other faiths.

In the early 1800s, Muslim religious leaders called for a jihad, or holy war, to restore the purity of Islam. Muslims believe that a Muslim killed in a jihad is assured a place in heaven. With armies inspired by this belief, several Islamic states in West Africa conquered large empires.

Among the best known of these Islamic empires was the Hausa-Fulani Empire located in what is today northern Nigeria. In 1804, Usuman dan Fodio, a Muslim scholar, unified the nomadic Fulani people. The next year, he led them in a jihad against the Hausa people because he thought the Hausa had corrupted Muslim practices. Usuman's forces seized control of the Hausa cities.

Usuman then organized the new lands into a strong Islamic state.

European Conquests

As you read earlier, new technology and European exploration sparked European expansion into West and Central Africa. The scramble for colonies began in the 1870s when Belgium concluded treaties with African rulers along the Congo River. As you read, Henry Stanley explored the Congo River basin. He also negotiated treaties with local rulers for the right to exploit the mineral wealth of the region. Stanley hoped that Britain would send settlers to the Congo, but Britain was not interested. Thus, Stanley turned to King Leopold II of Belgium, who agreed to set up Belgian settlements there. Belgium thereby gained control of the region, which became known as the Congo Free State.

The brutal treatment of the local people in the Congo Free State has come to symbolize the worst aspects of European imperialism in Africa. King Leopold II ruled the

In 1815, an Italian artist painted this picture of a village at the mouth of the Congo River. Europeans established an outpost here, but village life remained largely unchanged until the Age of Imperialism. In the late 1800s, Europeans in the Congo uprooted Africans from their homes and their traditional ways of life and forced them to work on rubber plantations and in copper mines.

Congo Free State as his own private possession. The area was rich in rubber and copper and other minerals. Leopold granted monopolies to European companies and earned handsome profits for himself.

The European companies ruthlessly exploited both the land and the people in the Congo Free State. To ensure maximum profit, company managers forced Africans to work long hours and punished them brutally if they did not produce enough. They also imprisoned African women to make their husbands work harder. Workers had their hands or ears cut off if they protested.

When Christian missionaries in the Congo revealed these atrocities, the Belgian government began an investigation. Eventually, in 1908, the government took over the administration of the Congo Free State, which then became known as the Belgian Congo.

France, too, began taking a greater interest in Africa in the 1870s. In 1879, the French built a railroad from Dakar, on the coast, into the interior. Britain felt threatened by French expansion into West Africa and took control of Nigeria and the Gold Coast, present-day Ghana. Germany, Portugal, and Spain also annexed territory. However, France acquired the largest part of West Africa.

African Resistance

Europeans used persuasion, force, and bribery to convince individual African rulers to sign agreements giving them economic and political rights. Once they established a foothold, Europeans often ignored the agreements and simply took what they wanted. If African rulers resisted, well-armed troops were sent in to crush them. Still, many African rulers vigorously opposed European expansion.

Samori Touré, ruler of an empire in what is today Senegal, signed an agreement with the French in the 1890s. When the French broke the agreement and tried to seize control of his land, Touré fought back. For seven years, he led his army against the French. Finally, in 1898, the French captured Touré and exiled him to Gabon, where he died two years later.

In Dahomey, King Behanzin battled the French until 1894, when he was captured and exiled to Algeria. The Ashanti, who had established a powerful state in the forest region of what is today Ghana, stubbornly resisted the British. However, not all West and Central African people fought the Europeans. Some accepted agreements that gave them minimal levels of self-rule. Others did not fight because resistance against European weapons appeared to be hopeless.

SECTION REVIEW

1. Locate: Sierra Leone, Liberia, Nigeria, Belgian Congo.
2. Identify: West African Patrol, Usuman dan Fodio, Leopold II, Samori Touré.
3. Describe two ways in which African slavery differed from slavery in the Americas.
4. (a) Why did the British found the colony of Sierra Leone? (b) Who established Liberia?
5. Why did Muslim leaders call for holy wars in West Africa?
6. What resources did the Congo Free State have?

4 Southern and Eastern Africa

In 1652, the Dutch founded Cape Town at the southern tip of Africa. The settlers supplied water, fresh meat, and vegetables to Dutch ships traveling to the East Indies. In the Cape area, the Dutch came in contact with local African herders. The Dutch gradually enslaved some of these people and forced others into the desert region to the north. However, by the early 1800s, the migration of other African peoples into southern Africa radically changed conditions there.

Settlers in Southern Africa

For almost 1,000 years before 1800, groups of Africans had been migrating into eastern and southern Africa. These peoples are known as Bantu-speaking peoples because they spoke languages that were related. However, their cultures were different.

Zulu expansion. The Zulu were one of the Bantu-speaking peoples migrating into southern Africa. By the early 1800s, the Zulu king Shaka had built a strong military empire northeast of the Orange River. Shaka introduced new fighting methods among the Zulu. He replaced the long throwing spears they had been using with short, stabbing swords. He reorganized the Zulu army into a powerful fighting force that expanded the Zulu empire.

The Zulu expansion created turmoil in southern Africa. The people defeated by the Zulu left their traditional homelands and retreated across southern and central Africa. They displaced other African groups, who then migrated northward.

The Boer republics. At about the same time as the Zulu were expanding their empire, the Boers, descendants of the Dutch who had founded Cape Town, were migrating north from the Cape Colony. The Boers were on the move because the British had gained control of the Cape Colony in 1814.

The Boers resented British rule because they felt that the British threatened their way of life. The British made English the official language of the colony and abolished slavery, which the Boers believed God had ordained. To preserve their way of life, about 10,000 Boers left the Cape Colony in the 1830s. They headed north in a vast migration of covered wagons, called the Great Trek. In the interior of southern Africa, the Boers set up two independent republics, the Transvaal and the Orange Free State. (See the map at right.)

The Boers soon came into conflict with the Zulu. For years the two groups fought for control of the land. Neither side was able to win a decisive victory. Finally, in 1879, the British became involved in these wars with the Zulu. The Zulu defeated the British in several battles, but the superior weapons and numbers of the British eventually led to the destruction of the Zulu empire.

The Boer War

The British officially recognized the independence of the Boer republics in 1852. But continued British interest in southern Africa worried the Boers. In the 1880s, gold and diamonds were discovered in the Transvaal and the Orange Free State. British adventurers flocked north from the Cape Colony to seek their fortunes in the mines.

By the end of the century, the British decided that control of all of South Africa was vital to their empire because South Africa was on the sea route to India. Moreover, Cecil Rhodes, the prime minister of the Cape Colony, had a grand plan to build a "Cape to Cairo" railroad, linking these British outposts in Africa.

■ *The movement of peoples into South Africa led to conflict after 1830. The Zulu, who had created a large empire, clashed with the Boers. The Boers had moved north from the Cape Colony after the British gained control of that area.*

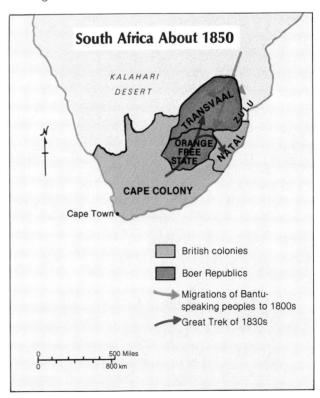

South Africa About 1850

KALAHARI DESERT

TRANSVAAL

ZULU

ORANGE FREE STATE

NATAL

CAPE COLONY

Cape Town

- British colonies
- Boer Republics
- → Migrations of Bantu-speaking peoples to 1800s
- → Great Trek of 1830s

0   500 Miles
0   800 km

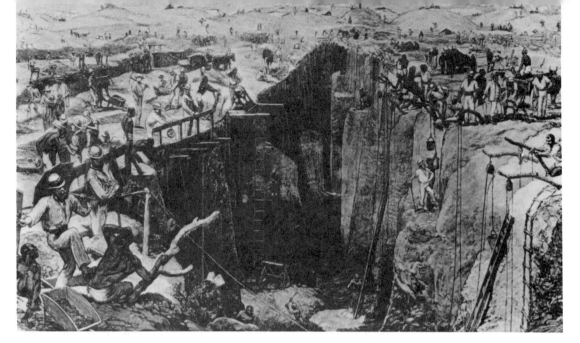

The discovery of diamonds at Kimberley in 1871 sent thousands of fortune hunters to South Africa. Kimberley soon grew into a sprawling mining town of 50,000 people. This print shows open-shaft mining at Kimberley. The diamond mines of South Africa were a source of wealth for European investors. But African mine workers were harshly treated, as you can see in this picture.

Finally, in 1899, tension between the British and the Boers exploded into war. The Boer War lasted for nearly three years before the Boers surrendered. The war left the Boers with bitter memories because the British placed thousands of Boers in concentration camps, where many died. After the war, the Boers had to accept British rule, but the British promised them self-government as soon as possible. In 1910, The British united their South African colonies into the Union of South Africa.

Under the constitution of the new nation, only white men had the right to vote. The British felt that the Africans might eventually be given the right to vote. The Boers opposed such a move because they believed black Africans were inferior to whites. The Boers were a majority of the white population of South Africa. As a result, they won control of the government.

Powerful States in East Africa

In East Africa, a profitable slave trade had developed by the 1700s. Arab traders who lived in the cities along the east coast used slaves to carry ivory and gold from Central Africa to the coast. As the slave trade expanded, the Arabs extended their control to include the inland trade routes.

In the 1800s, several African rulers challenged Arab authority over these trade routes and the growing slave trade. Mirambo, leader of the Nyamezi people, carved out an empire in part of what is today Tanzania. Because he controlled a vital trade route, Mirambo demanded large sums of money from traders to assure safe passage. He used this wealth to buy weapons and further increase his power. However, Mirambo's empire was based on his personal leadership, and it collapsed soon after his death.

Another African leader, Tippu Tib, created a strong state in what is today eastern Zaire. Like Mirambo, Tippu Tib controlled a vital trade route from the interior to the east coast. He built a strong army and conquered new lands. But Tippu Tib's empire, too, was based on personal leadership, and it crumbled after his death.

The rise of empires such as Mirambo's and Tippu Tib's disrupted the traditional way of life in East Africa and in some ways made European expansion in the late 1800s easier. The slave trade weakened many African societies and made African peoples suspicious of each other. When Europeans arrived in East Africa, they often gained support of Africans who wanted protection from the slave-trading states.

European Rivalries in East Africa

European trade along the East African coast increased in the early 1800s. After the American Revolution, ships from Boston and Salem carried cotton cloth to East African ports. The word for cotton cloth in East Africa is still "merikani" because of that trade. German, French, and British merchants also sought trading rights from local rulers.

By the 1870s, Britain and Germany were the chief rivals in East Africa. A latecomer to the scramble for colonies, Germany wanted what it called "a place in the sun." It wanted to win colonies in East Africa, the only part of the continent that was still largely unclaimed by other European powers. At the same time, British imperialists felt that control of East Africa was vital if Britain were to extend its empire from South Africa to Egypt. Also, both Portugal and Belgium claimed parts of East Africa in an effort to extend their colonial empires across the continent from the Atlantic Ocean to the Indian Ocean.

At the Berlin Conference, European nations settled their rival claims in East Africa. They recognized British and German rule over large parts of East Africa. Mozambique became a Portuguese colony, and Belgium took two small states in the interior. (See the map on page 122.) No Africans were consulted about these arrangements.

Fighting Colonial Rule

Many Africans resisted European colonization in East Africa. The Shana and Matabele in what is today Zimbabwe fought two major wars against the British. The Germans suppressed rebellions in their colony, but at considerable cost. The Uhehe (yoo HEE hee)

won fame by successfully fighting the Germans for seven years. Like so many other African people, the Uhehe were defeated by European cannons and machine guns.

Two factors, however, limited African resistance in East Africa. First, as you read, the slave states had disrupted many African societies and made some Africans sympathetic to European expansion. Second, the outbreak of rinderpest, a cattle disease, caused a disastrous famine that affected people's ability to fight the invaders.

Rinderpest was brought into Africa accidentally in the late 1880s. Cattle infected with the disease were imported from southern Europe to feed Italian troops in Somaliland. Because East African cattle had no previous exposure to rinderpest, they had no resistance to the disease. In some areas, 95 percent of all cattle died.

The epidemic spread south with terrible consequences because most East African people were cattle herders. Almost overnight their wealth and way of life were destroyed. Many people died of starvation. Others suffered severe malnutrition. Malnutrition made people vulnerable to diseases such as smallpox and malaria. Crushed by this disaster, many people lacked the resources and the will to fight the foreigners who took their lands.

SECTION REVIEW

1. Locate: Cape Town, Transvaal, Orange Free State, Uganda.
2. Identify: Zulu, Boers, Shaka, Great Trek, Cecil Rhodes, Union of South Africa, Tippu Tib.
3. (a) Why did the Boers move inland from the Cape Colony? (b) Who did they fight for control of the land?
4. Give two reasons why the British took a greater interest in South Africa in the late 1800s.
5. How did Mirambo build a strong state in East Africa?
6. What European countries claimed land in East Africa?
7. How did rinderpest affect the cattle-herding peoples of East Africa?

5 European Rule in Africa

European imperialism in Africa lasted about 100 years, from the 1870s to the 1970s. Compared to Africa's long history, this period was short. However, the impact of colonial rule on Africa was immense.

Colonial Governments

Once European nations had carved up Africa, they faced the question of how to rule their new colonies. They developed two types of colonial government: direct rule, practiced by France, Germany, Belgium, and Portugal; and indirect rule, used by Great Britain.

Direct rule. Through direct rule, the European nation controlled government at all levels in its colony. It appointed its own officials to replace local African leaders. It cast aside traditional African ways of governing in favor of its own methods.

Direct rule reflected the European belief that Africans were incapable of ruling themselves. Europeans used this belief to justify *paternalism*, the system of governing their colonies as parents would guide their children. Europeans thought they had to teach their African subjects the "proper" way to live, by which they meant the European way.

The form direct rule took varied among the different European colonies. France practiced a policy of *assimilation*. Assimilation meant that the colonies would be absorbed politically and culturally into the parent nation. Africans in the French colonies were expected to exchange their own heritage for French culture. Once the colonies became truly French, they would be made provinces of France, not just overseas territories. But until Africans adopted French culture, white French officials controlled the colonies.

To achieve assimilation, colonial schools, businesses, and law courts were patterned after those in France. Some Africans were sent to school in France and eventually gained minor government positions in the French colonies.

Portugal also followed a policy of assimilation, but it exerted rigid control over its colonies. It wanted the Africans in its colonies to become Portuguese Christians. Although some Africans converted to Christianity, very few were allowed to become Portuguese citizens.

Paternalism was the main characteristic of direct rule by Germany and Belgium. Germany looked on its African colonies as a source of wealth and labor. It exercised strict control over its colonial subjects, claiming that Africans could never learn to rule themselves. Belgium wanted to make Europeans forget the atrocities committed in the Congo during Leopold's rule. Therefore, it tried to make the Congo a model colony. The Belgians claimed to protect the interests of their African subjects by making all decisions for them.

Indirect rule. Britain was the only colonial power to rely on indirect rule. Under the system of indirect rule, a British governor and council of advisors made laws for each colony. But local rulers loyal to the governor retained some of their traditional authority. Thus, indirect rule differed from direct rule because it did not replace traditional rulers with European officials. Yet local rulers had only limited power and did not influence government decisions.

The British had practical reasons for using indirect rule. Even before the European scramble for Africa, Britain had more colonies than any other European nation. During the late 1800s, it acquired one third of the African continent, with sixty-four million people to rule. A small nation, Britain did not have enough officials or soldiers to control its huge empire without the help of local leaders.

Making Colonies Profitable

Although the European nations developed different methods of governing their colonies, their policies had a common goal. They all believed their colonies should be self-

A European Visits Africa: Identifying Cultural Bias

As you have read, eyewitness accounts are not always completely objective or accurate. Often, the writer has a point of view that influences his or her description of an event or development. (Review "Analyzing Conflicting Sources," page 32.) Eyewitness accounts are also affected by *cultural bias*, or the way the writer's culture shapes his or her attitude toward an event.

During the Age of Imperialism, Europeans who visited Africa judged the diverse peoples and cultures they saw in terms of European civilization. The following excerpt is from *The Lake Regions of Central Africa*, the journal British explorer Sir Richard Burton kept as he traveled through East Africa in 1858. Read the excerpt. Then use the following steps to identify the writer's cultural bias.

1. **Identify the nature of the document.** Ask yourself the following questions: (a) What type of document is it? (b) Who wrote it? (c) When was the document written? (d) Under what circumstances was it written?

2. **Review the contents of the document.** Answer the following questions about the excerpt: (a) What does the writer say about the early morning activities of people in the African village? (b) What does the writer say about the way the people spend the rest of the day? (c) What does the writer say about the activities of women and girls?

3. **Study the source to discover the writer's cultural bias.** You can do this by looking at the words the writer uses and the tone of the excerpt. (a) What word does the writer use to describe the dwellings in which the people live? (b) What word is used to describe the chief occupation of the people? (c) What seems to be the writer's attitude toward the people he is describing? (d) How might this attitude have affected his description of the village?

4. **Evaluate the document as a historical source.** Answer the following questions about the excerpt: (a) What parts of the description are most likely to be accurate? (b) What parts of the description reflect the writer's cultural bias? (c) Would you use this document as evidence about life in East Africa? Why or why not?

From Richard Burton's Travel Journal

The African rises with the dawn from his couch of cowhide. The hut is cool and comfortable during the day, but the barred door impeding ventilation at night causes it to be close and disagreeable. The hour before sunrise being the coldest time, he usually kindles a fire and addresses himself to his constant companion, the pipe. When the sun becomes sufficiently powerful, he removes the reed screen from the entrance and issues forth to bask in the morning beams. The villages are populous, and the houses touching one another enable the occupants, when squatting outside . . . to chat and chatter without moving. About 7 A.M., when the dew has partially disappeared from the grass, the elder boys drive the flocks and herds to pasture with loud shouts. . . . At 8 A.M., those who have provisions at home enter the hut to eat porridge; those who have not, join a friend.

After breaking his fast, the African repairs, pipe in hand, to the *iwanza* [the village inn], where he will spend the greater part of the day talking and laughing, smoking, or torpid [sluggish] with sleep. . . .

After eating, the East African invariably indulges in a long fit of torpidity, from which he awakes to pass the afternoon as he did the forenoon. . . . Toward sunset, all issue forth to enjoy the coolness: the men sit outside the *iwanza*, whilst the women and the girls, after fetching water . . . from the well, collecting in a group upon their little stools, indulge in the pleasures of gossip. . . . As the hours of darkness draw nigh, the village doors are carefully closed, and after milking his cows each peasant retires to his hut or passes his time with his friends in the *iwanza*.

---

sufficient. That is, each colony should pay all its own expenses, including salaries for government officials and the military and the costs of building roads, railroads, and schools. These expenses were immense, and most African societies could not pay for them. But European powers found ways to make their colonies both self-sufficient and

Europeans were fascinated by African wildlife, as this painting by artist Thomas Baines shows. Baines accompanied David Livingstone on his expedition up the Zambezi River. Paintings such as this one and written accounts of Europeans who traveled in Africa often emphasized the aspects of African life that differed the most from life in Europe.

profitable. They tapped the mineral and agricultural resources of their colonies, built up trade by exporting these resources, and developed internal transportation networks.

In some colonies, Europeans found valuable mineral resources, including copper in the Belgian Congo and gold in South Africa. Where mineral resources were lacking, Europeans developed cash crops such as rubber, palm oil, and peanuts.

Colonial governments also imposed taxes on Africans, which had to be paid in cash. The only way Africans could earn cash was to work for individual Europeans or for the colonial government. Thus, many Africans had to work on large plantations or in factories and mines owned by Europeans.

Europeans made their colonies more profitable by encouraging investment in enterprises such as railroad building. Investors put up the money to build railroads and received profits from the fees people paid to use the trains.

Railroads served both political and economic goals. Politically, they helped colonial governments impose their authority by providing a reliable transportation system. Economically, they gave Europeans a relatively cheap means of moving cash crops and other products to ports for shipment overseas. In Uganda, for example, many British farmers established cotton plantations in the interior. They depended on the railroad to send the cotton to the coast so it could be shipped to factories in Britain. Because investors were interested in high profits, they built railroads only in those areas where Europeans had settled or had businesses.

The Impact of Colonial Rule

Colonial rule profoundly affected the political, economic, and social structure of African societies. Europeans believed Africans were primitive people. They generally refused to recognize the customs and traditions that had shaped African societies. Furthermore, impressed by European wealth and power, many Africans rejected their traditional rulers and accepted European paternalism.

Breakdown of traditional culture. During the Age of Imperialism, many African economic and social traditions were destroyed. As colonial cities grew, some families moved to the cities, hoping to improve their positions. Others were forced to seek jobs in European-owned factories or businesses in order to pay taxes. Still others became migrant workers, leaving their villages for long periods to work in distant mines and plantations. As a result, the close-knit village, once the center of African life, declined. People no longer had the same concern for helping each other as they had in the past.

Christian missionaries actively tried to convert Africans to Christianity. As some Africans became Christians, however, conflicts developed within communities. Christian converts rejected the religious practices and beliefs of their families and neighbors.

Education contributed further to the breakdown of traditional African cultures. Colonial schools were run by Europeans. They presented a negative view of African cultures. African children were taught that their parents' beliefs and traditions were backward. In school, children studied European, not African, history.

Educated Africans who became successful under the colonial governments continued to be affected by European paternalism. Europeans held the most important positions and made all the major decisions. Africans found they had to conform to European ways to succeed. For example, if they wore their traditional flowing robes to work, they would lose their jobs. Only European clothes were considered correct.

The benefits. Although colonial governments helped destroy traditional patterns of life in Africa, some people argue that colonial rule brought important benefits. Europeans exploited the rich natural resources of Africa. They used the wealth they obtained from mining diamonds, gold, copper, and iron ore to develop their colonies economically. They built roads, railroads, and harbors. This economic development created jobs in which Africans acquired new skills.

Europeans increased literacy, the ability to read and write, among Africans, although there were literate societies in Africa before the Age of Imperialism. Christian missionaries were particularly active in setting up schools and developing written alphabets for some African languages.

Colonial governments and missionaries also introduced improved medical care and better methods of sanitation. New crops, tools, and farming methods helped increase food production. In addition, colonial rulers ended the local warfare among Africans, which had grown out of the slave trade.

A New Generation of African Leaders

By 1914, many Africans had graduated from colonial schools. Some had completed their education at European universities. At first, some educated Africans imitated everything European and denied their African traditions. After a time, however, a new generation of educated Africans emerged. They accepted some of the benefits of European civilization. However, they also recognized the importance of their own heritage.

These Africans came to appreciate their own culture, in part because of their experiences in Europe. There, they discovered more about their colonial rulers. In Africa, they had been taught that Europeans were superior and did not work with their hands. As a result, many Africans who went to

By the early 1900s, Europeans had established schools and colleges in their African colonies. This photograph shows an African medical school in Uganda, a British colony.

Paris, London, and Berlin were shocked to see Europeans employed as street cleaners and factory workers. In addition, in European universities, Africans studied the ideas of self-government expressed by philosophers such as John Locke and Thomas Jefferson.

On their return to Africa, these western-educated Africans experienced a sense of frustration. Colonial governments continued to treat them as inferiors. They realized that Europeans would never view them as equals no matter how westernized they became. In the early 1900s, this new generation of African leaders began to organize nationalist movements aimed at ending colonial rule.

SECTION REVIEW

1. Define: paternalism, assimilation.
2. (a) Describe two features of direct rule. (b) What European nations used direct rule in Africa?
3. (a) How did indirect rule differ from direct rule? (b) What nation governed through indirect rule? Why?
4. How did colonial governments try to make their colonies self-sufficient?
5. How did colonial rule affect traditional African culture?
6. Why did educated Africans organize nationalist movements?

IN PERSPECTIVE

Between 1870 and 1914, European nations carved up most of Africa. A variety of motives, including nationalism, economic rivalries, and humanitarian concerns, sent Europeans to Africa in ever-increasing numbers.

Europeans turned their attention to Africa just when important internal changes were taking place there. For example, Muhammed Ali had built a powerful Egyptian state in the early 1800s. The end of the slave trade and the revival of Islam altered the relationships among the peoples of West Africa. At the same time, Zulu expansion disrupted societies in southern Africa. In East Africa, new states had emerged under the leadership of strong individuals. People in many parts of Africa resisted European expansion. Yet their resistance failed, in part because Europeans were better armed.

Rivalries over Africa brought various European powers to the brink of war. However, they generally settled their differences peacefully. European powers ruled their colonies differently, but they shared similar attitudes toward African peoples and their cultures. Moreover, they believed their colonies should provide economic benefits, and they set about tapping the agricultural and mineral resources of Africa.

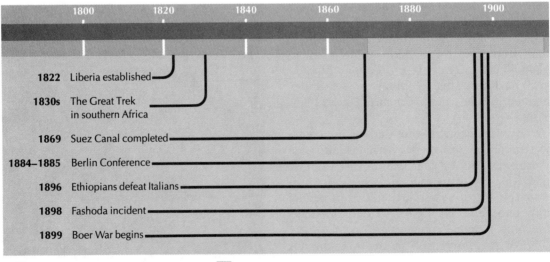

1822	Liberia established
1830s	The Great Trek in southern Africa
1869	Suez Canal completed
1884–1885	Berlin Conference
1896	Ethiopians defeat Italians
1898	Fashoda incident
1899	Boer War begins

■ **Industrial Revolution in Europe**   **Age of Imperialism**

Decide if the following statements are true or false. If a statement is false, rewrite the statement to make it true.

1. European nations divided up Africa at the Berlin Conference.

2. Christian missionaries wanted to preserve traditional African culture.

3. David Livingstone helped open up Central Africa to Europeans.

4. Under Muhammed Ali, Egypt increased its exports of cotton.

5. The Suez Canal was built by a German company.

6. The Congo Free State was owned by the king of France.

7. The Boers set out on the Great Trek to escape British control.

8. Britain established direct rule in its African colonies.

1. (a) Describe the major causes of European imperialism in the 1800s. (b) How did exploration lead to increased interest in Africa? (c) What advantages did Europeans have over the people they conquered?

2. (a) How did Muhammed Ali strengthen Egypt? (b) Why did his policies eventually result in greater European influence in Egypt? (c) What kind of control did the British establish in Egypt?

3. (a) How did Algerian resistance affect France's policies toward its colony? (b) How did Ethiopia prepare its defense against European imperialism? (c) Was it successful? Explain.

4. (a) Describe the slave-gun cycle. (b) How did the increased demand for slaves affect West Africa? (c) What effect did the abolition of the slave trade have on West Africa?

5. Explain how the expansion of each of the following groups in South Africa led to conflict: (a) Zulu; (b) Boers; (c) British.

6. (a) What powerful leaders ruled in East Africa in the 1800s? (b) How did they gain power? (c) Why were their empires short-lived?

7. (a) What attitude did most Europeans have toward the African peoples they ruled? (b) How did this view affect the kinds of government Europeans established in their colonies?

8. Explain how colonial rule affected each of the following areas of African life: (a) government; (b) farming; (c) village life; (d) religion.

1. *Relating Past to Present* (a) Why did the British want control over the Suez Canal? (b) Do you think the Suez Canal is as important today as it was in the late 1800s? Explain.

2. *Analyzing a Quotation* A British poet, Rudyard Kipling, wrote the following lines in 1899:

   Take up the white man's burden—
   Send out the best ye breed—
   Go bind your sons to exile,
   To serve your captives' need;
   To wait in heavy harness,
   On fluttered folk and wild—
   Your new-caught sullen peoples,
   Half devil and half child.

   How do these lines express European paternalism in the Age of Imperialism?

3. *Synthesizing* (a) Describe three ways in which Africans responded to European imperialism. (b) Why were Africans generally unable to prevent European expansion?

1. *Making a Review Chart* Make a chart with two columns and six rows. Title the columns Areas Claimed in Africa and European Rival. Title the rows France, Italy, Britain, Germany, Portugal, Belgium. Fill in the chart with information from your reading and the map on page 122. Then answer the following questions: (a) Which countries claimed lands in North Africa? (b) What areas of Africa did Germany claim? (c) How do you think the scramble for Africa affected relationships among European nations?

2. *Classifying* Make a chart with two columns. In the first column, describe the benefits of European imperialism for African societies. In the second column, describe the disadvantages of European imperialism for African societies. After completing the chart, answer the following questions: (a) What economic benefits resulted from imperialism? (b) What economic problems were caused by imperialism? (c) How did imperialism affect African cultures? (d) In your opinion, which were greater—the benefits or the disadvantages of imperialism? Explain.

See page 204 for suggested readings.

8 Asia and the West

(1650–1920)

A Chinese emperor granting an audience.

In 1793, King George III of Britain sent an ambassador to the Chinese emperor, seeking an exchange of diplomats and expansion of trade with China. Although Britain was one of the most powerful nations in Europe, the Chinese emperor, Ch'ien-lung, considered it a weak, uncivilized nation. Ch'ien-lung therefore replied to George III in these words:

"You, O King, have yearned from afar after the blessings of our civilization, and in your eagerness to come into touch with our converting influence have sent an Embassy across the sea bearing a memorial [diplomatic request]. I have already taken note of your respectful spirit of submission and have treated your mission with extreme favor and loaded it with gifts. . . .

"Yesterday, your Ambassador petitioned my Ministers . . . regarding your trade with China, but his proposal is contrary to the usage [custom] of our dynasty and cannot be entertained. Hitherto, all European nations, including your own country's barbarian merchants, have carried on trade with our Celestial Empire at Canton. Such has been the procedure for many centuries, although our Celestial Empire possesses all things in prolific abundance and lacks no product within its own borders. There was, therefore, no need to import the manufactures of outside barbarians in exchange for your own product."

The emperor's refusal to treat Britain as an equal was due in part to the Chinese belief that no nation could match Chinese achievements. In 1793, Emperor Ch'ien-lung did not foresee that Britain and other western nations would soon challenge China. During the Age of Imperialism, India, China, Japan, Southeast Asia, and Latin America would all feel the foreign influence.

1 India Under British Rule

After the Portuguese sailor Vasco da Gama reached India in 1498, English, French, Portuguese, and Dutch merchants established trade with India. Europeans at first posed no threat to Indian rulers because the *Mogul* Empire was at the height of its power. In the mid-1700s, however, the Mogul Empire was collapsing.

An Empire in Decline

For almost 200 years, from 1526 to about 1712, able Mogul emperors ruled a powerful empire. But during the 1700s, the empire suffered from a lack of strong rulers. Government efficiency declined, and provincial governors became increasingly independent.

In the early days of the Mogul Empire, both *Hindus* and *Muslims* had rallied behind the emperor. As the emperor's prestige faded, however, war broke out between the two religious groups. In addition, a growing number of people saw the Mogul government as extravagant and oppressive. In the mid-1700s, rival Indian princes competed for power. Europeans took advantage of these internal struggles to advance into India.

The English East India Company

As the Mogul Empire collapsed, French and British trading companies battled for control of trade with India. During the 1700s, the English East India Company successfully promoted its interests on the subcontinent. The East India Company had been founded in 1600 as a joint stock company. Its aim was to make money by selling Indian products such as cotton cloth, silk, sugar, and jute in world markets. However, as rivalry with France and the turmoil in the Mogul Empire threatened its profits, the East India Company became increasingly involved in political and military affairs.

In 1756 at the outbreak of the Seven Years War in Europe, Robert Clive, an employee of the East India Company, raised an army and led it against French outposts in India. Clive ousted the French. He then used his army to ensure that a government favorable to the East India Company ruled the Indian state of Bengal. Clive and his successors continued to interfere in local Indian affairs until the East India Company became the most powerful authority in India.

The East India Company practiced *commercial colonialism*—that is, it controlled India's foreign trade and used its army to keep friendly local rulers in power. To protect its interests, the company built forts and maintained an army of *sepoys*, Indian soldiers who served in European armies. During the late 1700s and early 1800s, the East India Company gained direct political control over some parts of India.

Establishing British Rule

The British government regulated some activities of the East India Company, but the company had a fairly free hand in India until the mid-1800s. By this time, many members of Parliament felt that the British government should assume responsibility for India. In 1857, an uprising known as the Sepoy Rebellion gave Parliament the excuse it needed to end the rule of the East India Company in India.

The Sepoy Rebellion. The immediate cause of the Sepoy Rebellion was rumors that bullet cartridges used by sepoys were greased with beef or pork fat. These rumors angered both Hindu and Muslim soldiers. Hindus were forbidden to touch beef, and Muslims were forbidden to touch pork. The sepoys were also bitter because they felt the British were forcing them to accept Christianity and adopt European customs. These grievances sparked a rebellion among the sepoys. The rebellion spread across India.

Hindu and Muslim princes supported the Sepoy Rebellion because they saw the British as a threat to their power. Peasants joined the uprising in protest against the severe hardships of their lives. British troops suppressed the rebellion, and in 1858 the

British Parliament took control of India from the East India Company.

Colonial government. After 1858, the British government established full colonial rule in India. A cabinet minister in London was responsible for Indian affairs. A British viceroy in India carried out government policies. British governors ruled about two-thirds of India, including the parts that the East India Company had controlled directly. Local Indian princes stayed on as rulers in the rest of the country. But British officials called residents closely supervised these Indian rulers. In 1877, British Prime Minister Benjamin Disraeli had Queen Victoria recognized as Empress of India.

In 1890, about one thousand British officials ran a colonial government that ruled some two hundred and eighty million Indians. During the Age of Imperialism, the British had a

clear idea of what they thought India should become. Unlike the East India Company, which had encouraged its officers to learn Indian languages and observe local customs, the British colonial government tried to impose British culture on India. British officials encouraged the Indian people to abandon their traditions and learn to speak, dress, and live like Europeans. These colonial officials believed that by adopting European ways, Indians would improve their lives.

Impact of British Rule

British rule affected Indian life in various ways. In countless Indian villages, the coming of the British had little direct impact. Farmers tilled their fields as they had for centuries. The *caste* system dominated village life, and the people observed traditional religious practices. However, British colonial policies opened the door to major economic and social changes.

Economic changes. The Industrial Revolution in Britain influenced British economic policies toward India. The East India Company had sold Indian-made luxury items abroad, but the British government saw India as a source of cheap raw materials for British factories. It also felt that India, which had a large population, would serve as a market for British manufactured goods. Britain, therefore, tied the Indian economy closely to its own.

The British discouraged local Indian industries. They encouraged Indian farmers to shift from growing food crops to raising cotton. Factories in Britain then used the Indian cotton to produce finished goods, some of which were sent back to India to be sold. Although this policy benefited British manufacturers, it hurt local industries in India. Village artisans could not compete with the cheaper, mass-produced British imports.

Moreover, British efforts to encourage the production of export crops, such as cotton, reduced the amount of food that was grown. As a result of reduced food supplies, famines killed millions of Indians during the 1800s.

British rule in India led to better communication and increased trade. By building

■ *Britain controlled all of India after 1858, but its method of rule varied from region to region. In the areas colored blue and purple on this map, British officials ruled directly over the Indian people. In the areas colored pink, they governed through local Indian rulers.*

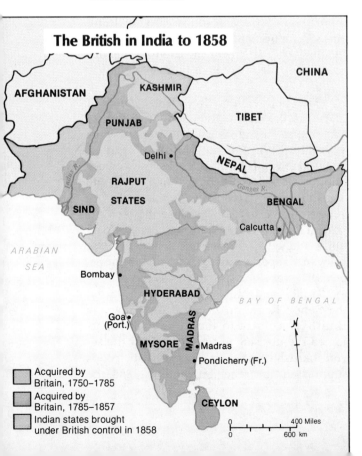

The British in India to 1858

CHINA

AFGHANISTAN

KASHMIR

TIBET

PUNJAB

Delhi

NEPAL

RAJPUT STATES

Ganges R.

SIND

BENGAL

Calcutta

ARABIAN SEA

Bombay

HYDERABAD

BAY OF BENGAL

Goa (Port.)

MYSORE

MADRAS

Madras

Pondicherry (Fr.)

N

CEYLON

☐ Acquired by Britain, 1750–1785
☐ Acquired by Britain, 1785–1857
☐ Indian states brought under British control in 1858

0   400 Miles
0   600 km

This 1870 Indian woodcut shows one of the effects of British rule—the building of thousands of kilometres of railroads. Notice that the last car, known as the "purdah carriage," was reserved for women and children.

new canals, roads, and railways, the British opened up India's vast interior to trade. The opening of the Suez Canal in 1869 made trade faster and easier between Europe and India as well as between Europe and the rest of Asia. Telegraph lines also made communications easier between Britain and India. These developments resulted in a tremendous increase in exports from India.

Social changes. The British sponsored programs to improve health care and control epidemics, which occurred frequently. They built hospitals and trained doctors to work in the countryside. Improved medical care contributed to a rapid growth of the Indian population. In some regions, population growth combined with inadequate food supplies resulted in famine. At the same time, the building of railroads helped reduce the effect of famine since food could be transported quickly from one region to another.

India's growing population made Indian cities among the largest in the world. British determination to introduce their own culture in India was especially evident in the cities. There, British rule created a class of British-educated professionals and businesspeople.

Young Indians, mainly from higher-caste families, attended British-run schools and colleges. They studied the same courses in science, mathematics, history, literature, and philosophy as students in Britain. These doctors, lawyers, professors, civil servants, and businesspeople became a new upper class in India. British officials depended on them to carry out colonial policies. By the late 1800s, however, some members of the new upper class began voicing discontent with British rule.

Indian Nationalism

Opposition to British rule was not new in India. Economic hardships in the countryside had touched off periodic uprisings. On occasion, British troops faced thousands of enraged peasants. However, these revolts did not threaten British control. The peasants were too poorly armed and organized to defeat the British.

In 1885, a group of well-educated, middle-class Indians formed a political party called the Indian National Congress. Known as the Congress, this party led the nationalist movement in India. At first, the Congress did not seek independence from Britain. It campaigned for reforms such as free compulsory education for boys and girls and greater Indian representation in local government.

In the early 1900s, Indian nationalists began calling for an end to British rule. They urged Indians to boycott, or stop buying, British goods. At the same time, Indian writers published books that restored people's pride in India's ancient heritage.

The best known nationalist leader was Mohandas Gandhi, born into the Vaisya, or

143

merchant, caste. Gandhi rallied widespread popular support for the independence movement. India should be free, he said, so that Indians could restore their village life and live according to their ancient traditions. Gandhi wanted to restore Indians' pride in their culture. He eventually united the Hindu population behind the call for Indian independence.

British leaders did not take the independence movement seriously in the early 1900s. They knew that both Hindus and Muslims in India wanted an end to colonialism. But they also knew that the two groups were so deeply divided that they would not cooperate against the British. Therefore, Britain refused to give in to the demands of Indian nationalists.

SECTION REVIEW

1. Identify: Robert Clive, Sepoy Rebellion, Indian National Congress, Mohandas Gandhi.
2. Define: commercial colonialism, sepoy.
3. Give one reason why the Mogul Empire declined in the 1700s.
4. What Indian goods did the English East India Company sell?
5. What was the main result of the Sepoy Rebellion?
6. List three ways in which British rule affected India.
7. (a) What reforms did the early Indian nationalists want? (b) How did their demands change in the early 1900s?

2 Conflict Between China and the West

In 1793 when the emperor Ch'ien-lung wrote the letter at the beginning of this chapter, China was probably the wealthiest, most powerful country in the world. A strong central government was successfully administering a vast empire. Yet within 100 years, this prosperous empire would be torn apart by internal rebellion and the growing influence of western nations* in Asia.

The Manchu Dynasty

In the early 1600s, invaders from Manchuria swept into China and overwhelmed the Ming dynasty, which had ruled China since the 1300s. The victorious Manchu, as the invaders were called, established their capital at Peking. They adopted the customs and traditions of the Chinese and won the support of the *Confucian* official class. The Manchu, claiming they had received the Mandate of Heaven, founded a new dynasty. The Manchu dynasty ruled China from 1644 to 1911.

The Manchu presided over a powerful and prosperous empire. Western merchants reaching China in the 1600s and 1700s were amazed at the splendor of Chinese civilization. They began arriving in ever greater numbers to buy Chinese tea, silk, and porcelain.

In the 1600s, the Chinese had restricted foreigners to trading at one city, Canton. Europeans had to pay for Chinese products with gold and silver because they had few European manufactured goods that the Chinese wanted. If foreign merchants did not observe Chinese customs, the Chinese expelled them. Although the restrictions irritated foreign merchants, they accepted the restrictions because huge profits could be made selling Chinese goods in Europe and North America.

In the 1800s, domestic turmoil disrupted life in Manchu China. This turmoil had several sources. Under the Manchu, the Chinese population had grown to about three hundred million people. Such large numbers strained food resources. A flood or drought could cause mass starvation. During times of famine, peasants in many parts of China rebelled against the government.

---

*The term "western" refers to the nations of Western Europe and North America.

Chinese porcelain was highly prized by westerners who went to China to trade. Gradually, all glazed pottery—no matter where it originated—became known as chinaware or simply china. In this Chinese print from the 1800s, skilled artisans are shown making pottery in a shed. Outside the shed, pots are set out to dry on long tables.

Furthermore, like earlier dynasties, the Manchu eventually became corrupt. Even during the reign of a powerful emperor, Ch'ien-lung, official corruption undermined Chinese strength. For 30 years, a court official and friend of the emperor, Ho-shen, ran wild with government money. It is estimated that Ho-shen skimmed a personal fortune equal to about one thousand million dollars from taxes. Throughout the empire, officials enriched themselves with public funds. To offset the loss of these revenues, officials raised the taxes peasants had to pay. Unbearable taxes led to more peasant uprisings.

Beginning of European Imperialism

While the Manchu government struggled to suppress these uprisings, Europeans were pressuring China to end its trade restrictions. European governments also demanded that China receive their diplomats and treat them as equals. The Chinese saw their land as the center of civilization, and they thought China should receive only "tribute bearers" from states they considered inferior.

The Opium War. Tensions between China and European powers increased until they flared into violence over the opium trade. In the early 1800s, British merchants discovered that they could make huge profits trading opium from India and Turkey for Chinese goods. While the opium trade enriched many foreign and Chinese merchants, the Chinese government was outraged as opium smoking spread throughout China. Not only was opium harmful to the Chinese people, but the opium trade drained China of silver, which was used to pay foreign merchants who imported the drug.

The Chinese decided to end the opium trade. In 1839, the government destroyed six million dollars worth of opium the British had brought to Canton. To China's surprise, the British responded with military force. In 1840, the British seized Canton and attacked Chinese forces along the coast. In this conflict, often called the Opium War, the British used their navy and superior weapons to defeat the Chinese.

The unequal treaties. In 1842, the Chinese were forced to accept humiliating terms in the Treaty of Nanking. Under this treaty, China had to accept foreign diplomats and open more ports to foreign trade. Britain won the island of Hong Kong and received compensation for the opium destroyed by the Chinese.

Other provisions limited China's ability to govern itself even more seriously. For example, China agreed to let Britain determine its tariffs, or taxes on imports. The Chinese also granted the British the right of *extraterritoriality*—that is, the British would be protected by the laws of their own nation, not the laws of China. Extraterritoriality meant that China would have little authority over foreigners.

The Treaty of Nanking was the first of the "unequal treaties" that China was forced to make with foreign powers. Other nations soon demanded and received most of the rights that the British had won in the Treaty of Nanking. In later struggles with western powers and Japan, China gave up still more rights.

China was unable to defend itself against these demands in part because its military technology had fallen behind that of the foreign powers. For centuries, the Chinese had believed in the superiority of their civilization. However, by the 1800s, European advances in science and technology had, for the first time, made European nations more powerful than China.

The Taiping Rebellion

Internal unrest continued to weaken the Manchu dynasty. In 1850, discontent with Manchu rule erupted into a widespread peasant uprising known as the Taiping Rebellion. The rebels were inspired by a mixture of ancient Chinese traditions and ideas learned from Christian missionaries. Their leaders promised reforms such as the redistribution of land to poor peasants, an end to high taxes, and equality for men and women.

The rebels seized the central region of China and nearly toppled the government. They sought the aid of European nations by claiming to be Christians. But in the end, the Europeans helped the Manchu emperor since they had already signed favorable treaties with him. After 14 years of fighting, the government finally defeated the Taiping rebels. However, the rebellion weakened the Manchu dynasty further and created a strong wish for reform within China.

During the Taiping Rebellion, European powers forced China to grant them more concessions. The Chinese government had to open additional ports to foreign trade and make the opium trade legal. It also had to allow foreign diplomats to live in Peking.

Spheres of Influence

In 1860, the Russians seized a large stretch of land on China's northern border and built the port of Vladivostok on the Pacific coast. Japan, too, took advantage of Chinese weakness to increase its influence in Korea, a country that China had dominated. In 1894, China tried to stop the Japanese advance in Korea, and war broke out. Japan quickly defeated China. China was forced to recognize Korean independence, and Japan won several islands from China, including Formosa, present-day Taiwan.

Toward the end of the century, China lost still more power. Russia, Germany, France, and Britain each acquired a sphere of influence in China. (See the map on page 147.) Each nation won special economic privileges in its sphere of influence, including the right to invest in mines, railways, and factories. These four European powers also forced China to lease them land so they could build naval bases to protect their spheres of influence.

The United States did not acquire a sphere of influence in China, but the American government insisted that it receive the same commercial rights as other foreign powers. It demanded equal access to trade in China for all nations. This Open Door Policy, as it was called, was meant to prevent foreign powers from carving China up into colonies. In letters addressed to the foreign powers in China, the United States called on these countries to allow free trade in their spheres of influence and to maintain Chinese political unity. The American policy did help preserve an open door to trade in China, but it did little to keep China from foreign domination.

Chinese Efforts at Reform

Chinese leaders were outraged at the sad condition of their country. As early as the 1860s, after the defeat of the Taiping rebels, the government had adopted a policy known as "self-strengthening." It hoped to reestablish government control over both the Chinese and the foreigners living in China.

This "self-strengthening" policy involved finding ways to modernize China while retaining Confucian traditions. The government tried to introduce modern weapons and began construction of telegraph and railroad lines. Chinese students were sent abroad to study western ideas. The government also tried to weed out corrupt officials. Many officials opposed these reforms, however, so the policy had little success.

Hundred days of reform. In 1898, as foreign interference increased, a young and idealistic Manchu emperor made another attempt to save China. On the advice of reformers at court, he decided to send diplomats and other officials abroad to study. He issued decrees to reform schools, added practical subjects to the curriculum, and translated foreign books into Chinese.

Known as the "hundred days of reform," this program introduced many changes that challenged the traditional Confucian order. Conservatives at the imperial court turned to the dowager empress Tz'u-hsi (tsoo shee) for help. Tz'u-hsi strongly opposed the new reforms. In 1898, she ousted the reformers from power and had the emperor imprisoned. For the next ten years, Tz'u-hsi ruled China and prevented any major reforms.

The Boxer Rebellion. The dowager empress faced two serious problems: foreign

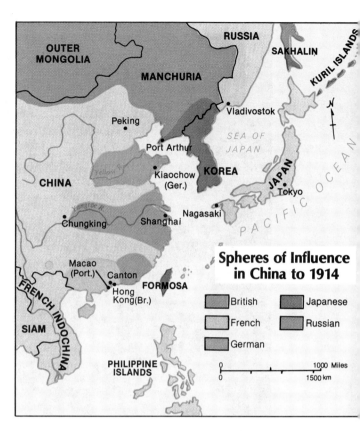

■ By the early 1900s, several European nations and Japan had acquired spheres of influence in China. Within its sphere of influence, each nation claimed exclusive trading rights. What relationship do you see between the spheres of influence and the rivers in China?

imperialism and a growing Chinese belief that the Manchu dynasty had lost the Mandate of Heaven. In 1899, a group of Chinese founded a secret society called the "Fists of Righteous Harmony" or "Boxers." The Boxers wanted to expel the Manchu and all foreigners from China. But Tz'u-hsi negotiated with the Boxers and agreed to aid them secretly against foreigners.

In 1900, the Boxers moved through northern China attacking foreigners. They then besieged foreign diplomats in Peking. The foreigners responded by organizing an international army to march on Peking and rescue the diplomats. The army defeated the Boxers and forced Tz'u-hsi to grant them concessions. China agreed to allow foreign

The battle cry of the Boxers was: "Overthrow the Manchu; destroy the foreigners." The Boxers attacked Chinese who had adopted foreign ideas such as Christianity. In June 1900, they surrounded foreign areas in Peking. This painting shows an international force of American, Japanese, and British troops attacking the Boxers in an attempt to rescue the trapped foreigners.

troops to be stationed on Chinese soil and to allow foreign naval vessels to patrol Chinese rivers and coastal waters.

The Revolution of 1911

In 1908, Tz'u-hsi died. She had named a two-year-old prince to succeed her. Three years later, revolutionaries overthrew the young Manchu emperor and proclaimed a republic.

The leading figure in the Revolution of 1911 was Dr. Sun Yat-sen. Sun had led revolutionaries in earlier uprisings against the Manchu. However, he was living in the United States when the revolution broke out in 1911. Sun returned to China at once and was named the first president of the Chinese Republic. He also helped found the Kuomintang (KWOH mihn TANG), or Nationalist party.

The new republic faced civil war in the provinces. Military leaders known as warlords fought each other and looted the countryside. Amid this confusion, Sun worked to build a united, powerful, and independent China. He set out a revolutionary program called "Three Principles of the People." The principles were political unity, democracy, and a basic living for all Chinese.

Sun was influenced by his travels in the United States and Western Europe. He wanted China to have the same high standard of living he saw in these nations. Sun believed that China should be thoroughly reorganized in order to achieve this goal. In the years ahead, Sun and the Kuomintang would struggle to make China a powerful modern nation.

SECTION REVIEW

1. Locate: Manchuria, Canton, Vladivostok, Formosa.
2. Identify: Manchu, Treaty of Nanking, Taiping Rebellion, Open Door Policy, Tz'u-hsi, Boxer Rebellion, Sun Yat-sen, Kuomintang.
3. Define: extraterritoriality.
4. Give two reasons for the decline of the Manchu dynasty.
5. (a) What was the immediate cause of the Opium War? (b) What was the outcome of the war?
6. What rights did foreigners gain in the "unequal treaties"?
7. (a) Which nations had spheres of influence in China? (b) What privileges did each nation acquire in its sphere of influence?
8. What were the Three Principles of the People proposed by Sun Yat-sen?

Sun Yat-sen despised the corrupt Manchu dynasty that ruled China. In the early 1900s, he wrote: "Today we are the poorest and weakest nation in the world and occupy the lowest position in international affairs. Other men are the carving knife and serving dish; we are the fish and the meat." Sun Yat-sen led the Chinese nationalist movement after the overthrow of the last Manchu emperor.

3 Modernizing Japan

In the 1600s, the rulers of Japan, the Tokugawa *shoguns*, expelled Europeans from their land and forbade Japanese to leave the country. Only one Dutch ship was allowed to visit Nagasaki each year. For 200 years, the Tokugawa shoguns were strong enough to enforce this policy of isolation. However, in the mid-1800s, they encountered serious domestic and international challenges.

Tokugawa Japan

The Tokugawa shoguns created a strong unified government in Japan. They established a system of centralized *feudalism* that rested on a rigidly controlled economic and social order. The *samurai* were the highest class. Below them were the peasants. The lowest social class was the merchant class.

During 200 years of peace under the Tokugawa shoguns, commerce and trade within Japan expanded. As a result of this economic growth, Japanese merchants often acquired more wealth than the samurai. Increasingly, wealthy merchants resented their low social status.

At the same time, some samurai organized revolts against the Tokugawa shogun. They were encouraged by a number of scholars who claimed that the shogun had no right to govern. These scholars argued that the shogun had unlawfully seized power from the emperor, who should be the true ruler of Japan. In the 1800s, these opposition forces became a serious threat to the Tokugawa because the once-powerful government lacked able leaders. The movement against the government was strengthened in the 1850s when foreigners reappeared in Japan.

An End to Isolation

In 1853, the United States government sent a naval mission to Japan under the command of Commodore Matthew C. Perry. The United States wanted to negotiate a treaty to protect American sailors shipwrecked in Japanese waters, to open Japanese ports so American ships could take on food and water, and to grant the United States the right to trade with Japan. Fully aware of the Japanese attitude toward foreigners, the United States decided to back up its request with a show of force. Therefore, Commodore Perry arrived in Tokyo Bay with a fleet of steam-powered warships.

The Japanese did not want to negotiate a treaty with the Americans, but they remembered China's defeat in the Opium War. Fearing a similar fate, Tokugawa officials argued:

> If we try to drive them away, they will immediately commence hostilities, and then we shall be obliged to fight.... In time, the country would be put to an immense expense, and the people be plunged into misery. Rather than allow this, as we are not the equals of foreigners in the mechanical arts, let us have relations with foreign countries, learn their drills and tactics ... and it will not be too late then to declare war.

Thus, in 1854, Japan signed the Treaty of Kanagawa with the United States. The treaty opened up two Japanese ports to foreign trade and met the other American demands.

This treaty marked the end of Japanese isolation. Japan, like China, soon had to grant further concessions to foreign powers. In the 1850s and 1860s, the Tokugawa government signed "unequal treaties" with the United States and the major European powers. The treaties gave these foreign countries control over Japanese tariffs, extensive trading rights in Japan, and the right of extraterritoriality.

The Meiji Period

The treaties granting privileges to foreigners aroused fierce opposition to the shogun among the Japanese. In southern Japan, samurai leaders bitterly denounced the for-

During the Meiji period, the Japanese sent many people to study western governments and technology. In 1871, Prince Iwakura, shown here, sailed from Yokohama at the head of the first diplomatic mission to the West. Iwakura's main purpose was to revise the "unequal treaties" with western nations. He failed to achieve this goal. But he did bring back detailed information about the Industrial Revolution taking place in the West.

eigners, who were arriving in growing numbers. The samurai rallied around the emperor in Kyoto and proclaimed that they had restored imperial rule.

In 1868, the last Tokugawa shogun resigned, and the emperor, who was only 15 years old, moved his capital from Kyoto to Tokyo. He took the name Meiji (may jee), meaning "enlightened government." During the Meiji period, from 1868 to 1912, the Japanese government embarked on a course that transformed the country from a feudal state into a modern industrialized nation.

Abolition of feudalism. Leaders of the Meiji government were determined to save Japan from foreign domination by building up its political, military, and economic strength. The government decided to abandon the centralized feudalism of the Tokugawa period. The abolition of feudalism affected the political and social structure of Japan. Large landowners were persuaded to turn their fiefs, or vast estates, over to the emperor. In return, they received financial compensation and high level positions in government.

Other changes introduced at this time affected all classes in Japan. The samurai class lost power and prestige because the Meiji government made all classes equal before the law. Moreover, in 1872, Japan introduced a system of universal military service. This meant peasants and merchants as well as samurai might serve in the armed forces. Their exclusive military service had been a major source of power and prestige for the samurai.

Constitutional government. In 1884, the emperor asked Ito Hirobumi, a Japanese official, to draft a constitution for Japan. Ito visited the United States and several European nations to study their constitutional governments. He met with Bismarck and was especially impressed with the constitutional system of government in Germany. On his return to Japan, Ito drafted a constitution based in part on the German model.

In 1889, the emperor presented the constitution to the Japanese people. The Meiji constitution established a two-house diet, or parliament. But the diet had limited power because the emperor had the greatest authority. He could issue laws, veto laws passed by the diet, and declare war. In practice, however, ministers appointed by the emperor did the actual governing.

A Japanese View of Europe

Yukichi Fukuzawa, a Japanese scholar, made many trips to Europe and the United States during the late 1800s. Fukuzawa enthusiastically supported modernization in Japan. In these excerpts from his autobiography, he expresses his interest in western ideas.

From Fukuzawa's Autobiography

During this mission in Europe, I tried to learn some of the most commonplace details of foreign culture. I did not care to study scientific or technical subjects while on the journey, because I could study them as well from books after I had returned home. But I felt that I had to learn the more common matters of daily life directly from the people because the Europeans would not describe them in books as being too obvious. Yet to us those common matters were the most difficult to comprehend.

For instance, when I saw a hospital, I wanted to know how it was run—who paid the running expenses; when I visited a bank, I wished to learn how the money was deposited and paid out. By similar firsthand queries [questions], I learned something of the postal system and the military conscription [draft] then in force in France but not in England. A perplexing institution was representative government.

When I asked a gentleman what the "election law" was and what kind of an institution the Parliament really was, he simply replied with a smile, meaning, I suppose, that no intelligent person was expected to ask such a question. But these were the things most difficult of all for me to understand. In this connection, I learned that there were different political parties—the Liberal and the Conservative—who were always "fighting" against each other in the government.

For some time it was beyond my comprehension to understand what they were "fighting" for, and what was meant, anyway, by "fighting" in peace time. "This man and that man are 'enemies' in the House," they would tell me. But these "enemies" were to be seen at the same table, eating and drinking with each other. I felt as if I could not make much out of this. It took me a long time, with some tedious thinking, before I could gather a general notion of these . . . mysterious facts.

Economic and Social Changes

During the Meiji period, Japan moved rapidly to strengthen its economy. In the late 1800s, the government led the effort to modernize Japan by sponsoring new industries. Once again, the Meiji government borrowed ideas from abroad. Japanese visited factories in Europe and North America. The government hired thousands of foreign engineers to teach their skills in Japan.

The government built defense industries such as shipyards and munitions plants. It also encouraged mining of coal and iron and developed a modern communication system by building railroads and stringing telegraph lines. Finally, it sponsored consumer industries such as textile manufacturing.

In the 1880s, the Meiji government decided to sell some of its factories and mills to private businesspeople. A few wealthy families, known as *zaibatsu* (ZĪ baht SOO), bought the chief industries and thereby came to dominate the Japanese economy. Families such as the Mitsubishi and Mitsui owned many large companies and controlled whole industries.

In Japan, cooperation among companies was more important than competition, so companies were often merged to increase efficiency. By 1914, the combination of government support and private initiative had made Japan a powerful industrial nation.

Industrialization transformed Japanese society. Millions of people abandoned farming and moved to the cities to work in factories. Because the samurai no longer enjoyed their old privileges, many of them became officers in the Japanese army and navy. Others went into business or government.

As part of its program of *modernization*, the government created a new educational system. By 1900, almost all children were enrolled in elementary schools. Some students continued their education in middle schools and high schools. The government also organized commercial and technical schools. At the top of the system were prestigious imperial universities, which admitted only a small number of outstanding students.

Japanese Expansion in the Pacific

By 1900, Japan was reaping the benefits of modernization. It negotiated new treaties with western nations. It also withdrew privi-

Under Meiji rulers, Japan modernized rapidly. It financed the building of modern factories. It also imported textile machinery and other western inventions. This 1883 print shows people stopping to watch the first electric street lamps being lighted in Tokyo.

leges such as extraterritoriality. In addition, Japan regained full control over its own tariffs.

As Japan increased its military strength, it participated in imperialist ventures. As you read earlier, Japanese expansion in Korea led to war with China in 1894. After defeating China, Japan acquired Taiwan and the same trading privileges enjoyed by western powers in China.

Ten years later, Japan surprised people in the West by winning a stunning victory over Russia. The Russo-Japanese War broke out in 1904 over rival Russian and Japanese claims in Manchuria. The Japanese army forced the Russians to retreat from Manchuria, and the Japanese navy defeated two Russian fleets.

In 1905, President Theodore Roosevelt invited Japanese and Russian diplomats to meet in Portsmouth, New Hampshire, where they worked out a treaty ending the war. Japan acquired Port Arthur and concessions in southern Manchuria from Russia. Japan thus gained a foothold for an empire on the Asian mainland. Furthermore, the Russo-Japanese War showed the world that an Asian power could defeat a major European nation. Nationalists in many parts of Asia applauded the Japanese victory.

SECTION REVIEW

1. Identify: Matthew C. Perry, Treaty of Kanagawa, Ito Hirobumi, Russo-Japanese War.
2. Define: shogun, samurai, zaibatsu.
3. (a) Which groups in Japanese society opposed the Tokugawa shogun in the 1800s? (b) Why?
4. Why did the United States want a treaty with Japan in 1853?
5. Describe two ways in which the Meiji leaders changed Japan.
6. List two results of the Russo-Japanese War.

---

4 Imperialism in Southeast Asia and the Pacific

Southeast Asia was another area of interest to western powers during the Age of Imperialism. During the 1500s, several European nations competed for control of the spice trade in the East Indies. Later, European nations extended their influence over most of Southeast Asia.

Peoples of Southeast Asia

Southeast Asia includes the area of the Asian mainland south of China. This area stretches from present-day Bangladesh in the west to present-day Vietnam in the east. Southeast Asia also includes the Philippine Islands, the East Indies, and Indonesia.

Southeast Asia is home to peoples with different languages, customs, and political systems. Geography has influenced the peoples of Southeast Asia. The language and customs of people in a mountainous region usually differ from those of nearby people in a lowland area.

The early civilizations of India and China influenced the peoples of Southeast Asia. Traders and *Buddhist* missionaries from India helped spread both Hindu and Buddhist beliefs. Indian culture had its greatest impact on the area that today includes Burma, Thailand, Laos, Kampuchea, and the southern part of Vietnam. During the T'ang dynasty, China began extending its influence into the northern part of Vietnam. In the 1200s, Arab and Indian Muslims carried *Islam* to Indonesia.

The political diversity among the peoples of Southeast Asia was evident to Europeans when they first arrived. In some areas, powerful monarchs united the people. Today, the ruins of Angkor Wat, an enormous temple built in the 1100s, recall the splendor of the Khmer Empire in Kampuchea. In other parts of Southeast Asia, there was no strong central authority. For example, when the Spanish reached the Philippines in the 1500s, they found only minor local rulers.

In the 1500s, when Europeans entered the spice trade, there were many separate states with their own cultural, social, and political traditions in Southeast Asia. Geography, trade rivalries, and religious differences further divided the peoples of the region, so they did not respond in a united fashion to the coming of the Europeans.

The Spice Trade

The early spice trade had little direct impact on the peoples of Southeast Asia. Portuguese, Spanish, and Dutch traders tried to drive Arab, Indian, and Chinese merchants

■ *The spice trade orginally attracted Europeans to Southeast Asia in the 1500s. In the 1800s, Europeans were more interested in cash crops such as sugar and rice and in natural resources such as oil and rubber. Which European nations claimed territory on the mainland?*

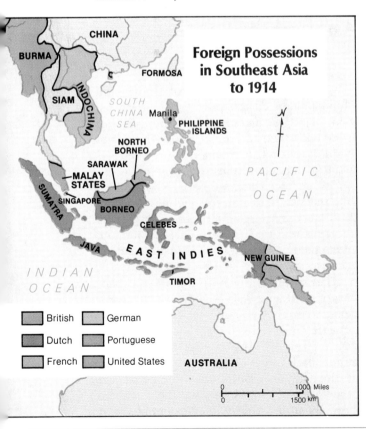

out of the spice trade. They also competed fiercely with each other. They established trading posts along the coasts but did not extend their influence inland.

Only in the Philippines did Europeans have an immediate impact. In 1571, the Spanish conquered the Philippine Islands and sent a Spanish governor-general to rule the colony. For the first time, the Philippines were united under a single government. Catholic missionaries entered the islands with Spanish officials and converted many of the people to Christianity.

The Spanish seized the Philippines because they wanted to establish a direct trade route between Asia and their empire in the Americas. Spanish ships carried silver from the New World to the Philippines. They then sailed to China to buy porcelains and silk or to the Spice Islands to buy spices.

Scramble for Colonies in Southeast Asia

In the 1700s, European interest in Southeast Asia shifted from spices to crops such as sugar, coffee, and rice. To ensure production of these crops, Europeans took control of large parts of the region and set up huge plantations. As European nations industrialized, they also looked to Southeast Asia as a source of raw materials such as tin, rubber, and oil.

During the 1800s, the Dutch converted their trading outposts in Southeast Asia into a colony called the Dutch East Indies. By this time, however, Britain and France had become the chief European rivals in the region. It was the fierce competition between these two nations that led to a scramble for colonies on the mainland of Southeast Asia.

To protect the eastern frontier of India, Britain acquired Burma piece by piece between 1820 and 1890. Britain also established control over Malaya and the island of Singapore, which commands an important sea route to China. While Britain extended its influence in these regions, France established the colony of French Indochina. Both the British and the French hoped to use their colonies as stepping stones to southern China.

During the scramble for colonies, only Siam, today called Thailand, escaped European domination. During the 1800s, Siamese rulers imported western technology to modernize their country. They also encouraged trade with western nations. Furthermore, the Siamese skillfully exploited the rivalry between Britain and France. By establishing their kingdom as a neutral buffer between the British in Burma and the French in Indochina, the Siamese guaranteed their freedom from foreign control.

Western Expansion in the Pacific

Several western powers seized control of various Pacific islands before the Age of Imperialism began. Spain conquered the Philippines, and Britain established colonies in Australia and New Zealand. In the late 1800s, Britain, Germany, and the United States seized other islands.

United States expansion in the Pacific region began after the Civil War as more and more American merchant ships began trading with China and Japan. American ships needed friendly ports where they could stop and take on fuel. In addition, the United States navy wanted bases to protect American trade. Thus, the United States began to take control of islands scattered through the Pacific. American interest in Southeast Asia and the Pacific grew as a result of a war the United States fought to free Cuba from Spain.*

The Spanish-American War began in 1898. The first American target in the war was a Spanish fleet in Manila Bay, the chief harbor in the Philippines. The American fleet commanded by Commodore George Dewey destroyed the Spanish ships and paved the way for American victory in the war. As part of the peace settlement, the United States acquired the Philippine Islands and Guam. In 1898, the United States also annexed Hawaii, where American mer-

chants and sugar growers had extensive interests.

Southeast Asia Under Colonial Rule

Western imperialism greatly affected Southeast Asia. Almost everywhere, local leaders were replaced by foreign administrators. The economic structure of the region also changed. Colonial powers emphasized the production of cash crops and the export of raw materials. As a result, the people of Southeast Asia became dependent on international markets, where prices could rise and fall sharply.

A few independence movements developed in Southeast Asia. The first nationalist revolution began in the 1880s in the Philippines. In fact, Filipinos who were rebelling against Spanish rule helped American forces in the Spanish-American War. After the war, Filipino nationalists were bitterly disappointed when the United States refused to grant them independence at once. They then turned their struggle against the United States. Other colonial powers faced rebellions in Southeast Asia. However, western powers were confident that they could continue to rule their colonies indefinitely.

SECTION REVIEW

1. Locate: Philippine Islands, Burma, Malaya, Indochina, Siam.
2. What different civilizations influenced the peoples of Southeast Asia?
3. Why did Spain seize the Philippine Islands in the late 1500s?
4. (a) What products did Europeans want from Southeast Asia during the Age of Imperialism? (b) What countries established colonies in Southeast Asia?
5. How did the United States acquire the Philippine Islands?
6. Describe two effects of colonial rule in Southeast Asia.

---

* You will read more about the causes of the Spanish-American War in the next section of this chapter.

5 Strengthening the New Nations in Latin America

During the wars of independence in Latin America (see pages 53 to 57), Simón Bolívar dreamed of uniting the Spanish colonies into a single nation. Other nationalist leaders shared this dream. They hoped that a common political and religious heritage would help unite the peoples of Latin America. But in the years after independence, the dream of unity faded as bitter rivalries surfaced.

Barriers to Unity

The new nations of Latin America faced numerous problems that prevented unity. During the wars of independence, many different groups had banded together against Spain. However, after independence, these groups disagreed over what kind of government should be organized. Power struggles broke out among rival leaders, triggering violent civil wars.

Another barrier to unity was the diverse geography of Central and South America. Rugged mountains, high plateaus, the arid Atacama Desert, and the rainforests of the Amazon region limited contact between people. Rough terrain made trade and transportation difficult and encouraged *regionalism*, loyalty to a small geographic area.

Differing interests led to the establishment of 18 separate nations in Latin America. The Republic of Great Colombia, which Bolivar had organized, splintered into three separate countries: Colombia, Venezuela, and Ecuador. South America was further divided when Peru, Bolivia, Argentina, Chile, Paraguay, Uruguay, and Brazil also set up their own governments. After gaining independence, the United Provinces of Central America broke up into five separate nations. On the island of Hispaniola, the Dominican Republic declared its independence from Haiti. (See the map on page 57.)

The Colonial Heritage

The newly independent nations of Latin America became republics and adopted constitutions modeled on the Constitution of the United States. Putting these constitutions into effect, however, proved to be difficult.

Unlike the 13 British colonies in North America, the Spanish colonies had no experience with representative government. During the colonial period, they had been under the absolute rule of the Spanish viceroy. In many of the new nations, ambitious leaders won the backing of the army and installed themselves as military dictators. These dictators, known as *caudillos* (kaw DEE yohs), stayed in power by force and ignored constitutions that called for elections.

Social structure. The nations of Latin America inherited other problems from their colonial past. The rigid social structure of the colonial period remained largely unchanged after independence. Social and racial divisions created a stumbling block to representative government. Many creoles who had led the struggle for independence did not want to share political power once they had ousted the peninsulares.

Mestizos were angry at being excluded from political power, as were Indians and blacks. Slavery was abolished, but neither blacks nor Indians had many rights. The majority of mestizos, Indians, and blacks worked on plantations and in mines owned by wealthy creoles. They deeply resented the social and political system that kept them in poverty.

Role of the Catholic Church. The Catholic Church was a powerful political and economic force in Latin America during the colonial period. It remained so after independence. The church owned huge tracts of land and controlled education. During the wars of independence, some members of the clergy, including Father Hidalgo in Mexico, had fought for liberal ideas. However, high church officials often favored the interests of creole landowners over other classes. After independence, the church was generally a conservative force.

Economic problems. Economic conditions remained relatively unchanged after independence. Although Latin America was rich in natural resources, the wealth was controlled by a handful of people. The church and a few powerful families owned most of the land. The majority of the people were landless and poor.

The economies of most Latin American nations remained closely tied to Europe. They supplied raw materials to Europe and were a market for European manufactured goods.

Many nations became dependent on the export of one or two products. Haiti, for example, relied mainly on the export of sugar. Chile exported silver and copper. When these products sold for high prices on world markets, the nations benefited. But when world demand dropped, as it often did, they suffered. Thus, Latin American nations had little control over their own economies.

Changing Economic and Social Conditions

Despite many problems, some nations, including Argentina, Brazil, Chile, Uruguay, and Costa Rica, made progress toward achieving stable governments in the 1800s. In these nations, governments worked to improve economic conditions. Chile, for example, diversified its economy by growing a broad range of agricultural products, developing new exports such as nitrates, and building its own industries. Brazil increased its foreign trade by establishing coffee and

Exporting sugar was the basis of the economies of many Caribbean nations. Single-crop economies left these countries at the mercy of the world demand for sugar. This picture shows men and women bringing sugar cane to the mill. At the mill, rollers crushed the cane and squeezed out the juice. The juice was then made into sugar.

The Gauchos of Argentina

Gauchos were the cowboys of Argentina. They lived on the pampas, open grassy plains, and made a living selling the hides of wild cattle and horses. Gauchos were daring and skillful horsemen. They rode in swift pursuit of cattle and horses using a boleadora—three stones or iron balls lashed together with a long leather thong—to entangle the legs of the animals.

Life on the pampas was scarcely glamorous. Gauchos lived in one-room mud huts that were shingled with grass mats. They slept on heaps of hides. Their traditional costume was a pair of wide-legged trousers, high boots, and a long woolen poncho that protected them from the cold and rain.

The introduction of barbed-wire fencing and refrigerated ships marked the end of the gaucho's way of life. Refrigerated ships allowed people to raise cattle for meat instead of hides. Soon, cattle were fed in stalls rather than on the pampas. Barbed-wire fencing allowed farmers to settle on the pampas and turn the open spaces into wheat and alfalfa fields.

As the gauchos gave way to the farmers, their way of life passed into folklore. Payadors, guitar-playing cowboys, composed songs praising the adventurous deeds of the gauchos. One of the most popular figures in Argentine literature is the fictional gaucho hero Martin Fierro. His life was summed up in these lines:

A son am I of the rolling plain,
A gaucho born and bred;
For me the whole great world is small,
Believe me, my heart can hold it all,
The snake strikes not at my passing foot,
The sun burns not my head.

---

rubber plantations. Argentina attracted many European immigrants who raised cattle and wheat.

Economic development led to urban growth and some social change. Rio de Janeiro, Buenos Aires, and Santiago became major cities. Although the class system remained fairly rigid, new economic opportunities favored the growth of a middle class. In Argentina, Brazil, Chile, and Mexico, the middle class accounted for about 10 percent of the population. Elsewhere, it remained smaller.

A Century of Change in Mexico

Mexico, you will recall, won its independence in 1821. During the next century, it struggled to achieve political, economic, and social stability. These struggles were similar in some ways to those that occurred in many other Latin American countries during the 1800s.

Clashes between conservatives and liberals shaped political developments in Mexico. Conservatives wanted to maintain the traditional social and economic structure. Liberals favored greater democracy. They supported such goals as reducing the size of large estates and redistributing land to small farmers. They also wanted to curb the power of the army and church.

During the power struggles between conservatives and liberals, several strong leaders emerged. In the 1830s and 1840s, General Antonio Santa Anna was in and out of power many times. At first, he supported liberal reforms. Later, he won the backing of conservatives and ruled as a military dictator.

War with the United States. During this troubled time, Mexico became involved in a war with the United States. Many people from the United States had settled in Texas, an area that belonged to Mexico. In 1836, these settlers defeated Santa Anna's forces and declared Texas an independent republic. In 1845, Texas, by treaty, became part of the United States. Soon after, disputes along the Texas-Mexico border led to war between the United States and Mexico. The war, which lasted from 1846 to 1848, ended in defeat for Mexico. It lost almost half its territory to the United States, including what is today California, Nevada, and Utah as well as parts of Arizona and Colorado.

An era of reform. In the following decades, Mexico introduced liberal reforms under the leadership of Benito Juárez. Born to a poor Indian family, Juárez earned a reputation as a brilliant lawyer and was elected president. Juárez extended political power to more people, thereby reducing the influence of the creoles. During the 1860s, he reduced the power of the Catholic Church by selling its lands. He also established a system of public education and made the state, not the church, responsible for marriage laws.

Soon after the death of Juárez, Porfirio Díaz was elected president. Although Díaz promised to continue the reforms of Juárez, he gradually became more conservative. He rigged elections so that he remained in power for 35 years. During this time, Mexico made important economic progress. Landowners and businesspeople reaped huge

Women in the Mexican Revolution

In 1910, Mexico was plunged into an era of revolution and social change that uprooted the old class structure and improved living conditions for the vast majority of Mexicans. Women took an active part in the revolution, although it was unusual for women to be involved in politics at all.

Women in Mexico, as elsewhere in Latin America, were expected to remain at home and raise large families. They were taught to be subordinate to men and to obey their fathers or husbands in all matters. By the early 1900s, however, some Mexican women were working in factories. Some upper class women had become teachers and journalists. Women journalists were often outspoken in their opposition to the dictator Porfirio Díaz.

Juana Belen Gutiérrez de Mendoza began her career as a teacher. She become increasingly concerned with educating poor Indian children and gaining rights for farm and factory workers. Gutiérrez sold a few goats she owned in order to buy a printing press and founded the newspaper *Vesper*. Eventually, she was jailed for criticizing Díaz in her newspaper. In prison, Gutiérrez met other women who shared her hopes for reform. She even managed to direct the publication of another newspaper while in prison. Later, Gutiérrez joined the rebel forces of Emiliano Zapata during the Mexican Revolution and earned the rank of colonel.

Other women also gained distinction in the Mexican Revolution. Carmen Alanis commanded 300 troops that helped capture Ciudad Juárez. Ramona Flores, a wealthy widow, used her inheritance to buy arms for rebel troops and later became chief-of-staff to a rebel general. Many women also served as soldiers. They trained and fought alongside

men. In 1911, *The New York Times* reported to its readers that "women have taken a spectacular part in the revolution." In addition to fighting, women served as train dispatchers, telegraph operators, nurses, and spies.

By the time the Mexican Revolution was over, women's place in Mexican life had changed permanently. The Constitution of 1917 guaranteed women basic legal rights, free education, and access to all professions. It also provided for maternity leave and equal pay for equal work. However, the Constitution did not grant women suffrage. Although some Mexican states gave women the vote in the 1920s, women did not win that right nationally until 1953.

159

profits from mining and the building of railroads. But the poor gained little, and large landowners took control of many Indian lands.

The Constitution of 1917. In 1910, a revolution broke out against Díaz. The Mexican Revolution plunged the nation into years of chaos and swept away most of the traditional order. Finally, in 1917, a new constitution was adopted. It passed into law many reforms that people had been demanding for decades.

Under the Constitution of 1917, large estates were broken up and sold to peasants. Over half the farmland in Mexico changed hands in this way. The new constitution reduced the creoles' power and enabled the mestizos and Indians to participate fully in government. It ensured the separation of church and state and set up a labor code dealing with hours and wages. Although many provisions of the constitution were not carried out right away, the constitution gave Mexico a stable government and enabled the country to achieve economic growth.

SECTION REVIEW

1. Locate: Ecuador, Bolivia, Argentina, Paraguay, Uruguay.
2. Identify: Santa Anna, Benito Juárez, Porfirio Díaz.
3. Define: regionalism, caudillo.
4. How did geography contribute to disunity in Latin America?
5. (a) What group or groups had the most political power in Latin American nations after independence? (b) What group or groups had little political power?
6. How did stable governments in some countries improve economic conditions?
7. Describe three reforms included in the Mexican Constitution of 1917.

6 Imperialism in Latin America

After winning independence, the nations of Latin America concentrated on solving internal problems. Yet the new nations also faced external threats. In the 1820s, Spain asked its allies in Europe to help it reconquer its former colonies. Although Prince Metternich of Austria was willing to support Spain, both Britain and the United States opposed any intervention in Latin America.

The Monroe Doctrine and the British Navy

Britain and the United States each had their own reasons for opposing intervention in Latin America. Britain wanted to bolster its trade with the newly independent nations. A return of Spanish rule would prevent new commercial ties. The United States had recognized the independence of Latin American nations early. It wanted to prevent European countries from regaining influence in the Western Hemisphere.

In 1823, the British asked the United States to make a joint declaration against European intervention in Latin America. Instead, the American President James Monroe decided to make a statement of his own. In his annual message to Congress in December 1823, Monroe announced the policy that the United States intended to follow toward Latin America.

"The American continents," Monroe declared, "are henceforth not to be considered as subjects for future colonization by any European powers." His policy, which became known as the Monroe Doctrine, further stated, "With the governments who have declared their independence and maintained it, we would consider any European intervention the manifestation of an unfriendly disposition [attitude] toward the United States. . . ."

The United States lacked the military strength to enforce this policy. However, Britain, which agreed in principle with the Monroe Doctrine, let other European powers know that it was prepared to use its strong navy to prevent foreign intervention in Latin

America. Thus, the Monroe Doctrine, backed up by British seapower, freed the nations of Latin America from the threat of reconquest.

Foreign Interests in Latin America

Britain and the United States were determined to prevent other powers from establishing colonies in Latin America, but they did not oppose foreign investment. During the 1800s, the United States and the industrial nations of Europe turned to Latin America as a source of raw materials and a market for their manufactured goods. Moreover, they invested heavily in building mines, railroads, bridges, and ports in Latin America.

By the early 1900s, Britain had invested five thousand million dollars in Latin America. The United States and France each had invested over one thousand million dollars. Germany was close behind. Although the nations of Latin America were technically independent, extensive foreign investment gave European nations and the United States economic and political influence. This type of influence is known as economic imperialism.

Some foreign investments were in the form of loans to governments for building railroads and ports. A corrupt dictator might use the money for personal enrichment instead of for the building project. If the dictator were overthrown, the new government might default, or refuse to repay the loan. In 1861, France used the excuse that Mexico had defaulted on foreign loans to send its army and install as emperor Maximilian, brother of Franz Joseph of Austria.

Similar situations arose frequently in the 1800s. When investors thought their loans were in danger, they appealed to their governments to protect their investments. Foreign warships would arrive and foreign governments would force their demands on the Latin American government.

Nevertheless, foreign investments did lead to economic growth in some Latin American nations. In politically stable nations, loans were used to develop new industries. For example, in Argentina, the number of industrial businesses grew from 41 to nearly 50,000 between 1869 and 1914.

In addition to investing, many Europeans settled in parts of Latin America. In the 1800s, about three million immigrants poured into Argentina, Brazil, and Chile.

The United States and Latin America

In 1783, a Spanish official made the following prediction about the United States:

> We have just recognized a new power in a great region where there exists no other to challenge its growth. ... The day will come when it grows and becomes a giant and even a colossus [a gigantic power] in those regions. Within a few years we will regard the existence of this colossus with real sorrow.

A century later, people in many Latin American nations were convinced that this prediction had come true. They called the United States "the Colossus of the North."

Relations between the United States and the nations of Latin America began on a friendly note with the Monroe Doctrine. But Latin American governments came to believe that the United States was using the Monroe Doctrine to dominate the Western Hemisphere.

In 1895 during a dispute between Venezuela and Britain, American Secretary of State Richard Olney invoked the Monroe Doctrine. Olney informed Britain that the United States "was sovereign on this continent," by which he meant the Western Hemisphere. His words disturbed many people in Latin America.

The Spanish-American War

Three years later, the United States fought a war with Spain that involved it even more deeply in Latin America. In 1898, Cuba and Puerto Rico were still Spanish colonies. However, Cuban rebels were fighting for independence. Journalists in the United States whipped up public sympathy for the Cuban cause. The United States sent the battleship *Maine* to Havana to protect American citizens and property in Cuba. When the *Maine* was destoyed in a mysterious explosion, people in the United States clamored for war with Spain.

In April 1898, the United States recognized Cuban independence, and Spain declared war. During the Spanish-American War, the United States won quick victories in the Caribbean and the Pacific. (See page 155.) In December, Spain agreed to a peace treaty, giving the United States control of Puerto Rico as well as the Philippines and Guam in the Pacific. The United States ruled Puerto Rico directly through an American governor and an American-appointed executive council.

Cuba became an independent nation. When Cubans drafted a constitution in 1900, however, the United States forced them to add a document known as the Platt Amendment. The Platt Amendment gave the United States the right to intervene in Cuban affairs to protect American lives and property. It put limits on Cuba's right to borrow from foreign powers, and it allowed the United States to establish two naval stations in Cuba.

Many Latin American nations looked on the expansion of the United States into the Caribbean with alarm. They feared that the United States had imperialist ambitions that would threaten their independence.

Roosevelt Corollary to the Monroe Doctrine

In the early 1900s, Venezuela and the Dominican Republic defaulted on loans from Britain, Germany, and Italy. Once again, Eu-

■ *In the early 1900s, some Caribbean areas were still under foreign rule, as you can see on this map. In addition, independent nations were subject to foreign influence. Governments of European nations and the United States often intervened when Caribbean nations were unable to pay their foreign debts.*

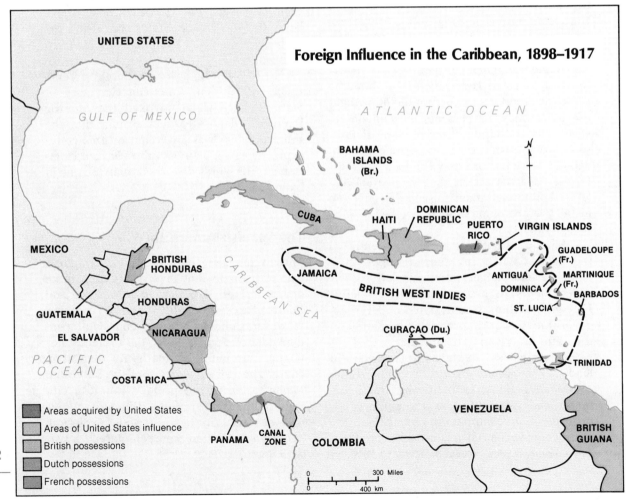

Foreign Influence in the Caribbean, 1898–1917

Areas acquired by United States
Areas of United States influence
British possessions
Dutch possessions
French possessions

President Theodore Roosevelt was fond of quoting a West African proverb: "Speak softly and carry a big stick; you will go far." Roosevelt used a "big stick" in the form of American economic and military strength in his dealings with Latin America. In this cartoon, Roosevelt, once police commissioner of New York City, is portrayed as the world's policeman.

ropean warships menaced Latin American nations. President Theodore Roosevelt invoked the Monroe Doctrine and sent American battleships to force the Europeans to withdraw their ships. The European nations protested. They insisted that if they could not send warships to make nations pay their debts the United States must take that responsibility.

To satisfy this demand, Roosevelt announced the Roosevelt Corollary to the Monroe Doctrine in 1904. In this policy statement, Roosevelt declared that the United States would exercise "international police power" to get Latin American nations to honor their financial commitments.

Over the next 20 years, several American presidents used this police power. President William Howard Taft sent troops to Nicaragua and Honduras in order to guarantee repayment of foreign debts. On other occasions, United States troops occupied parts of Latin American nations to protect American and European investments.

The Panama Canal

During the Age of Imperialism, the United States competed with the industrial nations of Europe for international markets. As the United States expanded its interest in the Pacific, it wanted to be able to move its fleet easily from the Atlantic Ocean to the Pacific Ocean without making the voyage around South America. President Roosevelt proposed building a canal across the narrow Isthmus of Panama, an area that belonged to Colombia.

Colombia was reluctant to grant the United States the right to build a canal, fearing it would lose control of the region. In 1903, however, the United States encouraged the people in Panama to revolt against Colombian rule. The rebels quickly won independence for Panama. Three weeks later, they signed an agreement allowing the United States to build a canal.

Construction on the Panama Canal began in 1904. First, workers drained swamps

163

and marshes, the breeding grounds of mosquitoes that carried yellow fever. Next, they moved millions of tonnes of earth to create the "big ditch." Finally, in 1914, the first ship traveled through the Panama Canal.

The United States was in a position to benefit most from the Panama Canal, although the new sea route helped the trade of many nations. Despite the advantages of the canal, many Latin American nations remained bitter about what they saw as United States imperialism in the region.

SECTION REVIEW

1. Locate: Cuba, Puerto Rico, Panama.
2. Identify: Colossus of the North, Monroe Doctrine, Spanish-American War, *Maine*, Platt Amendment, Roosevelt Corollary.
3. Why did the United States announce the Monroe Doctrine?
4. Which industrialized nations invested heavily in Latin America?
5. Why were Latin American nations suspicious of the Monroe Doctrine?
6. (a) Why did the United States want to build the Panama Canal? (b) Why was Colombia hesitant about letting the United States build the canal?

IN PERSPECTIVE

Between the 1500s and the 1800s, Europeans established limited contacts with the civilizations of Asia. In the 1800s, the Industrial Revolution and the decline of powerful governments in Asia allowed Europeans to gain influence in Asia. The Manchu government in China, while struggling to suppress internal rebellions, was pressured by Europeans into ending foreign trade restrictions. In 1858, India became a British colony. Western powers, such as the Dutch and the Spanish, also controlled much of southeast Asia.

In 1853, the visit of an American naval squadron to Japan resulted in a trade treaty and the end of Japanese isolation. Japan became a modern industrial nation, competing with western powers for a colonial empire in Asia.

In Latin America, the newly independent nations faced many problems. They had little experience in self-government. Strong rulers often seized power and set themselves up as military dictators. In addition, the industrial nations of Europe and the United States invested heavily in Latin America and were prepared to use force to protect their investments.

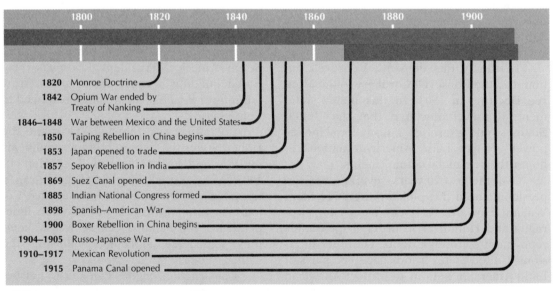

1820	Monroe Doctrine	
1842	Opium War ended by Treaty of Nanking	
1846–1848	War between Mexico and the United States	
1850	Taiping Rebellion in China begins	
1853	Japan opened to trade	
1857	Sepoy Rebellion in India	
1869	Suez Canal opened	
1885	Indian National Congress formed	
1898	Spanish–American War	
1900	Boxer Rebellion in China begins	
1904–1905	Russo-Japanese War	
1910–1917	Mexican Revolution	
1915	Panama Canal opened	

■ **Manchu dynasty in China**　■ **Meiji period in Japan**

Indicate whether each of the following statements refers to India, China, Japan, or Southeast Asia.

1. Meiji leaders introduced a program for modernization.
2. Grievances against the British touched off the Sepoy Rebellion.
3. The Opium War resulted in the first of the "unequal treaties."
4. Boxers attempted to expel foreigners from their land.
5. A strong army and navy were used to defeat Russia in 1905.
6. Sun Yat-sen worked to build a unified country.
7. Britain encouraged farmers to grow cotton for its factories.
8. Europeans sought tin, rubber, and oil.

1. (a) Why was the East India Company able to gain control in India in the 1700s? (b) Why did the British government end the East India Company's control of India? (c) How did the policies of the British government differ from those of the East India Company? (d) How did British rule affect Indian life?
2. (a) What attitude did the Manchu dynasty take toward European merchants in the 1600s and 1700s? (b) How did the Opium War affect relations between China and western powers?
3. Describe how each of the following events affected the Manchu dynasty: (a) Taiping Rebellion; (b) Open Door Policy; (c) Revolution of 1911.
4. (a) Why did Commodore Perry visit Japan? (b) What effect did his visit have on Japan?
5. (a) What steps did the Japanese take to modernize their nation? (b) How did these steps affect Japan's social structure and economy?
6. (a) Which European nations were the main competitors in Southeast Asia during the 1800s? (b) Why did they want to control this region?
7. (a) Why were the Spanish colonies poorly prepared for self-government? (b) What social problems did they face after independence?
8. (a) Why did industrial nations invest in Latin America? (b) How did foreign loans lead to economic imperialism in Latin America?

1. *Analyzing* Benjamin Disraeli called India "the brightest jewel in the British Crown." (a) What do you think he meant by this statement? (b) Why do you think he felt that India was important to Britain?
2. *Synthesizing* In the 1700s, China was the richest and strongest nation in the world. Yet within less than 100 years it was carved into spheres of influence. How did this happen? Give specific reasons to explain your answer.
3. *Comparing* (a) How were the Chinese and Japanese responses to Europeans and Americans similar? (b) How were they different? (c) What might explain the similarities and differences?
4. *Relating Past to Present* (a) Why do you think Japan was able to industrialize so quickly in the 1800s? (b) How do you think the Japanese policy of selective borrowing from other nations affected its rapid industrialization? (c) What present-day examples of Japanese success in industry can you cite?
5. *Understanding Economic Ideas* (a) Describe the economic ties between Latin America and Europe after Latin Americans won independence. (b) Why did most Latin American nations have little control over their own economies?

1. *Analyzing a Primary Source* Reread the special feature on page 151. Then answer the following questions: (a) What is the nature of the document included in the feature? (b) Who is the author? (c) What type of information did the author want to learn on his trip to Europe? (d) What did he find most perplexing during his trip? Why? (e) Do you think the document is a good source of information about Japanese attitudes toward Europe in the late 1800s? Why or why not?
2. *Map Reading* Compare the maps on pages 147 and 154. Then answer the following questions: (a) What nation's sphere of influence included Korea? (b) What three nations possessed New Guinea? (c) What nations had spheres of influence in China? (d) Which of these nations had possessions in Southeast Asia? (e) Based on both maps, which nation do you think was most powerful in eastern Asia? Explain your answer.

See page 204 for suggested readings.

Unit Four

The World Today

Unit Overview The second half of the twentieth century has been a time of tremendous change around the world. Western powers gave up their colonies, although western power and influence have remained strong. At the same time, other centers of power emerged. Since 1945, many new nations have gained independence in Africa, the Middle East, and Asia. These nations, as well as the developing nations of Latin America, have experienced rapid growth and change. They have undergone scientific, political, and industrial revolutions similar to those that had occurred earlier in Europe.

Science and technology, especially, are transforming the world today. They have helped to knit the world together in many ways. For example, people today quickly adopt new inventions of the machine age. The photograph at left shows a paper mill built in Japan being towed up the Amazon River in Brazil. The paper mill, equipped with the latest technology, had been towed across the seas to Brazil. The ready-made factory has helped Brazil tap its vast timber resources.

Industrialization and social and political changes have created challenges for every nation. As in the past, however, individual nations have developed their own distinctive patterns to meet the challenges of a changing world.

Chapter 9 A New Age of Exploration
(1945–Present)

9 A New Age of Exploration

(1945–Present)

Canada's first astronaut, Mark Garneau.

Before dawn on April 12, 1981, crowds gathered at Cape Canaveral, Florida. As dawn brightened the sky, they watched white clouds of exhaust billowing up from the launch pad, where the space shuttle *Columbia* stood ready for liftoff. At 7:00 a.m., *Columbia* lifted off with a thunderous roar.

On board the space shuttle, pilots John W. Young and Robert Crippen monitored the successful liftoff. Captain Young had already flown four missions in other spacecraft. He had oribited the moon in 1969 in *Apollo 10.* Three years later, he had landed on the moon. Captain Crippen was on his first space flight. His pulse raced to 130. The pulse of the more experienced Young remained its usual 85.

Six minutes into the flight, the main engines shut down on schedule. "Confirm shutdown," a voice from mission control in Houston, Texas, told the pilots. "*Columbia,* the gem of this new ocean, now in space, not yet in orbit," the voice added.

The voyage of *Columbia* was indeed a historic mission. Astronauts Young and Crippen were testing a new type of spacecraft. Unlike earlier spacecraft, *Columbia* was designed to be reused. Earlier space vehicles had been made for a single flight. They burned up during reentry into the earth's atmosphere. Designers of *Columbia* had equipped it with 31,000 heat-resistant ceramic tiles to shield the vehicle on reentry. The spacecraft was scheduled to glide to a gentle landing in the Mojave Desert, which it did after two days in space.

After its first successful flight, *Columbia* was repaired and prepared for another flight that took place seven months later. A third flight followed in March 1982. Scientists hope these flights mark the dawn of a new era—the day that space flights will be routine. They see *Columbia* as the forerunner of space cargo ships. Their job will be to ferry people and equipment to and from orbiting space satellites and laboratories.

Canada became a participant in the space shuttle program when the Canadarm was installed in the shuttle *Challenger*. The Canadarm was used to retrieve satellites from orbit when they needed repair and to place other satellites in more precise orbits. One of the crew of the October 1984 flight of *Challenger* was Mark Garneau, Canada's first astronaut.

1 The New Scientific Revolution

Many major advances in science have occurred in the 1900s. Researchers have solved age-old puzzles in chemistry, physics, biochemistry, and medicine. In solving these puzzles, they have made technological advances that have revolutionized people's lives.

Advances in Science and Technology

Before World War II, research scientists usually worked alone. They were generally interested in pure science—that is, developing theories about the causes of events in the natural world. They left *applied science,* or putting their findings to practical use, to engineers and technicians.

During World War II, research scientists such as physicists and chemists worked alongside technicians to develop weapons, medicines, and other technologies needed to win the war. The combination of pure and applied science produced important results. For example, a team of British scientists developed radar, a device that uses radio waves to detect objects. In the United States, a group of scientists working together constructed the first atom bomb.

After the war, experts in science and technology continued to work together to solve complex problems. Most governments have spent large sums to pay for scientific research and development. In addition, industries have invested thousands of millions of dollars in scientific research. This research has resulted in thousands of new products and inventions.

Space Exploration

Advances in science and technology have been dramatically evident in the area of space exploration. During World War II, German scientists working with Wernher von Braun developed rockets as weapons. The V-2 rocket, for example, was a guided missile that could be launched against London from bases in Germany.

After the war, some German rocket specialists went to the Soviet Union. Others, including von Braun, went to the United States, where they helped develop an American missile and rocket program. By the 1950s, both the United States and the Soviet Union had built rockets powerful enough to overcome the earth's gravity and leave the earth's atmosphere.

The Space Age begins. In October 1957, the age of space exploration began when the Soviet Union launched the first satellite, *Sputnik I*, into orbit around the earth. The first American spacecraft, *Explorer I*, was sent into orbit in 1958. In 1961, Soviet cosmonaut Yuri Gagarin was the first person sent into orbit. His flight was soon matched by that of John Glenn, the first American to orbit the earth.

After these early successes, scientists set their sights on more distant goals. On July 20, 1969, American astronauts Neil Armstrong and Buzz Aldrin stepped out of their *Apollo 11* spacecraft onto the surface of the moon. "That's one small step for a man," noted Armstrong, "one giant leap for mankind." In five more moon shots, other teams of American astronauts gathered much useful data. In the 1970s, the Soviet Union launched permanent orbiting laboratories. Soviet scientists conducted experiments to determine the effects of prolonged space travel on humans. Two cosmonauts lived aboard one Soviet space platform for 185 days.

The United States and the Soviet Union launched hundreds of unpiloted spacecraft to explore the planets. Soon, scientists were getting clear photographs and accurate information about Venus and Mars as well as about the more distant planets of Jupiter and Saturn.

In 1981, the American *Voyager 2* photographed Saturn and returned data indicating

In 1972, Canada launched the first North American domestic satellite. Because it was first intended to help keep in touch with the Far North, it was called "Anik", meaning "brother" in Inuit. Today, Anik satellites provide less expensive television service than ground-level systems of broadcasting.

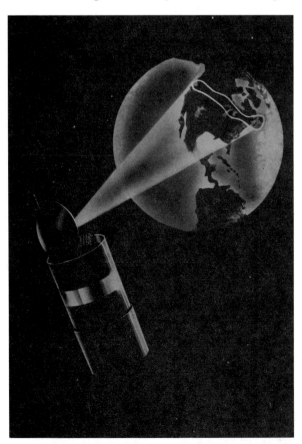

1,609 km/h winds on the planet. The spacecraft then flew toward its 1986 destination–Uranus. Eventually, *Voyager 2* will leave the solar system. It carries information about life on earth, including recordings of crickets and Beethoven's Fifth Symphony in case it encounters intelligent life beyond this solar system.

Putting satellites to work. By the early 1980s, the United States and the Soviet Union had launched more than 2,000 spacecraft. In addition, India, China, and Japan have each put satellites into orbit. Recently, a group of 11 European nations joined forces to build a permanent space laboratory.

Spacecraft have collected a vast amount of information and relayed it back to earth. Some satellites orbit the earth and provide a 24-hour watch on weather. Other satellites are used to transmit signals for radio, television, and telephone communication. Satellites have also provided useful data on crop yields. Today, space travel and communication are constantly expanding the horizons of scientific research.

The Computer Revolution

Computers have played a major role in space exploration. *Computers* are machines that process information at great speed. Computers on spacecraft, for example, relay information to computers on earth that in turn send data back to the spacecraft.

The development of computers dates back before World War II. Since the 1940s, their use has changed nearly every industry in the world. As faster airplanes were built during World War II, better ways were needed to track them. Engineers turned to a machine invented in 1930 by electrical engineer Vannevar Bush. Bush called his invention a differential analyzer. It was the grandparent of today's computers.

In 1941, Harvard University professor Howard Aiken developed the first workable digital computer. Digital computers solve problems by counting digits, or numbers. Mathematician John von Neumann made the next major advance when he invented a way to store a computer program in the machine. In 1951, engineers at the University of Pennsylvania built UNIVAC, the first large, mass-produced computer. UNIVAC was an enormous machine that filled an entire room.

The invention of the transistor in 1947 led to a revolution in computers. *Transistors* are devices used to control electric currents. Transistors are small, reliable, and relatively inexpensive. With them, scientists could make computers that were smaller, faster, and less expensive than UNIVAC. The invention of the integrated circuit, or chip, in the 1960s further revolutionized computers. Chips are units that contain many transistors. A single chip is very small, often no bigger than a fingernail. These tiny chips made still smaller, faster, and less expensive computers possible. As a result, computers came into use in many fields.

Today, computers are used to handle telephone communications, route airplanes, and store vast amounts of information needed by businesses and governments. In addition, computers are used by engineers and scientists to solve complex problems. The *Apollo 11* moon landing would not have been possible without computers. The development of handheld calculators and personal computers has brought the computer into homes and schools. At the same time, computer-controlled video games have become a popular form of entertainment.

Miracles in Medicine

Like many businesses, hospitals rely heavily on computers as well as on other advanced technology. The postwar era ushered in a "machine age" in medicine.

Medical technology. Some medical technology grew directly out of space research. For example, medical researchers wanted to learn the effects of liftoff and prolonged weightlessness on astronauts. As a result, technicians developed tiny sensors to measure the pulse, heartbeat, breathing, and body temperature of astronauts.

Today, similar monitoring devices are used routinely in modern hospitals. In in-

The Canadarm, used on American space shuttles, can remove a satellite from the cargo bay and put it into orbit. A camera at the "elbow" of the arm allows a viewer to examine the exterior of the space shuttle.

tensive care units, information from sensors is fed into a computer at a central nursing station. Warning bells ring if a patient's pulse falters or breathing stops. Doctors can also get a detailed 24-hour printout on a patient's vital signs.

Advances in medical technology have been used in surgery and other fields. In 1952, the first kidney transplant took place. The following year, surgeons performed the first open-heart operation. In the 1960s, heart care was improved by the development of the pacemaker. A pacemaker is a tiny electronic device that is implanted in the body to regulate a patient's heartbeat. Dr. Christiaan Barnard of South Africa performed the first successful human heart transplant in 1968. Recently, surgeons have pioneered in the field of microsurgery. Using microscopes and tiny instruments, they have operated on tiny areas such as the inner ear.

Antibiotics. Complicated surgery would be impossible without the medical advances made earlier in this century. These advances included the development of *antibiotics,* chemical substances that destroy bacteria and other microorganisms.

In 1928, British bacteriologist Sir Arthur Fleming accidentally discovered that a mold called penicillin killed bacteria. At first, his discovery was not put to much practical use. During World War II, however, the urgent need to prevent infection of battlefield wounds led to a program to mass-produce penicillin. The discovery of sulfa drugs, which also kill bacteria, was followed by their widespread use as antibiotics. Sulfa drugs and penicillin enabled surgeons to combat infection of wounds.

Vaccines. The first vaccines against viruses were developed in the late 1700s. Then, in the 1800s, Louis Pasteur developed vaccines against the viral diseases rabies and anthrax. But before the invention of the electron microscope in the 1930s, scientists had not seen viruses. With the electron microscope, scientists were able to study the structure of viruses. They were then able to develop vaccines against many viral diseases, including measles, mumps, diphtheria, typhoid, and cholera. Jonas Salk developed the first polio vaccine in the early 1950s. A few years later, Albert Sabin perfected an oral vaccine for polio.

Since World War II, agencies of the United Nations, national governments, and private health organizations have sponsored programs to vaccinate tens of millions of people. Epidemic diseases that once devastated populations have been wiped out or brought under control. In 1980, the World Health Organization announced that no new cases of smallpox had been reported anywhere in the world.

The growing record of medical successes has encouraged hopes that new ways can be found to prevent or cure other diseases such as cancer.

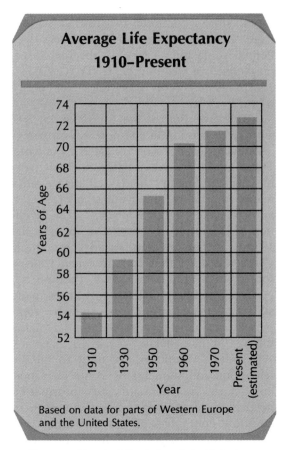

Average Life Expectancy 1910–Present

Based on data for parts of Western Europe and the United States.

Sources: *Historical Statistics of the United States;* OECD, *Child and Family;* and United Nations, *Demographic Yearbook.*

■ *Because of discoveries in medicine, people are living longer than ever before. Compare this graph with the graph on page 109 of life expectancy between 1850 and 1910.*

SECTION REVIEW

1. Identify: *Sputnik I,* Yuri Gagarin, John Glenn, Neil Armstrong, *Apollo 11,* Howard Aiken, Christiaan Barnard, Sir Arthur Fleming, Jonas Salk, Albert Sabin.

2. Define: applied science, computer, transistor, antibiotic.

3. How does pure science differ from applied science?

4. What kinds of information have satellites in space provided?

5. How have computers affected business and industry?

6. List three medical advances of the 1900s.

2 Resources for the Future

Satellites have taken many photographs of the earth from space. Scientists have used some of these photographs to map possible locations of important natural resources. They have found that the earth has abundant supplies of some resources but limited supplies of others.

The World Population

Population growth has accelerated in many parts of the world. The conquest of many diseases has contributed to this growth. Today, fewer babies die of disease. As well, people live much longer than they did in the past. In just 30 years, the world population has increased by 75 percent–from two thousand five hundred million in 1950 to about four thousand four hundred million in 1980. Recent estimates suggest that the world population will grow to at least six thousand million by the year 2000.

The greatest population growth has occurred in developing nations. Between 1950 and 1980, populations in developing nations grew from one thousand seven hundred million to three thousand three hundred million. (See pages 186 to 187.) The population explosion poses a number of challenges, especially to developing nations. Most governments want to ensure that their people have food, housing, jobs, and the education needed in today's world. But many developing nations have limited resources to meet these basic needs. As a result, poverty is widespread.

In 1980, China had a population of between nine hundred million and one thousand million. India had a population of six hundred and eighty-nine thousand million. Together, the Chinese and Indian populations accounted for one third of all the people on earth. Both nations have looked for ways to provide for and develop their vast human resources. In addition, to slow the rate of population growth, the Chinese government has encouraged peo-ple to marry later and have fewer children than in the past.

Rich Lands, Poor Lands

The population explosion has helped increase the gap between rich nations and poor nations around the world. Leaders

■ *The population of the world grew slowly for hundreds of years, but during the 1800s it began to grow more rapidly. How would you describe world population growth since 1900?*

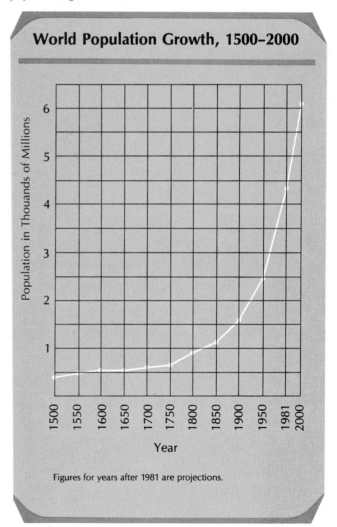

World Population Growth, 1500–2000

Population in Thouands of Millions (y-axis)

Year (x-axis): 1500, 1550, 1600, 1650, 1700, 1750, 1800, 1850, 1900, 1950, 1981, 2000

Figures for years after 1981 are projections.

Sources: *Atlas of World Population History* and the United Nations.

Today, there are nearly four thousand five hundred million people in the world. Some countries face a problem of overpopulation. This crowded scene shows the Ginza, the main shopping area of Tokyo, Japan.

Developing and Developed Nations: A Comparison

	Developing Nations	Developed Nations
Percent of World Population	67	33
Percent of World Farm Production	38	62
Hectares of Farmland per Farm Worker	1.3	8.9
Kilograms of Fertilizer Used per Hectare of Farmland	9	40
Daily Calorie* Consumption per Person	2,180	3,315

Source: **FAO**, *Agriculture: Toward 2000.*

■ *This chart shows the agricultural gap between developing and developed nations. Although two thirds of the world's people live in developing nations, those nations produce just slightly more than one third of the world's farm produce.*

from rich and poor nations have met to discuss ways that rich nations can help poor nations to develop. However, closing the gap between rich and poor lands poses many difficult challenges.

Rich lands include developed nations such as Britain, France, Japan, and the United States. These nations have the advantages of well-developed agriculture and industry, advanced technology, and strong education systems. Poor lands include many developing nations in Africa, the Middle East, Asia, and Latin America.

Developed nations have provided aid such as food, loans, and technical assistance to developing nations. But it will take time for developing nations to establish modern industrial economies. Moreover, worldwide inflation, natural disasters, and the population explosion have upset the plans of many developing nations.

Developing New Sources of Food

Bad weather in the early 1970s caused disastrous crop failures in India, China, and the Soviet Union. Also, drought ruined crops in the Sahel region of Africa. When nations faced with shortages competed to buy food abroad, prices shot up. The resulting food scramble focused attention on the growing problem of hunger around the world. Experts predicted that the food crisis would become worse in the decades ahead.

---

* One calorie is equal to 4.187 J.

About five hundred million people face hunger and malnutrition daily. In 1979, President Carter's Commission on World Hunger reported that one out of every eight people suffered from malnutrition. There was enough food grown in the 1970s and early 1980s to provide an adequate diet for every human being. The problem was the unequal distribution of food and people.

The United States and Canada produced about 80 percent of the world's grain. Yet these two nations have less than 6 percent of the world's population. While some countries produce surplus food, other countries, such as Bangladesh and Ethiopia, have not been able to grow enough to feed their populations. Moreover, some of these countries do not have enough money to buy food year after year on the world market.

Poor nations suffering from famine have received food aid from the governments of developed countries, the United Nations, and private relief organizations. But this type of aid does not solve the long-range problem of increasing food production.

Progress has been made in the area of food production. Efforts to increase food production have resulted in the "Green Revolution." This revolution began in the 1960s, when researchers found ways to double and even triple the amount of food produced on the same amount of land. "Yields which had been almost unchanged for centuries," a UN report noted, "leapt forward."

Experts developed new varieties of high-yield crops and taught farmers in developing nations better soil management methods. Control of plant diseases and increased

The World's Population: Synthesizing Evidence

Throughout this text, you have read, analyzed, and interpreted various kinds of historical evidence. In order to make the best use of evidence, however, you must be able to synthesize it—that is, pull several pieces together to form a whole pattern of a historical event or development.

You will use four pieces of evidence to practice the skill of synthesizing: the graph of world population growth on page 173, the table of large urban areas on page 182, the map of world population density on pages 186 to 187 in the Reference Section, and the picture on page 174. Use the following steps to study these pieces of evidence and synthesize the information they contain.

1. **Analyze each piece of evidence.** Answer the following questions about the pieces of evidence: (a) According to the graph on page 173, what was the approximate population of the world in 1800? In 1900? In 1980? (b) According to the table on page 182, what was the largest urban area in 1350 B.C.? In 1925? In 1980? (c) According to the map on pages 186 to 187, what is the population density in most of Europe? In most of North Africa? In most of Mexico? (d) What is the subject of the picture on page 174?

2. **Find relationships among the pieces of evidence.** Answer the following questions: (a) How does the information in the table support the information in the graph? (b) How does the picture illustrate the information in the table? (c) Find the place on the map where you think each of the largest urban areas in 1980 is located. Check your answers on maps in the Reference Section. (See pages 186 to 187.)

3. **Synthesize the evidence in order to draw conclusions.** Answer the following questions: (a) What conclusion can you draw about the change in the total world population since the early 1900s? Cite specific evidence to support your conclusion. (b) Does the evidence support the conclusion that world population is not very evenly distributed over the land surface? Explain. (c) What can you learn about world population from pictures such as the one on page 174 that you cannot learn from graphs, charts, and maps?

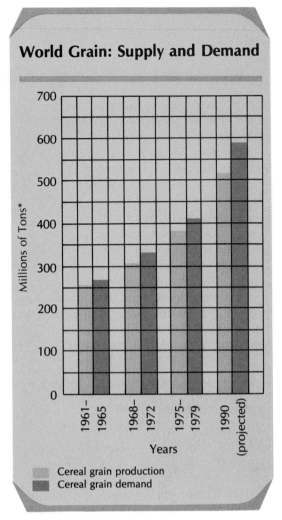

World Grain: Supply and Demand

Millions of Tons*

(vertical axis: 0, 100, 200, 300, 400, 500, 600, 700)

Years (horizontal axis): 1961–1965, 1968–1972, 1975–1979, 1990 (projected)

- Cereal grain production
- Cereal grain demand

Source: FAO, *Agriculture: Toward 2000.*

■ *The production of grain has increased since the 1960s, largely as a result of the Green Revolution. However, the demand for grain has grown even faster, as you can see from this graph.*

use of fertilizers and farm machinery helped boost food output. As a result, farm production in 1980 was two-thirds greater than it had been in 1960.

The Earth's Resources

The Green Revolution has had some undesirable side effects. Large amounts of chemical pesticides and fertilizers are needed to produce the high yields. These chemicals pollute the soil and local water supplies. In 1962, an American writer, Rachel Carson, published a book called *Silent Spring*. In this book, she described the devastating effects that pesticides used on crops have on the land and water, as well as on birds, insects, and fish.

Carson's book raised the issue of the environment. Since the 1960s, people around the world have warned of the dangers in abusing the earth's resources. As a result, scientists began paying more attention to *ecology*, the relationship between living things and their environments. Studies have revealed the delicate balance that exists in nature and how easily this balance can be upset.

In recent years, governments in some industrialized nations have taken steps to reduce air and water pollution. Developing nations have mixed reactions to environmental issues. They are anxious to industrialize quickly and cannot afford expensive programs to prevent pollution. In addition, many developing nations are willing to risk some pollution from pesticides in order to increase desperately needed food supplies. Yet some developing nations have moved to protect endangered wildlife and avoid the misuse of their resources.

In some desert areas, efforts to protect the environment are too late. Most desert regions are the result of natural causes such as prevailing winds or mountains that block rainfall. But in the past 50 years, people have contributed to the spread of deserts over land that was once productive.

In some areas, overgrazing has destroyed plants that held dry soil in place. Wind has blown this soil away, leaving land not suitable for growing plants. In other areas, poor irrigation methods have caused a build-up of salt in soil, creating "salt deserts." Parts of the Tigris-Euphrates Valley, once the "breadbasket" of the ancient Middle East, have become salt deserts. Deserts have spread in northern Africa, India, and the Arabian Peninsula. About 27,000 square miles (70,000 km²) of land has become desert in recent years. (See the map on page 188.)

At the same time, some people have successfully reclaimed desert land. For ex-

---

*One ton is equal to 907.185 kg.

The Giant Panda: An International "Treasure"

For years, people have flocked to zoos around the world to watch the antics of giant pandas. The Chinese have the most pandas in captivity. China is also the only place where giant pandas live in the wild. They inhabit the bamboo forests in a mountainous region of Szechwan (seh chwahn) province in south central China. Good-natured but shy, giant pandas have no natural enemies. They weigh between 90.8 to 136.2 kg. Chinese experts estimate that today fewer than 1,000 giant pandas live in the wild. Only about 50 giant pandas live in zoos.

Nearly every country has made efforts to save its wildlife from extinction. The Chinese government has declared pandas "national treasures" and has sent zoologists to study them in the wild. Zoologists know relatively little about the habits of the giant panda. They want to learn more about these bashful animals in order to protect their way of life.

A team of Chinese and American zoologists has recently traveled into the bamboo forests of Szechwan. There, they captured Long Long, a male panda, and outfitted him with a radio collar. They then released Long Long and listened for radio signals, which told them of his daily travels. The sensitive radio collar often picked up the sound of Long Long munching on bamboo shoots, the panda's chief source of food.

While some zoologists study giant pandas in the wild, others are trying to raise pandas in captivity. At birth, pandas weigh about 113.4 g and look like hairless white mice.

However, they soon gain weight and their distinctive coat of white and black fur.

The birth of a panda cub in a zoo is a cause for international celebration because so few pandas in captivity have produced offspring. About 12 panda cubs have been born in Chinese zoos over a 20-year period. In August 1981, a panda at the Mexico City Zoo gave birth to a cub named Cancun. Cancun is the first giant panda to be born and survive outside China. He is one indication that the international effort to save the giant panda might succeed.

ample, Israeli farmers have developed techniques for farming the desert. They have planted trees to form soil and push back the Negev Desert. They have designed irrigation pipes that carry droplets of water directly to plant roots, preventing evaporation. Other nations have adopted similar techniques to farm arid land.

The Energy Puzzle

Trucks arrive daily at a modern factory in Zurich, Switzerland, to deliver "fuel." The fuel is garbage. The factory burns the garbage to generate the energy it needs to operate. Burning garbage for energy was just one result of the energy crisis of the 1970s.

The energy crisis, brought on by OPEC price increases, focused world attention on several issues. First, it revealed the dependence of industrialized nations on imported oil. For example, like several other European nations, Switzerland had to import all the oil it consumed.

Second, the energy crisis made people aware that world oil reserves would someday be exhausted. Industrialized countries use vast amounts of energy to run factories, heat and light homes, and power cars, trucks, and airplanes. Since World War II, the chief source of energy has been petroleum.

Third, the energy crisis had vast economic consequences. Oil-importing nations had to pay billions of dollars more for energy when OPEC increased oil prices. In 1970, the United States spent three thousand million dollars to buy imported oil. By 1980, the bill had increased to a staggering sixty thousand million dollars. At the same time, oil-exporting nations acquired thousands of millions of dollars to spend on goods and services. Many OPEC members invested their wealth in the West. Thus, their economies and those of western nations became closely tied.

The abrupt end of cheap energy created a puzzling problem—how to produce enough energy for the world and how to pay for it. Part of the answer has been to conserve energy. Another part has been to harness energy from new sources, such as power from the sun.

New Sources of Energy

Governments in many nations have funded research into alternative sources of energy. Some researchers have explored water power, which was used to power machinery in the early Industrial Revolution. Today, they are trying to find ways to harness the energy of the oceans' tides. In addition, geothermal energy from deep in the earth has been used to produce electricity. As you have read, industries in some countries are using solid wastes, or garbage, to provide energy.

Experiments to find ways of producing inexpensive fuels from a variety of substances have been conducted. For example, in Brazil, researchers have found that a mixture of gasoline and alcohol made from sugar cane can be used to power cars and trucks. Other research has focused on developing equipment for collecting solar energy. This equipment traps energy from the sun's rays, which can then be used to heat homes and factories.

Much research has gone into exploring nuclear power. Nuclear power plants have been built in 22 countries. But breakdowns, accidents, and fears about the safety of nuclear power have raised questions about the future of nuclear plants.

Existing nuclear plants use nuclear fission, the splitting of heavy atoms to produce energy. But nuclear fission also produces radioactive wastes. Safe disposal of these wastes is a problem. As a result, for more

Since the energy crisis of the 1970s, much attention has been focused on possible uses of solar energy. Here, solar panels are being installed on the roof of a home. The panels use energy from the sun to heat the home.

than 30 years, researchers have been trying to master nuclear fusion, the joining of two light atoms. Nuclear fusion produces enormous amounts of power but much less radioactive waste than nuclear fission.

In 1981, scientists at Princeton University created the conditions for nuclear fusion—for one tenth of a second. But no one expects a working nuclear fusion plant before the year 2000. Nevertheless, the work of these scientists represents a step toward the development of a safe and unlimited source of energy for the future.

3 New Patterns of Culture

When Prince Charles married Lady Diana Spencer in July 1981, the wedding ceremony was beamed via communications satellites to 74 countries. An estimated seven hundred and fifty million people—nearly one out of every five people on earth—watched the wedding on television. This huge audience underscored the impact of mass communication on the world.

Mass Communication

Television, radio, and other forms of mass communication enable people to receive information and entertainment from around the world. When Pope John Paul II was shot in 1981, people rushed to radios and televisions to learn what had happened. Events such as the Olympics are seen on televisions worldwide. Such broadcasts enable people from many countries to share experiences.

In developed nations, especially, television has become an important part of daily life. One survey of American teenagers revealed that they spent 15,000 hours watching television during their high school years. Another survey showed that the average American adult spent nearly 30 hours a week watching television.

Like television, movies often have a worldwide audience. Hollywood movies such as *The Godfather* and *Star Wars* set new records for movie attendance. Since World War II, filmmakers in other countries have challenged American dominance in this field. Britain, France, Japan, Italy, India, and Sweden are among the nations that have produced film classics.

Worldwide distribution of films has enabled moviegoers to gain views of life in other lands. For example, Indian filmmaker Satyajit Ray made a series of movies that traced the life of one man from childhood through marriage and parenthood. These movies offered vivid insights into everyday life in India.

The Performing Arts

As movies, television, and radio have captured large audiences, some people have predicted that live performances in theaters would not survive. But the mass media has awakened a new interest in the performing arts. Often, people choose to attend a live performance of an artistic group they have seen on television.

In addition, newspapers and magazines carry frequent articles about trends in art, film, theater, and music. Directors and actors are interviewed on television. Individual

179

Today, many popular movies are seen by audiences in all parts of the globe. This photograph of a scene from Star Wars *shows imperial stormtroopers questioning two of the film's heroes about their robots. The extraordinary special effects created for this movie illustrate the high level of technology achieved by the film industry.*

performers whose work appeals to the public have become world famous.

The world of ballet. In recent years, audience enthusiasm has led to a major revival of classical dance, or ballet. In the 1950s, there were only a handful of outstanding ballet companies in the world. Two of the leading companies—the Bolshoi and Kirov—were in the Soviet Union. Generally, only people living in major cities could attend the ballet.

In 1961, while the Bolshoi Ballet was on a world tour, its leading male dancer, Rudolf Nureyev, defected to the West. Russian ballerina Natalia Makarova defected in 1970 and joined an American company. In 1974, Mikhail Baryshnikov, one of the greatest male dancers of the century, slipped away from the Kirov Ballet and sought artistic freedom in the West. Intense publicity surrounding the defection of these Russian dancers increased curiosity about ballet and helped build new audiences.

The music of youth. A new musical sound forged a vast youth audience in the postwar period. Fusing traditions of American country and western music and rhythm and blues, American musicians created rock 'n' roll in the 1950s. With its pounding beat, youth-oriented lyrics, and amplified sound, rock became a shared experience among young people around the globe. Today, rock groups throughout the world attract tens of thousands of people to a single concert.

New technology also played a part in creating a vast music industry. Long-playing records and stereophonic sound reproduction provided a truer sound than ever before. Electric instruments and electronic synthesizers created new possibilities in music. Transistor radios, cassettes, tape decks, and headphones made music portable.

Exploring the Past and Present

An information explosion has taken place in the second half of the twentieth century. For example, as you have read, scientists have gained vast stores of new knowledge in such fields as space and medicine. Mass communication has helped spread this knowledge. Schools and universities have expanded their courses of study to cover massive amounts of new information. In addition, an increasingly literate public is reading about the latest discoveries.

People are also taking a new interest in the past. Many records of the past have been stored in museums. These museums have opened their doors to millions of people. They have mounted well-planned, lively exhibits. Science museums have let people explore complicated space age technology. Museums of art and archaeology have allowed people to learn about other societies.

Proud of their ancient heritages, nations such as Egypt and China have allowed museums in other countries to display treasured artifacts. In the 1970s, an exhibit of treasures from Tutankhamon's tomb traveled to North America and Western Europe. A world tour of Chinese artifacts included 3,000-year-old Shang bronzes and terra cotta figures that had guarded the First Emperor's grave. These exhibits have increased people's curiosity about other people's cultures.

Museums have also collected modern works of art. People flock to see the works of twentieth century masters such as Pablo Picasso and Henri Matisse. Competition among museums and private collectors to buy modern works of art has caused prices of these pieces to skyrocket.

After the end of the second world war in 1945, the center of the art world shifted from Paris to New York. In New York, several new schools of painting developed, including abstract expressionism. Jackson Pollock, a leader of this movement, swirled and dripped paint across his canvasses. In another modern art movement, pop art, artists used images from the mass media. Pop artists based their work on such everyday images as soup cans. Amer-

In the 1970s, Chinese archaeologists discovered the tomb of the emperor Shih Huang Ti. The emperor, who died in 210 B.C., had ordered the building of the Great Wall of China. He also employed hundreds of workers preparing his tomb. Archaeologists have just begun to excavate the many life-sized terra cotta figures (left) that were buried in the emperor's tomb. The kneeling archer (right) was supposed to protect the emperor in the afterlife.

Population of the World's Largest Urban Areas

(in thousands)

1350 B.C.		1000 A.D.		1600 A.D.	
Thebes, Egypt	100	Cordova, Spain	450	Peking, China	706
Memphis, Egypt	74	Constantinople, Turkey	450	Constantinople, Turkey	700
Babylon, Iraq	54	Kaifeng, China	400	Agra, India	500
Chengchow, China	40	Sian, China	300	Cairo, Egypt	400
Khattushas, Turkey	40	Kyoto, Japan	200	Osaka, Japan	400
1925 A.D.		1980 A.D.		2000 A.D. (projected)	
New York, US	7,774	New York, US	20,400	Mexico City, Mexico	31,000
London, England	7,742	Tokyo, Japan	20,000	São Paulo, Brazil	25,800
Tokyo, Japan	5,300	Mexico City, Mexico	15,000	Tokyo, Japan	24,200
Paris, France	4,800	São Paulo, Brazil	13,500	New York, US	22,800
Berlin, Germany	4,013	Shanghai, China	13,400	Shanghai, China	22,700

All figures are estimates.

Source: United Nations.

■ *The centers of population have changed in the past 3,000 years. This table shows the five largest urban areas at five points in history. It also shows the urban areas projected to be the largest in the year 2000.*

ican artist Roy Lichtenstein used comic strip characters as subjects for his paintings. The painting "Three Flags" by pop artist Jasper Johns sold for one million dollars in 1981. This was the highest price ever paid for a work by a living artist.

Challenges for the Future

The period after the second world war has brought tremendous changes to people around the globe. New nations have emerged in Africa, the Middle East, and Asia. Since 1945, these nations and the developing nations of Latin America have taken a prominent role in world affairs. Improved communication and transportation have put people from different parts of the world in closer touch with each other than ever before. In addition, nations have been tied more closely together by such economic needs as access to energy resources.

In both developed and developing nations, education has contributed to widespread changes. In the United States and Western Europe, college attendance soared in the postwar period. Dozens of new colleges and universities were opened. In the same period, developing nations worked toward increasing literacy rates. Many students from these nations attended universities in the United States and Europe.

Important changes have occurred in the workplace. Working conditions, hours, wages, and fringe benefits have been improved. New inventions have led to the growth of new industries. Computers have begun to revolutionize industry. On farms, new high-yield crops and machinery have changed the way food is produced.

As you have read, the movement of people from rural areas to cities has been a worldwide phenomenon. In cities and their suburbs, people have easier access to education, jobs, and various forms of popular entertainment.

Patterns of change in the postwar era have also affected women. In developed countries, women have entered the workforce in increasing numbers. In 1982, for example, more than half of all adult women in Canada worked outside the home. Women in many countries have expanded their roles in public life.

These patterns of growth and change continue to pose challenges to all nations. As in the past, individual societies are developing their own ways of meeting these challenges.

SECTION REVIEW

1. Identify: Satyajit Ray, Rudolf Nureyev, Jackson Pollock.
2. (a) List three forms of mass communication. (b) What effect has mass communication had on people around the world?
3. How has new technology affected popular music?
4. What subjects did pop artists use in their work?
5. Describe three changes that have taken place in the workplace in recent years.

IN PERSPECTIVE

Since 1945, vast changes have occurred in many fields. Research scientists working with engineers and technicians have made many advances in technology. Space exploration has offered dramatic evidence of the advances in science and technology. Both the computer revolution and improvements in medicine have transformed the lives of people around the globe.

Scientists have explored ways of meeting the demands of the world's growing population. They have developed new sources of food and are looking for new sources of energy. Even so, world hunger and the need for energy remain among the major challenges for the future.

Mass communication has also had a dramatic effect on peoples' lives. Thanks to satellite communications, millions of people can watch a major event on television. Yet despite radio and television, audiences continue to flock to live artistic performances.

Today, people are taking a new interest in the heritage of the past along with the achievements of the present. Displays of ancient artifacts from different civilizations have drawn huge crowds to museums, while space shots have also attracted thousands of spectators.

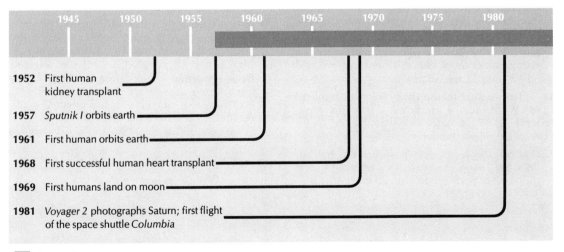

1952	First human kidney transplant
1957	*Sputnik I* orbits earth
1961	First human orbits earth
1968	First successful human heart transplant
1969	First humans land on moon
1981	*Voyager 2* photographs Saturn; first flight of the space shuttle *Columbia*

■ Space Age

Decide if the following statements are true or false. If a statement is false, rewrite the statement to make it true.

1. Applied science involves putting science to practical use.

2. The Space Age began during World War II.

3. John Glenn was the first American to orbit the earth.

4. Other nations in addition to the United States and the Soviet Union have launched satellites.

5. The development of radar allowed smaller computers to be built.

6. The use of vaccines has helped wipe out smallpox.

7. Populations are growing fastest in Western Europe.

8. The Green Revolution has helped increase food production.

9. Television and movies have led to reduced interest in live performances of theater and music.

10. The center of the art world today is Paris.

Chapter Checkup

1. (a) How did the need for better weapons during World War II help launch the Space Age? (b) What were the major Soviet achievements in space exploration? (c) What were the major American achievements in space exploration?

2. (a) Describe the development of computers. (b) How are computers used in business and industry? (c) How are they used in medicine?

3. (a) Why was the discovery of penicillin important? (b) How did the electron microscope affect medical research? (c) How have medical advances affected surgery?

4. (a) How widespread is the problem of hunger? (b) What are the major causes of this problem? (c) What steps have been taken to increase food production?

5. Describe how each of the following has influenced people's lives: (a) television and movies; (b) performing arts; (c) museums.

For Further Thought

1. *Relating Past to Present* Review the description of the Crystal Palace on page 61 and the liftoff of *Columbia* at Cape Canaveral on page 736. (a) What similarities do you see in these two events? (b) What differences do you see? (c) How might people living during the Industrial Revolution have reacted to the *Columbia* liftoff?

2. *Expressing an Opinion* (a) Why do some developing nations ignore warnings about pollution? (b) Do you agree with the position of these developing nations? Explain.

Developing Basic Skills

1. *Researching* Choose one of the advances in technology of the postwar period. Research how this advance was achieved. Then answer the following questions: (a) What earlier developments contributed to this advance? (b) Was this advance the work of a single individual or of many people? Explain. (c) What has been the major result of this advance?

2. *Graph Reading* Study the graphs on page 172 and page 109. Then answer the following questions: (a) How did average life expectancy in Western Europe and the United States change between 1910 and 1930? Between 1950 and 1960? (b) During which period between 1910 and the present did life expectancy increase the most? (c) How does average life expectancy in Western Europe and the United States today compare to average life expectancy in these areas in 1850?

3. *Forecasting Future Trends* No one can say exactly what will happen in the future. But people can make forecasts based on trends, or changes taking place in the present. Make a list of five major changes that have taken place since World War II. Next to each, note what aspect of people's lives it has affected. Decide whether this change is likely to continue. Then answer the following questions: (a) Describe a change that has affected political life. (b) Is it likely to continue? Explain. (c) What economic trends have affected people's lives? (d) Which trend do you think will have the greatest impact on future developments?

See page 204 for suggested readings.

Reference Section

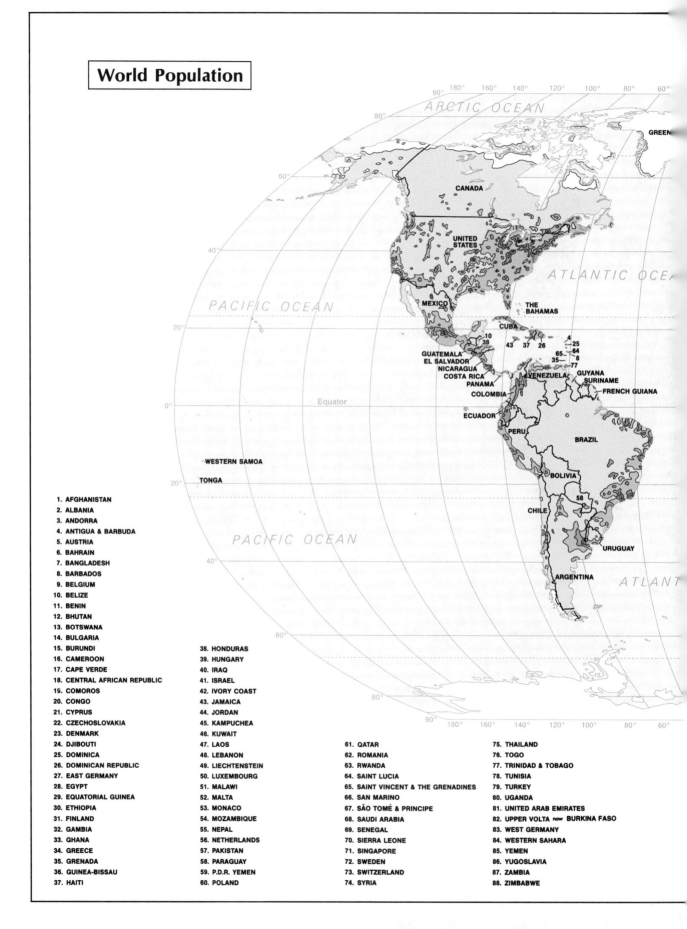

World Population

1. AFGHANISTAN
2. ALBANIA
3. ANDORRA
4. ANTIGUA & BARBUDA
5. AUSTRIA
6. BAHRAIN
7. BANGLADESH
8. BARBADOS
9. BELGIUM
10. BELIZE
11. BENIN
12. BHUTAN
13. BOTSWANA
14. BULGARIA
15. BURUNDI
16. CAMEROON
17. CAPE VERDE
18. CENTRAL AFRICAN REPUBLIC
19. COMOROS
20. CONGO
21. CYPRUS
22. CZECHOSLOVAKIA
23. DENMARK
24. DJIBOUTI
25. DOMINICA
26. DOMINICAN REPUBLIC
27. EAST GERMANY
28. EGYPT
29. EQUATORIAL GUINEA
30. ETHIOPIA
31. FINLAND
32. GAMBIA
33. GHANA
34. GREECE
35. GRENADA
36. GUINEA-BISSAU
37. HAITI

38. HONDURAS
39. HUNGARY
40. IRAQ
41. ISRAEL
42. IVORY COAST
43. JAMAICA
44. JORDAN
45. KAMPUCHEA
46. KUWAIT
47. LAOS
48. LEBANON
49. LIECHTENSTEIN
50. LUXEMBOURG
51. MALAWI
52. MALTA
53. MONACO
54. MOZAMBIQUE
55. NEPAL
56. NETHERLANDS
57. PAKISTAN
58. PARAGUAY
59. P.D.R. YEMEN
60. POLAND

61. QATAR
62. ROMANIA
63. RWANDA
64. SAINT LUCIA
65. SAINT VINCENT & THE GRENADINES
66. SAN MARINO
67. SÃO TOMÉ & PRINCIPE
68. SAUDI ARABIA
69. SENEGAL
70. SIERRA LEONE
71. SINGAPORE
72. SWEDEN
73. SWITZERLAND
74. SYRIA

75. THAILAND
76. TOGO
77. TRINIDAD & TOBAGO
78. TUNISIA
79. TURKEY
80. UGANDA
81. UNITED ARAB EMIRATES
82. UPPER VOLTA now BURKINA FASO
83. WEST GERMANY
84. WESTERN SAHARA
85. YEMEN
86. YUGOSLAVIA
87. ZAMBIA
88. ZIMBABWE

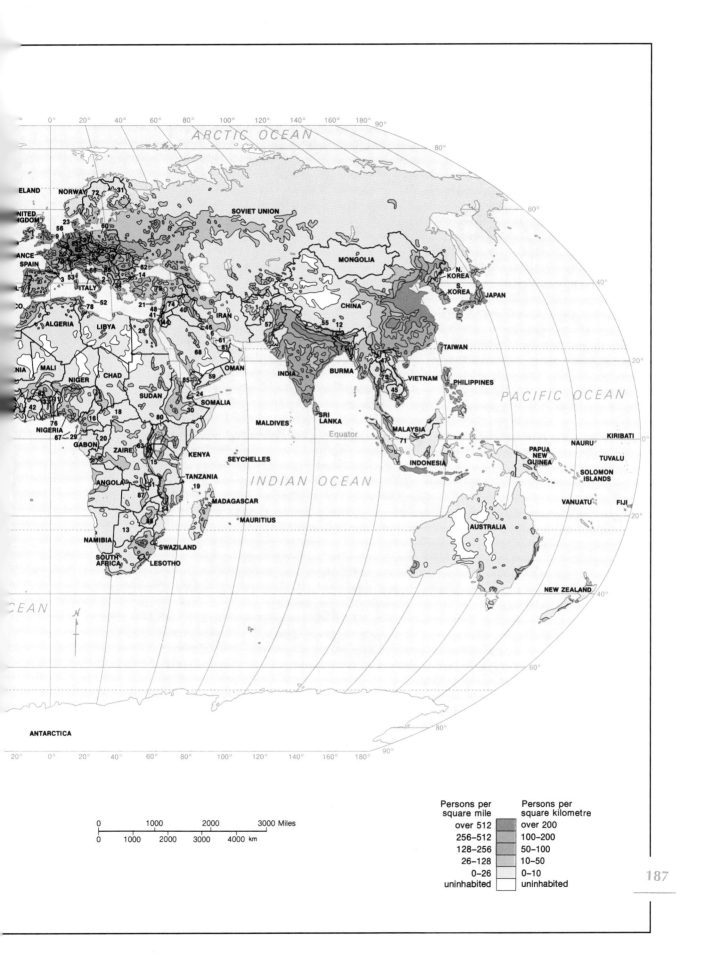

ARCTIC OCEAN

20° 40° 60° 80° 100° 120° 140° 160° 180° 90°

ELAND

NORWAY 72 31

UNITED KGDOM

SOVIET UNION

56 23
9

60

MONGOLIA

N. KOREA

ANCE
SPAIN

S. KOREA

JAPAN

3 53

ITALY

62
14

78 52

21 48 74
40
41

IRAN

CHINA

55 12

TAIWAN

ALGERIA

LIBYA

28

46
6
61
81
68

NIA

MALI

NIGER

CHAD

SUDAN

85

59

24

OMAN

INDIA

BURMA

PACIFIC OCEAN

SOMALIA

30

VIETNAM

PHILIPPINES

16

18

80

SRI
LANKA

45

NIGERIA

67 29

GABON

20

ZAIRE

63

15

KENYA

MALDIVES

Equator

MALAYSIA

71

NAURU

KIRIBATI

TUVALU

PAPUA
NEW
GUINEA

SOLOMON
ISLANDS

ANGOLA

51

87

TANZANIA

19

SEYCHELLES

INDONESIA

INDIAN OCEAN

VANUATU

FIJI

54

MADAGASCAR

MAURITIUS

13

48

NAMIBIA

AUSTRALIA

SOUTH
AFRICA

SWAZILAND

LESOTHO

NEW ZEALAND 40°

CEAN

N

ANTARCTICA

20° 0° 20° 40° 60° 80° 100° 120° 140° 160° 180° 90°

0 1000 2000 3000 Miles

0 1000 2000 3000 4000 km

Persons per square mile		Persons per square kilometre
over 512		over 200
256–512		100–200
128–256		50–100
26–128		10–50
0–26		0–10
uninhabited		uninhabited

187

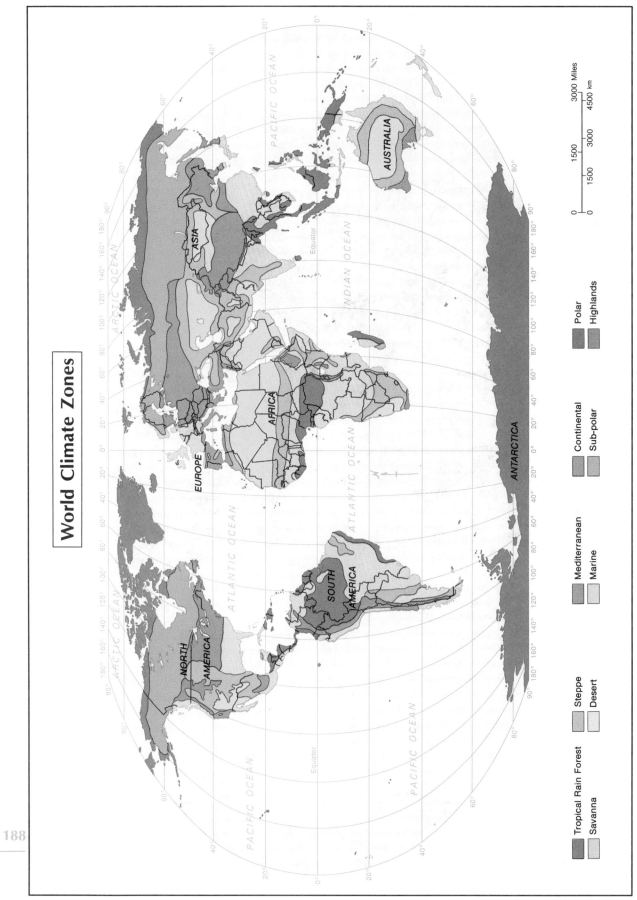

World Climate Zones

Legend:

- Tropical Rain Forest
- Savanna
- Steppe
- Desert
- Mediterranean
- Marine
- Continental
- Sub-polar
- Polar
- Highlands

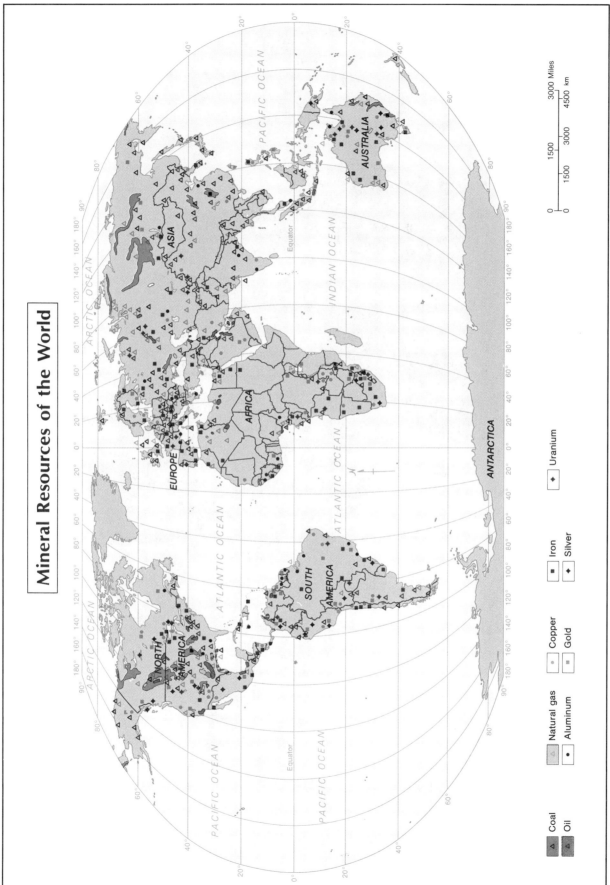

Mineral Resources of the World

Coal — ◁

Oil — ◁

Natural gas — ◁
Aluminum — ●

Copper — ●
Gold — ■

Iron — ■
Silver — ◆

Uranium — ◆

0	1500	3000	3000 Miles
0	1500	3000	4500 km

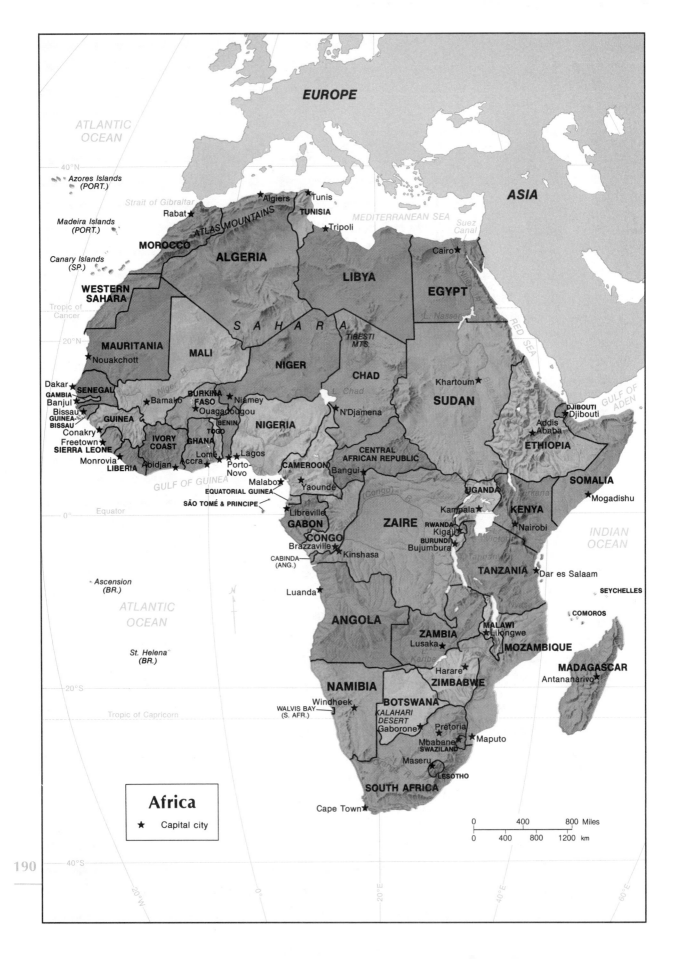

Africa

★ Capital city

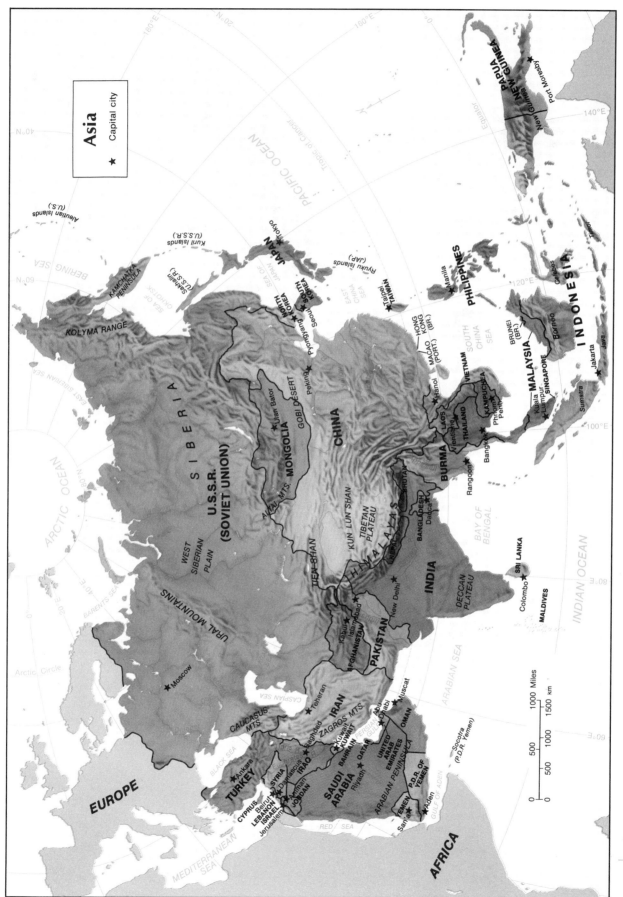

Asia

★ Capital city

EUROPE

ARCTIC OCEAN

Arctic Circle

★ Moscow

URAL MOUNTAINS

BARENTS SEA

KARA SEA

EAST SIBERIAN SEA

KOLYMA RANGE

KAMCHATKA PENINSULA

BERING SEA

Aleutian Islands (U.S.)

Kuril Islands (U.S.S.R.)

Sakhalin (U.S.S.R.)

SEA OF OKHOTSK

PACIFIC OCEAN

JAPAN ★Tokyo

SEA OF JAPAN

NORTH KOREA ★Pyongyang

SOUTH KOREA ★Seoul

Ryuku Islands (JAP.)

EAST CHINA SEA

★Taipei TAIWAN

HONG KONG (BR.)

MACAO (PORT.)

PHILIPPINES ★Manila

SOUTH CHINA SEA

BRUNEI (BR.)

Borneo

MALAYSIA

Kuala Lumpur★ ★SINGAPORE

Sumatra

Celebes

INDONESIA

Jakarta★

Java

Timor

PAPUA NEW GUINEA

New Guinea ★Port Moresby

Equator

SIBERIA

WEST SIBERIAN PLAIN

U.S.S.R. (SOVIET UNION)

ALTAI MTS.

Ulan Bator★

MONGOLIA

GOBI DESERT

★Peking

CHINA

KUN LUN SHAN

TIEN SHAN

Tibetan Plateau

HIMALAYAS

Tropic of Cancer

VIETNAM ★Hanoi

LAOS ★Vientiane

BURMA ★Rangoon

THAILAND ★Bangkok

KAMPUCHEA ★Phnom Penh

CAUCASUS MTS.

BLACK SEA

CASPIAN SEA

ZAGROS MTS.

IRAN ★Teheran

★Baghdad IRAQ

TURKEY ★Ankara

SYRIA ★Damascus

CYPRUS

Beirut★ LEBANON

ISRAEL

★Jerusalem

★Amman JORDAN

KUWAIT ★Kuwait

BAHRAIN

QATAR

PERSIAN GULF

UNITED ARAB EMIRATES

★Abu Dhabi

OMAN ★Muscat

ARABIAN PENINSULA

★Riyadh

SAUDI ARABIA

YEMEN ★Sanaa

P.D.R. OF YEMEN ★Aden

Socotra (P.D.R. Yemen)

GULF OF ADEN

RED SEA

MEDITERRANEAN SEA

AFRICA

AFGHANISTAN ★Kabul

★Islamabad

PAKISTAN

NEPAL

BHUTAN

BANGLADESH ★Dacca

★New Delhi

INDIA

DECCAN PLATEAU

BAY OF BENGAL

SRI LANKA ★Colombo

MALDIVES

ARABIAN SEA

INDIAN OCEAN

1000 Miles

0   500   1000

0   500   1000   1500 km

191

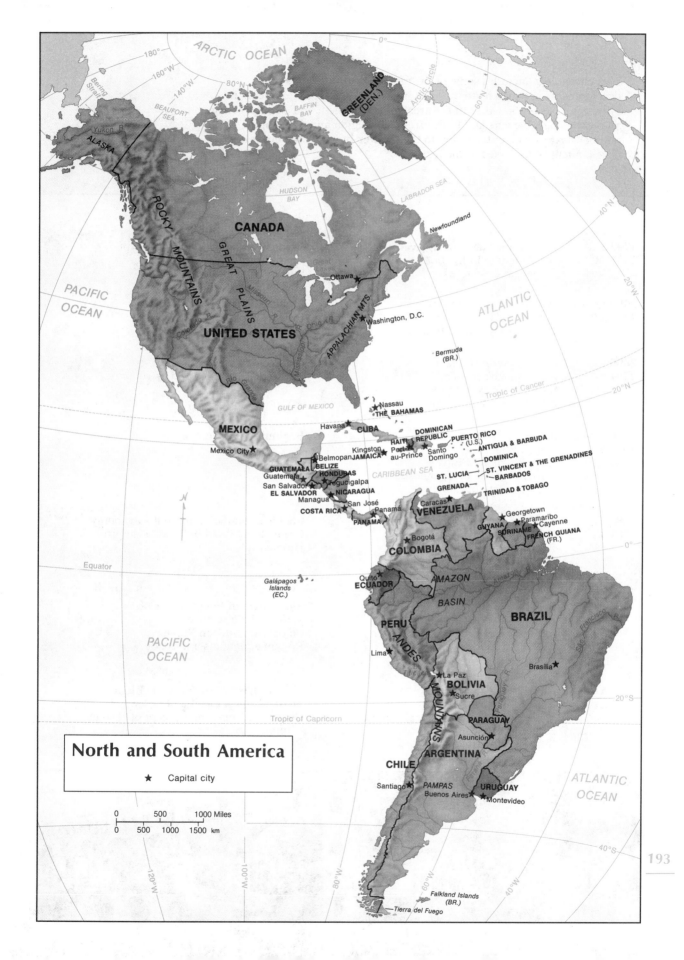

North and South America

★ Capital city

| 0 | 500 | 1000 Miles |
| 0 | 500 | 1000 | 1500 km |

A Chronology of World History

This chronology includes some of the most important events and developments in world history. It can be used to trace developments in different parts of the world in the areas of government and society, science and technology, the arts and literature, and religion and philosophy. The number next to each entry refers to the chapter in which the event or development is discussed in the text.

	Government and Society	Science and Technology
3000 B.C.– **2501 B.C.**	Civilizations develop in river valleys Old Kingdom in Egypt Sumerian city-states	Great Pyramid of Khufu in Egypt Egyptian calendar Sumerian arithmetic
2500 B.C.– **2001 B.C.**	Middle Kingdom in Egypt Sargon in Mesopotamia Indus Valley civilization	Chinese calendar Irrigation of Nile Delta
2000 B.C.– **1501 B.C.**	Minoan civilization Hammurabi's law code Shang dynasty in China New Kingdom in Egypt	Indus cities planned Shang mathematics and astronomy
1500 B.C.– **1001 B.C.**	Aryans in India Trojan War Tutankhamon in Egypt Dorians invade Peloponnesus Chou dynasty in China	Beginning of Iron Age
1000 B.C.– **501 B.C.**	Efficient government in Assyria Solomon's rule in Israel Persian Empire Caste system emerges in India	Chaldean mathematics and astronomy Great Royal Road in Persian Empire Hippocrates
500 B.C.– **1 B.C.**	Persian Wars Athenian democracy Alexander the Great Asoka in India Roman Republic	Alexandria in Egypt center of Hellenistic science Colosseum built in Rome Roman aqueducts and roads
1 A.D.– **500 A.D.**	Han dynasty in China Roman Empire Maya civilization in Central America Fall of Rome Gupta Empire in India	*Natural History* by Pliny the Elder Medical encyclopedia of Galen Decimal system and concept of zero in India Paper invented in China Maya develop calendar and zero

The Arts and Literature	Religion and Philosophy	
Gilgamesh Epic	Pharaohs as god-kings in Egypt Dumuzi and Inanna in Sumer	**3000 B.C.–** **2501 B.C.**
Temples at Luxor and Karnak Egyptian literature	Osiris worshipped in Egypt Mother goddess worshipped in Indus Valley	**2500 B.C.–** **2001 B.C.**
Chinese bronzes and silk Chinese writing Minoan frescoes	Ancestor worship and use of oracle bones in China	**2000 B.C.–** **1501 B.C.**
Temple of Hatshepsut in Egypt Obelisks built in Egypt	Vedas and Upanishads in India Hinduism develops Akenaton in Egypt Hebrew belief in one God	**1500 B.C.–** **1001 B.C.**
Library at Nineveh Phoenician alphabet *Ramayana* in India *Book of Odes* in China *Iliad* by Homer	Olympian gods in Greece Buddhism founded Zoroaster in Persian Empire Confucius in China	**1000 B.C.–** **501 B.C.**
Parthenon in Greece *Antigone* by Sophocles *Aeneid* by Virgil Stupas built in India	Socrates, Plato, and Aristotle in Athens Stoics and Epicureans in Greece Legalism in China	**500 B.C.–** **1 B.C.**

The Annals by Tacitus
Roman mosaics
Kalidasa in India
First Chinese dictionary
Ajanta cave paintings
	Christianity founded
	Christianity becomes official religion of
	   Roman Empire
	Confucianism influences Chinese
	   government
		1 A.D.–
		500 A.D.

	Government and Society	Science and Technology
501–1000	Charlemagne in Europe Emergence of feudalism in Europe Expansion of Islamic Empire Golden Age of T'ang in China Kingdom of Ghana in West Africa	Stirrup, heavy plow, three-field system in Europe Arab advances in science and mathematics Printing in China
1001–1499	Crusades Decline of feudalism in Europe Kublai Khan in China Fall of Constantinople to Turks	Flying buttress, clocks, glass in Europe Inca roads and terraces Printing press in Europe
1500–1599	Aztec and Inca empires conquered in New World Magellan rounds Cape Horn Height of Ottoman Empire Akbar in India	Scientific Revolution begins in Europe Copernicus studies planets Vesalius studies anatomy
1600–1699	Emergence of absolute monarchs in Europe Thirty Years' War Louis XIV in France Tokugawa shoguns isolate Japan English Bill of Rights	Galileo challenges traditional thinking Invention of microscope Newton develops mathematical laws Steam-driven engine developed
1700–1799	Enlightened monarchs in Europe American Revolution French Revolution	Agricultural Revolution in Europe Industrial Revolution begins in Britain Inventions in textile industry
1800–1899	Congress of Vienna Independent nations in Latin America Unification of Italy Unification of Germany American Civil War Age of Imperialism	Spread of Industrial Revolution Fulton develops steamship Telephone and electric light invented Advances in physics and chemistry Improvements in medicine
1900–Present	World War I Great Depression Rise of totalitarian states World War II Nations of Africa, Middle East, and Asia win independence	Assembly-line production Flight at Kitty Hawk Airplanes used in war Space Age begins Invention of computers

The Arts and Literature	Religion and Philosophy	
Santa Sophia built in Constantinople Illuminated manuscripts Carolingian minuscule T'ang porcelain and poetry Ife glazed pottery	Islam founded German tribes convert to Christianity Christian Church dominant in Europe Buddhism spreads to Japan	**501–1000**
Tale of Genji by Lady Murasaki Gothic cathedrals *The Canterbury Tales* by Chaucer *The Rubaiyat* by Omar Khayyám Beginning of the Renaissance	Christian Church splits into Roman Catholic Church and Eastern Orthodox Church Aztec temple at Tenochtitlán Islam carried to India	**1001–1499**
Da Vinci, Michelangelo, Raphael Dürer *Autobiography* by Cellini Pieter Bruegel	Reformation begins Calvin's *Institutes of the Christian Religion* Catholic Reformation	**1500–1599**
Don Quixote by Cervantes Shakespeare El Greco Velázquez Versailles built	*The Leviathan* by Hobbes *Two Treatises on Government* by Locke	**1600–1699**
Bach, Handel, Mozart Classical style in architecture Paris salons Scenes of French Revolution painted by David	Enlightenment Voltaire and Rousseau *Wealth of Nations* by Adam Smith Thomas Jefferson drafts Declaration of Independence	**1700–1799**
Frankenstein by Mary Shelley *Hunchback of Notre Dame* by Victor Hugo *Hard Times* by Charles Dickens Romanticism Impressionism	Liberalism and conservatism *The Communist Manifesto* by Marx and Engels Social Darwinism	**1800–1899**
All Quiet on the Western Front by Erich Maria Remarque Picasso *Dr. Zhivago* by Boris Pasternak Gabriela Mistral Movies and rock 'n' roll	Gandhi's philosophy of nonviolence Fascism *Mein Kampf* by Hitler *Thoughts of Chairman Mao* by Mao Tse-tung	**1900–Present**

Pronunciation Key

When difficult names or terms first appear in the text, they are respelled to aid pronunciation. A syllable in LARGE CAPITAL LETTERS receives the most stress. Syllables with a secondary stress appear in SMALL CAPITAL LETTERS. The following key lists the symbols used in respelling. Next to each symbol, the key provides examples of words that use the sound and shows how the examples would be respelled.

Symbol	Example	Respelling
a	hat	(hat)
ay	pay, late	(pay), (layt)
ah	star, hot	(stahr), (haht)
ai	air, dare	(air), (dair)
aw	law, all	(law), (awl)
eh	met	(meht)
ee	bee, eat	(bee), (eet)
er	learn, sir, fur	(lern), (ser), (fer)
ih	fit	(fiht)
ī	mile	(mīl)
ir	ear	(ir)
oh	no	(noh)
oi	soil, boy	(soil), (boi)
oo	root, rule	(root), (rool)
or	born, door	(born), (dor)
ow	plow, out	(plow), (owt)
u	put, book	(put), buk)
uh	fun	(fuhn)
yoo	few, use	(fyoo), (yooz)
ch	chill, reach	(chihl), (reech)
g	go, dig	(goh), (dihg)
j	jet, gently, bridge	(jeht), (JEHNT-lee), (brihj)
k	kite, cup	(kīt), (kuhp)
ks	mix	(mihks)
kw	quick	(kwihk)
ng	bring	(brihng)
s	say, cent	(say), (sehnt)
sh	she, crash	(shee), (krash)
th	three	(three)
<u>th</u>	then, breathe	(thehn), (bree<u>th</u>)
y	yet, onion	(yeht), (UHN-yuhn)
z	zip, always	(zihp), (AWL-wayz)
zh	treasure	(TREH-zher)

Glossary

This glossary defines many important historical terms and phrases. Many of the terms are phonetically respelled to aid in pronunciation. See the Pronunciation Key on the preceding page for an explanation of the respellings. The page number following each definition is the page on which the term or phrase is first discussed in the text. Most of the entries appear in italics the first time they are used in the text.

A

absolute monarch ruler who has complete authority over the government and the lives of the people (page 2)

artisan (AHR tuh zuhn) skilled craftsperson (page 24)

assembly line production method that breaks down a complex job into a series of smaller tasks (page 91)

assimilation (uh SIHM uh LAY shuhn) policy whereby an imperial power tries to absorb colonies politically and culturally (page 134)

autocracy (aw TAH kruh see) government in which the ruler has unlimited authority (page 74)

autonomy (aw TAHN uh mee) self-government (page 78)

B

bourgeoisie (boor zhwah ZEE) in the Middle Ages, the French word for townspeople; later, a term used to describe the middle class (page 24)

Buddhist (BOOD ihst) a follower of the religion and philosophic system founded in the sixth century B.C. by Siddhartha Gautama, known as the Buddha; Buddhists believe that self-denial enables the soul to reach Nirvana, the condition of wanting nothing (page 153)

bureaucracy (byoo RAH kruh see) system of organizing government by departments or bureaus (page 23)

C

cash crop crop that can be sold on the world market for money (page 124)

caste social group based on birth; in India, caste determined the jobs people could hold (page 142)

caudillo (kow DEE lyoh) during the 1800s in Latin America, a military dictator (page 156)

Christian (KRIHS chuhn) a person professing belief in Jesus as the Christ, or in the set of beliefs based on the teachings of Jesus (page 45)

Church of England, or **Anglican Church** the Protestant church of England which has the reigning monarch as its head; established by Henry VIII with the Act of Supremacy of 1534 (page 7)

colony territory that an outside power controls directly (page 2)

common law system of law in England based on decisions of royal courts that became accepted legal principles (page 9)

communism form of complete socialism in which there is public ownership of all land and all the means of production (page 105)

Confucian (kohn FYOO shuhn) a follower of the ethical teachings formulated by the Chinese philosopher Confucius, emphasizing devotion to parents, family, and friends, respect for ancestors, and the maintenance of justice and peace (page 144)

conservatism during the 1800s, a philosophy that supported the traditional order and resisted political and social change (page 43)

corporation business owned by investors who buy shares of stock in the business; investors risk only the amount of their investment (page 91)

creole (KREE ohl) descendant of Spanish settlers born in the Americas (page 53)

czar (zahr) Russian word for Caesar; title of the ruler of the Russian Empire (page 43)

D

domestic system system in which a merchant paid peasants in the countryside to do work such as spinning and weaving, thus bypassing guild regulations (page 84)

E

émigré (EHM uh gray) person who flees his or her country for political reasons (page 29)

enclosure movement during the 1700s in Britain, the practice of fencing off common lands by individual landowners (page 83)

Enlightenment name applied to the 1700s when philosophers emphasized the use of reason, which they believed would free people from ignorance and perfect society (page 2)

entrepreneur (AHN truh pruh NER) merchant willing to take financial risks in the hope of making large profits (page 25)

extraterritoriality (EHKS truh TEHR uh TAWR ee AL uh tee) the right of foreigners to be protected by the laws of their own nations (page 146)

F

factory system system in which workers and machines are brought together in one place to manufacture goods (page 85)

feudalism (FYOOD 'l ihzm) system of rule by local lords who were bound to a king by ties of loyalty; developed in Western Europe during the Middle Ages (page 149)

franchise (FRAN chiz) the right to vote (page 112)

free market market in which goods are bought and sold without restrictions (page 4)

G

guerrilla warfare (guh RIHL uh) from the Spanish word for little war; fighting comprised of hit-and-run attacks (page 39)

guild association of merchants or artisans that governed a town or craft in the Middle Ages (page 25)

H

hieroglyphics (HI er oh GLIHF ihks) system of writing developed by Egyptian priests in which pictures were used to represent words and sounds (page 35)

Hindu (HĪHN doo) a follower of Hinduism, a religion and social system developed from Brahmanism (page 141)

I

imperialism (ihm PIHR ee uhl ihzm) domination by one country of the political, economic, or cultural life of another country or region (page 121)

interchangeable parts identical component parts that can be used in place of one another in manufacturing (page 91)

Islam (IHS luhm) the Moslem religion, founded in the seventh century by Mohammed, its chief prophet; Allah is the supreme deity (page 153)

L

laissez faire (LEHS ay FEHR) French phrase meaning let people do as they choose; used to describe an economic system in which the government does not interfere with the economy (page 103)

legitimacy (luh JIHT uh muh see) Metternich's principle of restoring to power the royal families that had lost their thrones when Napoleon conquered Europe (page 43)

liberalism during the 1800s, a philosophy that supported guarantees of individual freedom, political change, and social reform (page 43)

limited monarchy government in which a monarch's powers are limited, usually by a constitution and a legislative body (page 2)

M

mass production method of manufacturing large quantities of goods in standard sizes (page 91)

mercantilism (MER kuhn tihl ihzm) economic philosophy maintaining that a nation's economic strength depends on exporting more goods than it imports (page 4)

mestizo (mehs TEE zoh)   person in Spain's colonies in the Americas who was of mixed European and Indian heritage (page 53)

Middle Ages   period of history in Europe following the fall of the Roman Empire and lasting from about 500 to 1350 (page 25)

modernization   creation of a stable society capable of producing a high level of goods and services (page 152)

Mogul (MOH guhl)   Mogul was the Persian word for Mongol; the Mongols were originally nomadic herders from central Asia, but in the thirteenth century they conquered an empire extending from China to Eastern Europe (page 141)

monarch (MAHN uhrk)   king or queen who heads a government (page 2)

monastery (MAWN a STEHR ee)   the place of residence of a group of people, especially monks, who have withdrawn from the world under religious vows (page 7)

monopoly (muh NAHP uh lee)   total control by one corporation of the market for a particular product (page 25)

Muslim (MUHZ lihm)   a follower of the religion of Islam (page 141)

N

nationalism   feeling of pride for and devotion to one's country (page 62)

P

paternalism (puh TER n'l ihzm)   system in which an imperial power governs its colonies closely because it believes that the people are not able to govern themselves (page 134)

peninsulare (peh NIHN suh LAHR ay)   official sent by Spain to rule Spanish colonies in the Americas (page 53)

philosophe (fee leh ZOHF)   French word meaning philosopher; person during the Enlightenment who believed that the use of science and reason would lead to human progress (page 3)

physiocrat (FIHZ ee uh KRAT)   philosophe who searched for natural laws to explain the economy (page 4)

pogrom (poh GRAHM)   violent raid on a Jewish community, often conducted by government troops (page 75)

prime minister   head of the cabinet in parliamentary governments, usually the leader of the largest party in the legislature (page 14)

proletariat (PROH luh TAIR ee uht)   the working class (page 105)

protectorate (pruh TEHK tuhr iht)   country with its own government that makes policies under the guidance of an outside power (page 121)

R

republic   system of government in which citizens who have the right to vote choose their leaders (page 10)

S

samurai (SAM uh RĪ)   warrior knights of Japan during the feudal period (page 149)

scientific method   an approach to the study of the natural world in which experiments, observation, and mathematics are used to prove scientific theories (page 4)

serfdom (SERF duhm)   feudal servitude in which a serf, or peasant, was bound to the lord's land and was transferable with the land to a new owner (page 24)

shogun (SHOH guhn)   after 1192, the chief general in Japan, who held more political power than the emperor (page 149)

socialism   economic and political system in which society as a whole rather than private individuals own all property and operate all businesses (page 48)

sphere of influence region in which a power claims exclusive investment or trading privileges (page 121)

status quo (STAYT uhs KWOH) existing state of affairs (page 46)

T

technology (tehk NAHL uh jee) tools and skills people use (page 2)

U

universal male suffrage right of all adult men to vote (page 49)

V

vertical integration form of business in which a corporation controls the industries that contribute to its final product (page 92)

Z

zaibatsu (ZĪ baht SOO) wealthy Japanese families who bought the chief industries of the country in the 1880s and thereby came to dominate the Japanese economy (page 152)

zemstvo (ZEHMST voh) local elected assembly created by the Russian government under Alexander II (page 75)

Suggested Readings

I

Chapter 1

Boas, Marie. *The Scientific Renaissance 1450–1630*. Harper. A description of the Scientific Revolution and its results.

Chidsey, Donald Barr. *The Birth of the Constitution*. Crown. An informal history of the issues and individuals that created the Constitution of the United States.

Gay, Peter. *The Age of Enlightenment*. Time-Life. A thorough, illustrated treatment of Enlightenment Europe.

Howell, Roger. *Cromwell*. Little, Brown. A well-written biography of Oliver Cromwell.

Roberts, Clayton and Roberts, David. *A History of England*. Prentice-Hall. A comprehensive survey of English history.

Chapter 2

Alderman, Clifford Lindsey. *Liberty, Equality, Fraternity: The Story of the French Revolution*. Julian Messner. A brief, readable account of the French Revolution.

Castelot, André. *Marie Antoinette*. Harper & Row. A profile of the young queen from her marriage at age 15 to her death at age 38.

Dickens, Charles. *A Tale of Two Cities*. Dutton. A classic novel that recreates the excitement and terror of the French Revolution.

Herold, J.C. *The Horizon Book of the Age of Napoleon*. Harper & Row. An illustrated history of the Napoleonic Age.

Chapter 3

Bernard, J.F. *Talleyrand: A Biography*. Putnam. A biography of Talleyrand, the arch rival of Metternich.

Brown-Baker, Nina. *He Wouldn't Be King: The Story of Simón Bolívar*. Vanguard. A readable biography of the famous South American liberator.

May, Arthur. *The Age of Metternich, 1814–1848*. Holt, Rinehart & Winston. A brief treatment of Europe during the time of Metternich.

Nicolson, Harold. *Congress of Vienna: A Study in Allied Unity*. Harcourt. An account of the Congress of Vienna and the problems European leaders faced after the defeat of Napoleon.

II

Chapter 4

Cowles, Virginia. *The Kaiser*. Harper & Row. An account of William II and his role in the growth of German unity.

Dill, Marshall. *Germany: A Modern History*. University of Michigan. A general history of Germany in the 1800s and 1900s.

Crankshaw, Edward. *The Shadow of the Winter Palace*. Viking. A comprehensive history of Russia under the Romanovs.

McLeon, R.A. *Cavour and Italian Unity*. Exposition. An account of the life of Cavour and his role in unifying Italy.

Chapter 5

Aiken, Joan. *Midnight Is a Place*. Viking. A fast-paced novel about children living in a factory town.

Ashton, T.S. *The Industrial Revolution: 1760–1830*. Oxford University Press. A brief, scholarly account of the early Industrial Revolution in Britain.

Eco, Umberto, and Zorzoli, G.B. *The Picture History of Inventions*. Macmillan. A collection of illustrations of major inventions from the Industrial Revolution to the present.

Hart, Roger. *English Life in the Nineteenth Century*. Putnam. An illustrated discussion of English life in the 1800s.

Zola, Émile. *Germinal*. Dutton. A novel about the lives of French miners.

Chapter 6

Curie, Eve. *Madame Curie*. Doubleday. A biography of Marie Curie written by her daughter.

deKruif, Paul. *Microbe Hunters*. Harcourt. A dramatic account of medical achievements, especially those of the 1800s.

Hugo, Victor. *Les Misérables*. Fawcett. A historical novel that realistically protrays French life in the 1800s.

Longford, Elizabeth. *Queen Victoria: Born to Succeed*. Harper & Row. An account of the life of Queen Victoria and British society in the 1800s.

Mackenzie, Midge. *Shoulder to Shoulder*. Knopf. An illustrated history of suffragettes in Britain.

Chapter 7

Davidson, Basil. *Black Mother: The Years of the African Slave Trade*. Little, Brown. A thorough treatment of the transatlantic slave trade from the 1500s to 1800s.

Eaton, Jeanette. *David Livingstone: Foe of Darkness*. Morrow. A readable biography of this famous scientist, missionary, and explorer.

McKown, Robin. *The Colonial Conquest of Africa*. Watts. A readable account of European imperialism in Africa.

Moorehead, Alan. *The White Nile*. Harper. An account of European explorers seeking the source of the Nile River in the late 1800s.

Ulli, Beier. *African Poetry: An Anthology of Traditional African Poems*. Cambridge University. A fascinating collection of poetry from all regions of Africa.

Chapter 8

Brown-Baker, Nina. *Juárez: Hero of Mexico*. Vanguard. A biography of Juárez.

Buck, Pearl S. *Imperial Woman*. John Day. A fictionalized biography of Tzu-hsi, last empress of the Manchu dynasty.

Edwardes, Michael. *Asia in the European Age, 1498–1953*. Praeger. An account of European imperialism in Asia.

Reischauer, Edwin O. *Japan: Past and Present*. Knopf. A comprehensive survey of Japanese history and culture.

Shafer, Robert J. *History of Latin America*. Heath. A general survey of Latin American history.

Waley, Arthur. *The Opium War Through Chinese Eyes*. Macmillan. A scholarly, readable account of Chinese reactions to the Opium War.

Chapter 9

George, Susan. *How the Other Half Dies: The Real Reasons for World Hunger*. Allanheld, Osmun. An examination of famine in developing nations.

Osborne, Adam. *Running Wild: The Next Industrial Revolution*. McGraw-Hill. A short survey of the effects of the computer revolution.

Robinson, Donald. *The Miracle Finders: The Stories Behind the Most Important Breakthroughs in Modern Medicine*. David McKay. An informative account of medical advances since 1945, with portraits of the physicians and scientists responsible for the breakthroughs.

Ward, Barbara. *Progress for a Small Planet*. Norton. A discussion of the challenges facing people around the world: energy, food, medicine, and industrialization.

INDEX

207

ILLUSTRATION CREDITS

Frequently cited sources are abbreviated as follows: AR, NY, Art Resource, New York; BA, The Bettmann Archive; CP, Culver Pictures, Inc.; GC, The Granger Collection; NYPL, New York Public Library; TBM, The British Museum.

Key to position of illustrations: *l*, left; *r*, right.

Cover: TBM

UNIT ONE: Page 1 Yale University Art Gallery; **2** Historical Society of Pennsylvania; **4** Wedgewood; **5** Snark/AR, NY; **6** TBM; **7** National Portrait Gallery, London; **8** Scala/AR, NY; **9** TBM; **10** NYPL; **16** American Antiquarian Society; **22** Bibliothèque Nationale; **25** Giraudon/AR, NY; **27** Scala/AR, NY; **29** Snark/AR, NY; **33** GC; **36** Scala/AR, NY; **42** Lauros/Giraudon; **44** AR, NY; **46** Copyright reserved to H.M. the Queen; **48** Snark/AR, NY; **52** AR, NY; **54** CP; **55** Caribbean Tourism Association; **58** The Phillips Collection, Washington.

UNIT TWO: Pages 60-61 TBM; **62** AR, NY; **64** Scala/AR, NY; **66** GC; **71** NYPL; **72** Courtesy of the Crupp Foundation; **75** NYPL; **76** AR, NY; **82** Scala/AR, NY; **84** NYPL; **85** AR, NY; **90** CP; **91** U.S. Dept. of the Interior, National Park Service, Edison National Historic Site; **92** BA; **95** NYPL; **96** AR, NY; **98** International Museum of Photography at George Eastman House; **99** Insurance Company of North America; **102** Scala/AR, NY; **104** NYPL; **105** Snark/AR, NY; **107** GC; **108** Pasteur Institute, Paris; **110** CP; **113** BA; **115** United Church Archives, Victoria University.

UNIT THREE: Pages 118-119 Peabody Museum of Salem, photo by Mark Sexton; **120** Biblioteca Mediceo Laurenziana; **124** CP; **126** American Museum of Natural History; **127** GC; **129** Scala/AR, NY; **132** Snark/AR, NY; **136** Royal Geographic Society, London; **137** The Mansell Collection; **140** Bibliothèque Nationale; **143** GC; **145** Scala/AR, NY; **148** Library of Congress; **149** BA; **150** Scala/AR, NY; **152** Scala/AR, NY; **157** TBM; **159** AR, NY; **163** Library of Congress.

UNIT FOUR: Pages 166-167 Manchete, Pictorial Parade; **168** National Research Council Canada; **170** Hughes Aircraft Co./Telesat Canada; **171** NASA; **174** United Nations; **177** Wally McNamee, Woodfin Camp & Associates, Inc., **178** William Hubbell, Woodfin Camp & Associates, Inc.; **180** Museum of Modern Art/Film-Stills Archive; **181** *l*, *r* Marilyn Grayburn.

REFERENCE SECTION: Page 194 *l*, *r* AR, NY; **195** *l* The Cleveland Museum of Art, Gift of George P. Bickford, *r* Scala/AR, NY; **196** *l* By Permission of The British Library, *r* AR; **197** *l* Scala/AR, NY, *r* AR, NY.

Photo coordinator: Michal Heron
Photo researcher: Helena Frost
Text maps, graphs, and charts: Lee Ames & Zak, Ltd.
Reference maps: R.R. Donnelley & Sons Company